DATE DUE

JAN 0 2 2002	
OCT 2 4 2002	

BRODART   Cat. No. 23-221

WHAT IS COUNSELLING?

WHAT IS COUNSELLING?

The Promise and Problem of the Talking Therapies

Colin Feltham

SAGE Publications
London • Thousand Oaks • New Delhi

Excerpt from 'This Be The Verse' from *Collected Poems* by
Philip Larkin © 1988, 1989 by the Estate of Philip Larkin.
Reprinted by permission of Farrar, Straus & Giroux, Inc and
Faber and Faber Ltd.

First published 1995

SAGE Publications Ltd
6 Bonhill Street
London EC2A 4PU

SAGE Publications Inc
2455 Teller Road
Thousand Oaks, California 91320

SAGE Publications India Pvt Ltd
32, M-Block Market
Greater Kailash – I
New Delhi 110 048

British Library Cataloguing in Publication data

A catalogue record for this book is
available from the British Library.

ISBN 0 8039 8856 7
ISBN 0 8039 8857 5 (pbk)

Library of Congress catalog record available

Typeset by Mayhew Typesetting, Rhayader, Powys.
Printed in Great Britain by Redwood Books, Trowbridge,
Wiltshire.

Contents

Foreword

What Should be Included in a Superb Overview and Introduction to a Non-existant Profession of Counselling and Psychotherapy?

I picture at least three kinds of people who read this book. One consists of those who receive or are given the counselling or psychotherapy, whether they are called patients, clients, counsellees, analysands, consumers, or whatever. A second consists of those who provide it, whether they have been doing it for a while or are just beginning, whether their way of doing it is called client-centred, Gestalt, psychoanalytic, eclectic, or whatever. The third and the main group I have in mind are those who are teaching and training it and those who are learning or being trained in it, both now and in the future. I am picturing all the people who are or will be learning how to be a counsellor or psychotherapist, and all those who are involved in teaching and training them.

Counselling and psychotherapy do not exist; there is no such profession

One reason that 'it' is not a profession, or a discipline, or a field of study, is that we don't even know what to call 'it' or what it is. In the very title of Colin Feltham's superb book, he calls it counselling in the title, therapy in the subtitle, and even goes further to call it the 'talking therapies'! So what is it that we are talking about? Is it counselling? Is it psychotherapy? Is it case work? Are psychoanalysis and analysis included or excluded in counselling, or in psychotherapy, or in whatever we are talking about?

If we wanted to make 'it' a profession or a discipline, would we have one for counselling and another for psychotherapy? Would we have one grand profession or discipline and call it counselling-psychotherapy-case work-analysis-psychoanalysis-talking therapies? Since we don't know what 'it' is we don't know what is to be included and excluded from the undefined 'it'.

But, whether it is called counselling or psychotherapy, it seems to me that it does not even exist because there is no such profession. Or, put differently, what we call counselling or psychotherapy is rightfully owned by lots of different professions, disciplines, fields, each of which can state their rightful claims to legitimate ownership.

Whereas law is owned by the profession of law, medicine is owned by medicine, engineering is owned and taught by the profession of engineering, dentistry is owned and taught by the profession, discipline, or field of dentistry, counselling and psychotherapy are owned and taught by such altogether different professions, disciplines and fields as medicine, health sciences, social work, psychology, nursing, education, theology, and lots of other professions, disciplines and fields. If you want training in medicine, go to medicine. If you want training in counselling and psychotherapy, lots of different professions can give you training. There is no existing profession of counselling and psychotherapy.

Regardless of which particular profession or field trains counsellors or psychotherapists or whatever they are called, there are probably more differences among its graduates than there are between its graduates and the graduates of those trained in any of the other professions that train counsellors or psychotherapists. Suppose that we take a look at what the graduates actually do, whether they were trained in psychology, education, medicine, theology, social work or nursing. Suppose we take a look at counsellors and psychotherapists whose training was in any one of these professions. My impression is that there would be more differences among those graduates than there would be between those graduates and those whose training was in any of the other professions. In other words, there seems to be no single profession of counselling or of psychotherapy or of whatever the non-existing profession is to be called.

If you go to a college or university and ask who teaches whatever is meant by counselling and psychotherapy, with few exceptions you may be directed to departments, faculties, professions, and schools of psychology, medicine, social work, theology, nursing, education, and so on. If you ask if there is a separate, distinct, independent profession, department, faculty, or school of counselling or of psychotherapy, the ordinary answer is no. In terms of teaching and training, a fair case can be made that there is no such thing as counselling and psychotherapy. Such a profession does not exist.

What book would you choose as the single best overview and introduction to counselling and psychotherapy?

Here is a challengingly practical question. It may be that very few counsellors and psychotherapists study the same text as a required overview and introduction to counselling and psychotherapy. But suppose that we were to help make such a decision. Suppose that we were to recommend a single text as the required overview and introduction for the training of most psychiatrists, psychologists, social workers, pastoral counsellors, and everyone else who is learning how to be a counsellor or psychotherapist.

What would that book be? Or, if you want to get somewhat more realistic, if there were a single course that was a required overview and introduction to counselling and psychotherapy, regardless of the profession or discipline, what texts might be included in that course?

I would nominate *What Is Counselling?* as one of a few volumes to provide the best overview and introduction to counselling and psychotherapy – and I would have to figure out what the other few volumes might be. Of course, I would like to invite Colin Feltham to alter the title just a wee bit to include both counselling and psychotherapy.

Why would I nominate this volume? What is so special about this volume? What makes this better than most others that try to provide a solid overview and introduction to the broad field of counselling and psychotherapy? Here are some answers that come straight out of my own bias:

1   This volume covers the important issues and topics that I believe ought to be covered. It covers the history of psychotherapy and counselling. The historical material is interesting, even exciting, and is done in a scholarly way. It covers the various models and approaches to counselling and psychotherapy. It puts counselling and psychotherapy in a workable context by relating the notions, ideas, concepts and basic thoughts of this field to those of such related fields as philosophy, religion, sociology, politics and so on. The person who has gained what this book offers has covered what I would regard as very important topics of a superb overview and introduction to the field.

2   This volume treats counselling and psychotherapy as a field that is worthy, inviting, respectable and profound, rather than straining to put a professional and scientific spin on the field. I confess to being unimpressed by most texts that strain to make our field seem so very professional and scientific. It is as if these texts are waging a fight to insist that counselling and psychotherapy is really a profession and a science based on solid research. Instead of straining in these ways, the present volume rises above those efforts by digging deeper into the issues, concepts and the basic ways of thinking in this field. It allows the reader to deal with issues of professionalism and science without trying to make a case that it either is or is not a worthy and deserved profession or science.

3   This volume is even-handed in covering the various approaches without betraying a bias in favour of certain approaches over others. So many texts are clearly written from the perspective of some approach, and the struggle is to be fair in covering the other approaches. In contrast, this book seems much more to come from a scholar, a teacher, a knowledgeable practitioner who is not especially a devout cognitive behaviourist or psychodynamicist or eclecticist who has to strain to be fair to the other approaches. I appreciate this.

If I were to suggest one book that most counsellors and psychotherapists should read before or after entering the world of practice, I would probably choose this volume.

There is a fourth reason why I like this book so much. The reason is so central to me that I prefer putting it into its own heading.

An overview–introduction should include the absolute truths in counselling and psychotherapy versus absolute truths are collectively held myths, and it is more useful to include positions on basic issues

One very common way of thinking in our field is based on the idea that there really are absolute truths. Our field is a science. Science is a way of getting closer to what is true. There is a cumulative body of knowledge. It is comprised of pieces and bits of rigorous research, empirical knowledge.

According to this very common mind-set, when Colin Feltham asks 'What is counselling?', we should find a conclusion somewhere. He will probably review what the authorities say, what has been found by the researchers and come to some conclusion that answers the question of what is counselling. The answer may not be the final definitive answer, but it should bring us closer to the true answer because there is some true answer that is knowable.

According to this attitude, if the author is going to tell us what counselling is, the contents should include absolute truths such as: interpersonal relationships, especially during childhood, largely account for the person's current interpersonal problems. Clients seek counselling mainly because of their difficulties and problems. Psychoanalysis is the deepest form of counselling. Being empathic is requisite for successful outcome. There are common, universal basic needs, drives, motivations. Therapists should ensure that patients are able to guard and control against the outbreak of basic impulses, needs and drives. There is a common set of basic skills for virtually all counselling approaches. The therapist should check signs of suicidal tendencies in depressed patients. There is a mental disorder called psychosis and therapists should know the signs and be able to diagnose psychosis. Counsellors should first diagnose the problem or mental disorder and then select and apply the appropriate treatment. Biological, neurological and physiological determinants are basic to psychological determinants. Counsellors' statements should not criticize, disapprove, or diminish a client's self-esteem. Patients with weak egos and inadequate defenses can be harmed by treatments that exert too much stress. There are stages of childhood development. Successful counselling involves insight and understanding. Psychopaths do not do well in intensive counselling. Behavioural approaches are the treatment of choice for simple phobias. There are hereditary and environmental determinants of mental illness. And on and on to loads of other absolute truths.

On the other hand, an alternative way of thinking is that the common

way of thinking is just one way of thinking. According to this alternative
way of thinking, absolute truths are generally collectively held myths, that
are 'true' largely because they are uncritically held to be true.

According to this alternative perspective, it is perhaps more useful to
think in terms of basic and fundamental issues and questions, and to try
and frame useful positions and answers. The criterion of a good position
or answer is that it is useful, helpful and effective, rather than how closely
it is taken as approximating some mythical truth. The criterion shifts from
what is true to what is useful. You think in terms of aims, purposes, and
goals, and what is useful to help move toward those aims, purposes, and
goals. You let go of thinking in terms of truth, of what is the truth.

Which is closer to the truth: a hammer or a screwdriver? If you want to
pound in a nail, which is more useful, a hammer or a screwdriver? Which
definition of counselling is closer to the truth? Which definition of
counselling is more useful? In the field of psychotherapy, we are typically
caught looking for what is true. Maybe there is another way of looking at
things. Maybe we can look at things in terms of what is useful, helpful,
practical.

According to this way of looking at things, there can be multiple
perspectives, various positions on issues and questions. Each of these
perspectives and positions can make sense. 'What is counselling?' Here are
some good answers. 'Which answer is correct, more accurate?' They all
can be. 'Which answer-perspective-position is more useful for this or that
purpose?' Ah, now you are thinking in a new way!

I prefer this new way of thinking, although by 'new' I mean new for the
field of counselling and psychotherapy.

This volume is cast within this new way of thinking. It is a different way
of providing an overview–introduction to counselling and psychotherapy.
I think it is a fine way. I suggest that you use this volume for its overview–
introduction to the profession of counselling and psychotherapy. Even if
there is no such profession.

Alvin R. Mahler
University of Ottawa

Acknowledgements

A book of this kind always owes debts to a great many other writers. I hope these have been duly acknowledged by references. In addition, I am grateful to the British Association for Counselling for allowing me access to its archives and to other organisations whose representatives have supplied me with helpful material. I am especially thankful to Hans Eysenck and Bettina Peterseil for their written contributions. The text has also benefited greatly from the advice of Windy Dryden and Tim Bond. Jill Aebi, Geoff Haines, Alex Howard, Brian Thorne and Sheelagh Strawbridge have given me valuable feedback on particular chapters. Warm thanks are also due to those who corresponded with me, sent me material, and/or who answered my elementary questionnaire, including Hans Hoxter, Alvin Mahrer, John Rowan and David Smith. Susan Worsey at Sage Publications has been especially understanding, encouraging and patient, as has Krysia Domaszewicz.

I have in some ways composed a kind of collage of descriptions, definitions, anecdotes and impressions. Accordingly, I have found it necessary to use many references and I apologise to those students in particular who find reference-ridden texts off-putting. I have also sought to place counselling in some sort of historical and interdisciplinary context and I therefore own, in advance, any errors or inadequacies in those intellectual territories where I am obviously a relative stranger. I believe the risk of error is outweighed by the need to attempt an overview, however imperfect, of the subject. I trust too that my switching sometimes from a broad brush perspective to a fine tooth-comb focus will be understood as an attempt to put the question of the book into pertinent perspectives.

As always, my wife Marie and sons Jack and Owen have provided more implicit support than they could know.

Formal acknowledgements are due to: Oxford University Press for permission to reproduce extracts from the *Shorter Oxford English Dictionary* and the *Oxford English Dictionary*; and to Faber and Faber Ltd and Farrar, Straus & Giroux, Inc for permission to reproduce an extract from 'This Be The Verse' by Philip Larkin.

For Marie, Jack and Owen

1

Introduction

My subtitle conveys, I hope, the message that counselling, however it may ultimately be defined, can be interpreted as both good and questionable news. At the very least, it is problematic and demands our critical attention. This book is intended to be a critical enquiry into the field of the talking therapies. I make it a priority to try to convince you that what you are about to read, far from being an irrelevant aside in the otherwise colourful literature of counselling, is of central importance. I write as a practising counsellor and a trainer and supervisor of counsellors, not as a cynical or ill-informed outsider. Yet I also write from a position of temperamental scepticism and with a passion, I hope, for engaging in what the psychotherapist Yalom (1989) has called 'at bottom a truth-seeking venture'. The psychological therapies and good critical enquiry, whatever else they may do, undoubtedly seek to uncover buried or obscured truths and to promote new perspectives on the way we conduct our lives and our work. It is better that counsellors fully embrace critical perspectives on their own work than deny that they are valid (Howard, 1995; Spinelli, 1994).

Counselling, along with psychotherapy, is a fast growing field, exciting hopes for remedies in its clients and for meaningful employment in trainees. Apparently, therefore, exactly what counselling *is* should be fairly widely understood. It may be the case that the general public roughly, intuitively, knows what counselling is, but I have become convinced as a counsellor and supervisor of other counsellors that the term 'counselling' and the activities that go on under that name are problematic. I am concerned about the low level of critical thought that is often brought to bear on questions such as 'What is counselling?', 'What is psychotherapy?', 'Who is to say what good practice is?', 'What is neurosis (or a 'problem in living')?' and also 'Who decides what counselling and mental health are?'. An activity that holds out hope to distressed people, that can involve a great deal of money passing hands, and that makes high moral, intellectual and emotional demands on its practitioners, cannot simply carry on pragmatically, enthusiastically and urgently 'enabling' its clients or 'curing souls' without addressing some of its own big questions.

One of the big questions presented to counsellors in training concerns the acquisition of mental disturbance and how it may, according to one theory and another, be remedied. This is the great implicit promise of counselling and psychotherapy, surely, that some sort of remedy is at hand. It is assumed perhaps that this question can be comfortably answered within traditional forms of discourse and the possibility that a kind of species pathology (more pervasive than individual human problems) may be involved is not usually taken seriously. This level of pathology is what Bohm (1994) refers to as a 'systemic flaw' in human thought itself. The novelist Luke Rhinehart, in *The Search for the Dice Man*, offers the following succinct summary of the human condition, which suggests that counsellors, among others, may be enmeshed in the problem itself:

> Somehow somewhere human beings seem to have built into them an unhappiness-creating mechanism. . . . Since the sickness permeates everything we do, it must be inherent in everything we do – in the very way we think about ourselves and our lives, in the way we make or don't make decisions, in the way see or experience life, *in the very way we try to cure ourselves.* There is something fundamentally wrong with the way we normally live our lives and we'd sort of like to find out what it is. (Rhinehart, 1994: 251, emphasis added)

In the writing of the *Dictionary of Counselling* (Feltham and Dryden, 1993) I began to realise just how thorny the issues are surrounding consensual understanding and definitions in this field. I also became intrigued with the subject of how new fields of knowledge emerge, or how and by whom they are invented and appropriated. I believe that in one sense the term 'counselling' simply validates the wish of one person to air and discuss their concerns, in a stressful and often unfriendly society, with another person. Consider how difficult it would be for most of us to say even to a close friend, 'Look, can I just talk seriously with you for a while about something that's troubling me, and will you please listen to me and not reassure or humour me?'. 'Counselling' as 'facilitated' by a 'counsellor' may often be no more than a good friend could offer, were he or she to assent to the above request.

It seems astonishing that in a field like counselling and psychotherapy, with all its psychological, socio-economic, epistemological and other ramifications, few people stand back to ask, 'What's going on here?'. You only have to ask a few counsellors or counsellors-in-training, for example, 'What is counselling?' to discover that any answers that may be forthcoming are quite likely to be muddled, vague, uncertain or defensive. If, as a client, you ask your counsellor or psychotherapist, 'What is counselling/psychotherapy?' you may well meet (a) an 'analytic' silence, (b) a 'rabbinic' question: 'What do *you* think it is?', (c) a negative reply: 'It's not me telling you what to do', or (d) a vague statement such as 'Well, it's an opportunity for you to explore any issues of concern to you'. Some counsellors opt for the cunningly congruent reply: 'Well, I know what *I* think counselling is, and I know that everyone has their own idea, but I'm most interested in what *you* think it might be, and how you think it could help you.' I hope these examples begin to demonstrate, at least, that what counselling is is not a straightforward matter. I believe it is a complex, problematic enterprise which, on ethical, political, philosophical and other grounds, deserves to be aired and discussed. Just think of it – at this very moment, an incalculable number of people are sitting in private rooms engaged in 'counselling' and 'psychotherapy', yet we cannot agree on what these are!

Transactional analysts sometimes like to adopt the attitude of 'thinking Martian', or visualising yourself observing an activity as if you were an extra-terrestrial trying to make sense of some earthling phenomenon. So, imagine that you are in outer space, looking through your advanced observational equipment at Planet Earth. Your lens is able to focus down on and into human houses. It picks up the scene of two people in a room, gesticulating and talking. One is talking more than the other. You activate your translation technology and learn that the speaker is recounting what his wife said to him yesterday and how that reminds him of the way his mother used to talk to him when he was five years old. He appears very absorbed in his narrative. Simultaneously, your observational probes pick up scenes of famine in other parts of the Earth, ecological damage, local wars, disease, immense suffering and rhetoric-spinning governments. You are able to tune into the goings-on in many households and you marvel at the domestic tensions and dramas. Thinking Martian, you try to relate the scene of the two people engrossed in their talking about the distant memories of one of them, to other Earth phenomena. The distressed speaker says, 'Well, I didn't know how much was inside me,' hands some bundled papers to the other person, and leaves the house. A few blocks away, a man beats his wife; a woman has a heart attack; just over the sea, a small village is destroyed by soldiers; and higher up, over there, a hole in a protective ozone layer is growing visibly larger.

This is, of course, a long way from 'What is counselling?' Or is it? As I hope to show in this book, counselling is integrally concerned with adaptation to conditions on Planet Earth. In fact, counselling which concerns itself explicitly with 'human potential', the 'transpersonal', 'deep ecology' and so on, is a far from rare phenomenon. In their book *We've Had a Hundred Years of Psychotherapy and the World's Getting Worse*, Hillman and Ventura (1992) make the far from flippant point that the psychological therapies appear to be encouraging many human beings to spend a great deal of their time, energy and money on internal, intra-psychic matters to the detriment of caring for the physical environment. Counsellors, if they are indeed engaged in a truth-seeking venture, might be asked 'What is counselling doing in relation to the deterioration of the world?' and 'May not the collectively deteriorating world be more sickening to your clients than their individual psycho-archaeologies?' Such questions are not posed to put counselling down but to challenge and enliven it. It is possible that one of the reasons for the expansion in the demand for counselling is that many people are, or feel they are, lost in a world without God, without any obvious moral authority or governmental integrity, without strong parents or educators and without any guiding philosophy. It *may* be that one of the main current premises on which counselling ideology rests (that individual autonomy is achievable, desirable and the key to happiness) is incorrect or off the mark. This possibility of error is one that will be examined later.

Most of us, counsellors and clients alike, do not spend our time thinking Martian. Let us now take another perspective on counselling, which we might call everyday thinking. Many of us experience our lives as a struggle from day to day; we semi-anxiously negotiate our way compromisingly through urban and domestic jungles of interpersonal, occupational and existential obstacles. Some of our lives turn into the kind of intolerable existence depicted with such searing poignancy in Munch's painting *The Cry*. Some of these sufferers turn to counsellors and other helpers; their distress is acute, possibly more maddening than hunger and certainly more preoccupying than distant problems with ozone layers. People who are so distressed are unable to think Martian or indeed to think anything that is beyond their own pain. It would be quite absurd and ineffective for anyone aiming to help them to attempt to call their attention to issues of global concern. There is without doubt a significant role for counsellors or others engaging in urgent, pragmatic responses to human suffering. People suffering with the intensity I have described may very well be uninterested in truth-seeking or in the state of the planet. The possibility of error here, then, is to think that all clients' problems must be related to higher concerns.

The word 'counselling', which may be used both by people ruminating on their relationship with the cosmos and by people agonising over how they can pay their mortgage, survive their divorce or stay out of prison, is clearly a word of many applications. Many of the possible definitions are given in Chapter 2. I must make it clear here that throughout this book I often shall use the words counselling, psychotherapy and therapy interchangeably, except when differentiation is crucial. When I refer to counselling, I am referring to the talking-and-listening therapies generally, and even to those therapies which deal with bodywork or psychodramatic phenomena. I am not, however, concerned in any depth with primarily somatic or physical medicines or therapies, whether homeopathic or allopathic. My main subject here is psychological problems, problems in living, and the therapies which claim to alleviate or radically transform them.

2

Defining Counselling

Counselling is hard to define but there is a great deal of it about

Timms and Timms (1982)

The importance and difficulty of defining counselling

For many people, what counselling is is apparently axiomatic, or so near-axiomatic that the question appears 'academic'. It may be considered quite obvious that counselling is a form of help for people who need it; that counselling usually involves two people discussing the problems or concerns that one of them has and the other is willing to listen to. This, no doubt, is obvious to some, but not to others. Counselling in the context of personnel management, for example, can still carry the meaning of interviewing in relation to disciplinary procedures, where the willingness of the 'counsellor' to be a listener may be very limited. Counselling still carries its traditional meaning of advice-giving and many dictionaries still define it in this way. Even more specifically, counselling, or 'counsel' has legal connotations. (I have a copy of an old book called *The Home Counsellor*, published by Odhams but carrying no publication date, which is entirely concerned with facts and advice on tenancies, motoring offences, marriage law, conveyancing, hire purchase agreements, and so on.) Advertisements appear in the press for 'camp counselors' in the USA which give the impression that a counsellor is some sort of childminder, playleader or games-organiser. Building societies and other financial institutions now claim to provide 'financial counselling' which on closer inspection appears usually to refer to selling. Counselling is not alone in lending its name to diverse activities; Clare and Thompson (1981) suggest that psychotherapy falls into a very similar semantic promiscuity. Of course, what all the talking therapies have in common is the confidential context in which they are carried out, a factor which may create undue secrecy, speculation, fantasy and misinformation around the attempt to clarify them.

There are myriad uses of the words 'counselling' and 'counsellor'. The British Association for Counselling (BAC) acknowledges that it has no proprietary rights over these terms. The American Counseling Association (ACA) has no official definition of counselling at all. Clearly, however, the kind of counselling which is of primary concern to organisations like BAC and ACA is the personal, emotional, psychological kind. You might think that it is a simple matter to define and describe counselling which is limited to the psychological kind but this is not the case. In the definitions and commentaries I present in this chapter, I wish to demonstrate that it is extremely difficult to define counselling in a way that fairly, unambiguously and accurately places it beyond misunderstanding and which reasonably distinguishes it from other similar activities.

This problem stems partly from historical factors (divorcing advice from counselling), from semantics (the intrinsic difficulties of defining concepts), from the complications of professionalisation (the need of an emerging profession to invent boundaries which exclude other activities) and also from subjective associationism. By this latter term I mean the tendency for words to 'produce effects in the mind' which 'mingle and interact' to yield variable, rich, often idiosyncratic meanings (Taylor, 1970). It has been said that 'counselling' has a more democratic ring to it, and a less pretentious, less medical tone than 'psychotherapy', for example. It can therefore appeal to those who are more comfortable with such associations. The converse of this is that counselling may be judged to be less rigorous, authoritative, effective or professional than psychotherapy. The point I am making here is that meanings may be infinitely coloured, enriched or misunderstood according to their emotional associations for each individual. A consensual definition of counselling may not be a possibility.

There is one area in which it is crucial to strive for an accurate and non-misleading definition. That is the point of delivery, where counselling is sold and purchased, directly or indirectly. Consumers should not be misled as to what counselling is, what it is based on, what it can and cannot achieve, and so on. Counselling is a service which affects its consumers economically and emotionally. All too frequently, it is not a service for which any measurements of satisfaction are offered. It is sometimes presented as a process by which desired results will *probably*, in some modest degree, be forthcoming. Clients may not be apprised of how long it will take, how much it will cost in the long run, or whether it will in fact work. I believe that any comprehensive definition or description of counselling should refer to these aspects. Providers of counselling should not imply that it is based on more scientific evidence than is warranted. They should not exploit the pain, confusion or neediness of clients by offering exaggerated promotional descriptions of counselling. They should certainly try to avoid seductively vague definitions which may imply that counselling is a sort of mystical panacea. Unfortunately, counselling and psychotherapy are all too often presented in just the ways I suggest they should not be. One of my aims here, then, is to identify such problems and highlight abuses and possible correctives.

Dictionary definitions

I believe that the following extracted definitions and sources of the term 'counselling' and closely related terms are worth gathering. The great variety of historical and contextual nuances add up to a fascinating understanding of the richness and problematic nature of the subject. The overall historical shift from legal to psychological meaning is apparent, along with an important shift from *telling* towards *listening*. At the same time, the broad field of contemporary counselling comprehensively (and sometimes conflictually) embraces many of these meanings.

The *Oxford English Dictionary* (Simpson and Weiner, 1989) defines counselling as:

> giving or taking of counsel; advising; . . . the giving of advice on personal, social, psychological, etc., problems as an occupation; [in psychology] a form of psychotherapy in which the counsellor adopts a permissive and supportive role in enabling a client to solve his or her own problems.

An interesting reference is given to Chaucer's *Wife of Bath's Tale* (1386). In The Prologue, she says:

> Men may conseille a womman to been oon [remain single]
> But conseillyng is no comandement.

This distinction foreshadows many of those being made in our own day between information-giving, advising, coercing, facilitating, and so on.

Under 'counsel', the OED includes the references:

> to counsel a person; to give or offer counsel or advice; . . . to counsel a course or purpose; . . . to advise its adoption or doing; to recommend (a plan, suggestion, etc.); to take counsel with oneself; . . . to take counsel with others; . . . to consider; to consult, deliberate.

We are reminded that 'counsel' has had and still has certain legal connotations. Thus, a counsel is, in the UK, 'a legal adviser; a counsellor-at-law, advocate, or barrister'. The word 'counsel' is linked etymologically with 'consult' and 'council' and has, therefore, a long historical association with the concept of decision-making in various settings.

Under 'counsellor', the OED refers to:

> one who counsels or advises; . . . an official counsellor; an adviser of the sovereign, a member of the King's Council; . . . one who specializes in the counselling of clients.

A reference is given to R. L'Estrange's *Fables*: 'Let All Men of Business be Councellors, Confidents, etc.' (xxi (1714): 29).

Reference is also made to Shakespeare's *Measure for Measure* (I.ii.109) in which Mistress Overdone, a 'bawd' (procuress, or brothel-keeper) is assured that 'Good Counsellors lacke no Clients'. This is a rather amusing reflection on counselling, since in its Shakespearean context it refers metaphorically to the idea that good prostitutes will never want for trade. The likeness between counselling and prostitution (a one-to-one, private, intimate, acceptant, customized service for the relief and satisfaction of one party by another) has been made often enough!

The OED also contains the rarely used word 'counsellable':

Open to counsel; willing to be counselled; . . . to be recommended; advisable.

A reference is given to J. Goodman's *Penit. Pardoned*: 'He requires a perswadable counsellable temper' (III (1713): 310). Such a usage anticipates our own contemporary debates about distinctions, or lack of them, between counselling and persuasion as well as the concept of client motivation, or readiness for and commitment to counselling.

The *Shorter Oxford English Dictionary* (Onions, 1983) offers the following definitions of 'counsel':

> consultation, plan, deliberating body; interchange of opinions; consultation, deliberation; . . . advice, direction, as the result of deliberation; . . . the faculty of counselling; judgement; prudence; sagacity; . . . a secret; a confidence.

We are reminded of the concepts of 'counsel of perfection'; 'evangelical counsels' (the obligations of poverty, chastity and obedience to a religious superior); 'in counsel' (in private, in confidence); 'to keep one's own counsel' (to be reticent about one's intentions, etc.). The popular document known as the *Desiderata*, mistakenly thought to date from 1692, but actually written by American poet Max Ehrmann in 1927, urges readers to 'Take kindly the counsel of the years, gracefully surrendering the things of youth'.

Timms and Timms, in their *Dictionary of Social Welfare* (1982), admitting that 'counselling is hard to define', refer to Sutherland's (1972) view that it is 'a personal relationship in which the counsellor uses his own experience of living to help his client to enlarge his understanding – and so make better decisions'. Timms and Timms point out that counselling is practised in many settings, often by non-professionals 'who have undergone the same or similar experience to those seeking comfort'. They mention the centrality of confidentiality and suggest that counselling is 'usually assumed to be non-directive'.

Dictionary of Counselling

In this, the first specialized dictionary of counselling (Feltham and Dryden, 1993), counselling is defined thus:

> a principled relationship characterised by the application of one or more psychological theories and a recognised set of communication skills, modified by experience, intuition and other interpersonal factors, to clients' intimate concerns, problems or aspirations. Its predominant ethos is one of facilitation rather than of advice-giving or coercion. It may be of very brief or long duration, take place in an organisational or private practice setting and may or may not overlap with practical, medical and other matters of personal welfare.

It continues:

> It is both a distinctive activity undertaken by people agreeing to occupy the roles of counsellor and client (see, for example, 'co-counselling') and it is an emergent profession. . . . It is a service sought by people in distress or in some degree of

confusion who wish to discuss and resolve these in a relationship which is more disciplined and confidential than friendship, and perhaps less stigmatising than helping relationships offered in traditional medical or psychiatric settings.

It goes on to note that 'there are many schools of counselling but all share respect for the client's autonomy' and that 'counselling aims to promote healthy functioning as well as having a problem-solving focus'. It further distinguishes between counselling and advice-giving, information-giving and psychotherapy. These latter distinctions are discussed fully in Chapter 3 of this present book.

This definition reflects features of the period in which it is written, when professionalization of counselling is spawning many debates, working parties and interest groups concerned with differentiating counselling from other activities. Counselling is viewed, therefore, as *principled* (an ethical endeavour with strict boundaries); which draws on theories of psychotherapy and personality (it is a serious, professional activity resting partly on knowledge from the social sciences); which is practised according to certain learned (not innate or casually acquired) interpersonal skills; but which none the less includes the values of practical, personal experience and intuition. It should not be confused with advice-giving, but neither should it be thought inferior to, or even essentially different from, psychotherapy. It is markedly different from friendship or psychiatry. It may be practised both professionally and simply by adult agreement between equals. Its main target group is the distressed and confused but it is also an educative endeavour.

Consider and compare one of Freud's early (circa 1917) descriptions of psychoanalysis:

> Nothing takes place in a psychoanalytic treatment but an interchange of words between the patient and the analyst. The patient talks, tells of his past experiences and present impressions, complains, confesses to his wishes and his emotional impulses. The doctor listens, tries to direct the patient's processes of thought, exhorts, forces his attention in certain directions, gives him explanations and observes the reactions of understanding or rejection which he in this way provokes in him. (Freud, 1974: 41)

Freud went on to qualify this by saying that words have magical power and that the analyst has a special insight, understanding and stature. In Chapter 3 I ask whether counselling really is different from psychotherapy, psychoanalysis and other forms of talking-and-listening which are dedicated to analysing and ameliorating human distress.

Clients' definitions and descriptions

Clients rarely, of course, formulate or publish definitions of counselling. Their overriding interest is in resolving their personal difficulties or crises, overcoming life-long preoccupations and traumas and gaining new levels of understanding and freedom. By their search for and acceptance of counselling or talking therapies generally, people do of course indicate that they believe in and value these activities to some extent. However, the fact that counselling is valued and desired by a small proportion of the public does not implicitly mean that it is understood. Let us suppose that many satisfied clients feel, without being able to articulate why, that their own experiences of talking with a designated counsellor have been helpful. This, I think, is one of the most common reactions of the satisfied: 'my counsellor just helped me to understand things better, to accept myself'. One of my own clients volunteered the statement that 'It's quite a relief to have someone listen to you who doesn't know you, and who doesn't have preconceived ideas about what you should do'. This is the appreciative, modestly positive kind of unsolicited testimonial that probably quite accurately summarises much of counselling.

Winmill (1994) argues that clients in fact have their own preconceived idea of what counselling is, which is very often that it is a prescriptive activity addressing particular problems and steering clear of uncomfortable emotions. 'No amount of postulation about what counselling and psycho-therapy are will be conclusive if . . . the frame of reference, wherein the definition lies, is with the prospective client' (1994: 256). This writer considers that first-time clients 'contain the introject (sent down by our western culture) that to bear witness to emotional pain is wrong'. Because of this, they seek comfort in labels like counselling, and counsellors and therapists should avoid colluding with them: the reality of a thorough-going therapy which deals necessarily with emotional depths avoids entrapment in intellectualisation. To seek to define is, in this view, to fall into a trap. Winmill is not alone in taking the view that, in effect, counselling and psychotherapy can only be defined authentically within the process itself: you will know what it is when you stop asking (defensively) and start experiencing.

There are positive reactions to counselling and psychotherapy which tend towards the hyperbolic in their praise. I refer here to the 'It saved my life' kind of statements. During the anti-psychiatry movement of the 1960s, for example, many published accounts appeared of people who had apparently experienced something akin to psychological rebirth after undergoing radical forms of talking therapy, when previous psychiatric treatment had either damaged them or simply failed to help them. In truth, these accounts are associated more often with the humanistic and existential psychotherapies than with the average analysand, although many of Freud's early cases read like minor miracles and Herman (1988) is in parts effusive in her praise of her Kleinian analyst, for example. Masson (1988) argues that no matter how positively clients describe their experiences in therapy, this is not objective evidence that it is a good thing, it demonstrates only that they are enthusiastic.

Reports of this nature often have a great deal to say about the person of the counsellor or therapist and their qualities of warmth, understanding and containment. Grierson (1990), speaking as a client, says how much she valued the counsellor's acceptance, strength, calmness, caring and understanding. Being believed, respected, understood and engaged with honestly seem to be important ingredients of successful counselling for the client. We might then say that counselling (when successful) is a relationship which is experienced as healing and it is a relationship which is offered and entered into formally, rather than casually or by chance. A typical client's inferential definition of successful counselling would seem to highlight relationship factors far above techniques. This is confirmed by Howe (1993), who argues from analyses of clients' experiences that they mainly seek the chance to talk with someone capable of understanding them, who is interested in them, who is warm, friendly and genuine. One partial definition of the non-verbal aspect of counselling might be simply that it is 'hearing another's pain'. Perhaps it should also be said to be about hearing another's experiences and differences. Clients appreciate having their feelings validated within a dialogue with a stranger. Oldfield's (1983) study of clients' experiences, good and bad, portrayed a mixture of hope, appreciation and bafflement.

What does counselling feel like to the counsellor during the counselling session itself? Obviously this varies greatly from counsellor to counsellor. My own experience is that it can be, by turns, deeply engrossing, frustrating, shapeless, complex and challenging. I bring what knowledge, experience and creativity I possess to every counselling encounter and sometimes it proceeds a little 'by the book', but more often I feel that I am negotiating highly idiosyncratic and unknown territory. Does this particular client need or want something resembling commonsense and reassurance? Is another client benefiting, as he or she appears to be, from open-ended exploration, sometimes painful, sometimes apparently aimless? Sometimes many weeks may go by with a sense of being in a fog, which gradually or suddenly clears to reveal a significant new focus and real progress. Counselling at such times may more resemble parenting or sculpting in progress than anything that can ever be well defined. There are, too, the performance aspects of counselling: at times the counsellor may be 'on the ball', full of presence of mind and healing creativity; at other times he or she may be struggling, somewhat preoccupied, or unable to find rapport, understanding or helpful techniques.

According to folklore, 'two heads are better than one' and 'a problem shared is a problem halved'. We have a 'heart to heart' about something of importance, or a 'tête-à-tête'. We understand the need to 'get it off your chest,' and 'not to bottle it up'. Weatherhead (1952) alludes to many poetical and literary references to the value of intimate conversations with confidants. Bacon said 'This communicating of a man's self to his friend . . . cutteth griefs in halfes'. Spenser, in the *Fairie Queen*, suggests that 'he often finds present help who does his grief impart'. Clearly, then, an understanding of the value of and perhaps need for unburdening to others, has existed over the ages. Anna O, the patient of Breuer whose treatment was so central to the formulation of psychoanalysis, says to Breuer, in

Freeman's (1990: 31) reconstruction of events, 'When I tell you everything on my mind, it's like chimney-sweeping'. Historically, this process has usually been an informal rather than formal one but often finds itself labelled in the present age as counselling or therapy.

Critics' definitions of counselling

I have outlined some of the more positive and generous definitions and descriptions of counselling and therapy. I now propose to look at some of the ways in which the critics of counselling perceive and write about it. Not all my examples are from commentators who regard themselves as negative critics of the talking therapies, so it would be more accurate to talk about critical definitions or views of counselling. The purpose of including these views is to gain as complete a picture as possible of what counselling may be, or of counselling as it is perceived by a range of observers at this moment in history.

Take, for example, the comment of Gaie Houston (1991), who is herself a counsellor/therapist:

> In counselling, what we are engaged in is, for the most part, guesswork. We do no more than guess at what makes people tick, however much we turn our guesses into grand-sounding, quasi-religious articles of faith.

Houston is not advocating uninformed guesswork, but a loving, listening kind of guesswork that is always prepared to learn from clients, colleagues and researchers; but guesswork, none the less. The accent here is on humility and a refusal to make dishonest claims. It is well acknowledged by counsellors and therapists that they are at least partly guided in their work by hunches and 'clinical conjectures'.

Raimy (1950) defined therapy as 'an unidentified technique applied to unspecified problems with unpredictable outcomes'. This view differs from Houston's in that it seems to espouse cynicism rather than humility, and fits roughly with Eysenck's perennial rebuttal of the claims of therapy and counselling. It is a negative definition, telling us that therapy is a non-method which can promise nothing with any certainty in relation to problems which are ill-defined. Counselling is a vague affair here, perhaps, but not necessarily pernicious or unwanted!

Friedrich (1975) reviewed the histories and remedies of many people suffering from mental illness and came to some sobering conclusions about therapy. He refers to group therapy as a *Kaffeeklatsch* (something like small-talk over coffee) and is very negative about the outcomes of therapy:

> All that any psychiatrist can really do is to listen to unhappy people and try to help them deal with their difficulties. Which means that even a wise psychiatrist is not very different from a wise priest or a wise parent or a wise friend. It also means that even a wise psychiatrist often can't do very much to solve the victim's problems. (1975: 355)

In Chapter 3 the alleged differences between counselling and psychotherapy are spelled out. According to many psychotherapists, counselling
may be negatively defined as a lesser form of psychotherapy. Ernest
Gellner (1992), in spite of his general scepticism regarding all talking
therapy, decides that counselling is 'Freud and water', a seriously diluted
form of psychoanalysis or perhaps even a dilletante's rendition of it.
Similar metaphors have been employed in an effort to bring psychoanalytically oriented psychotherapy into disrepute when compared with
pure psychoanalyis. The theme is that somewhere there is a pure, honest,
effective, original theory and practice of therapy which is appropriated,
watered-down and served up to deceive unsuspecting customers into
believing that they are imbibing the real thing.

Stafford-Clark (1952) aligns counselling with the kind of psychotherapy
which helps people adjust to their circumstances. He speaks of
'reassurance, support, understanding, and guidance, which can be said
to include general counselling of the Dutch uncle variety at the most
simple end of the scale' (Stafford-Clark, 1952: 168). Harris (1987) too
describes counselling as 'time, sympathy and a willingness to help' and
reminds us about 'quack remedies' for baldness and stammering as if
counselling is pretty much in the same camp. So, it is both simple 'tea and
sympathy' and also, more sinisterly, a form of deception.

Sutherland (1991), in the *Macmillan Dictionary of Psychology*, gives
many satirical or dismissive definitions. A psychoanalyst is 'a person who
takes money from another on the pretence that it is for the other's own
good' (1991: 352). Psychotherapy is defined in straightforward terms but
Sutherland suggests that of the many forms of therapy, 'most of them are
of doubtful value' (1991: 356). Sutherland approves to some extent of
cognitive therapy, but adds that 'in practice, it is often unclear how the
approach of the cognitive therapist differs from that of most laymen
confronted with mental disorder in others' (1991: 78); in other words, he
regards it as basically consisting of encouragement and commonsense.
Counselling is equated with advice-giving, and 'may be obtained on almost
every aspect of one's life from grooming to gardening, and from coping
with one's career to coping with leisure time' (1991: 99). Sutherland writes
not only as a psychologist but also as an arch-critic of therapy, following
his own experience of mental distress and a series of unsatisfactory
therapies (Sutherland, 1992).

I have seen and heard definitions which imply that counselling is
amateurish, well-meaning do-goodery, a form of social control, a quasi-
religious activity, and ordinary human helpfulness dressed up in the
emperor's clothes of professionalisation. Counselling and psychotherapy
have also been equated with brainwashing and cult phenomena (Sargant,
1957). An account of scientology in the *Guardian* (21.9.94) claims that
scientology's opponents warn: 'the cult gains a psychological hold over
people by the counselling process, called auditing'. Another newspaper
usage also puts counselling in a dubious light: 'Working-class communities

have always had their resident 'tellers' or 'speywifes', motherly kitchen
mystics who provide counselling as much as prediction for their clients.' In
the same article on the spuriousness of many New Age remedies, the writer
suggests that mass astrology and mass gambling (the National Lottery for
example) are 'sustained by a bottomless despair about controlling the
direction of one's life' (*Guardian* 4.1.95).

Roiphe's (1994: 9) challenge to feminism and political correctness
generally includes a description of current American university campus
life. 'There are fliers and counselors and videotapes telling us how not to
get AIDS and how not to get raped, where not to wander and what signals
not to send.' In this scenario, educative counselling is just one more part
of the contemporary landscape of political correctness and echoes
uncomfortably the pervasive voice of Big Brother or Sister.

3

Counselling's Cousins

There are many conversational and helping activities and relationships that resemble counselling. There are also activities which may appear different but have the same intentions or outcomes. These issues were analysed inconclusively by the American Psychology Association's Committee on Definition in the 1950s (Whiteley, 1984) and have received more recent attention by Russell et al. (1992) in Britain. Broadly speaking, there are two diametrically opposed views on this overlap factor. First, counselling organisations and training institutes increasingly seek to distinguish counselling from similar activities, arguing that it has a distinct professional identity. This viewpoint leads to, and fuels, much of the current thrust towards professionalisation in the form of counsellor accreditation and in the registration of psychotherapists. Interestingly, those seeking to make such distinctions seem clearer about the differences between counselling and advice-giving, befriending and so on, than about those between counselling and psychotherapy. I think it is fair to say that in a hierarchy of kudos and prestige, psychotherapy tends to rank more highly than advice-giving and befriending. Counsellors are often keen to distance themselves from advisers and to equate themselves with psychotherapists.

The second viewpoint, which has been put often enough by writers like Szasz (1988) and Howard (1992), is that counselling and psychotherapy are not ultimately distinguishable from other interpersonal activities or relationships like friendship, teaching, training, and so on. Any distinction which is claimed stems from a covert drive towards professionalisation and its benefits for practitioners, rather than from observable and significant actual differences, according to this argument. On the face of it, the debate between the critics of counselling and its proponents is an insoluble conflict, each party attributing dark motives to the other. In this chapter I wish to scrutinize alleged and actual differences between the talking therapies and other forms of helpful interpersonal relationship, in the hope of clarifying some of the issues further.

Advising and influencing

As we have seen, counselling has historically been largely associated with advice-giving in the domains of monarchy, law and everyday life. Advising, however, is not identical with commanding since advice can be heeded and acted upon, or ignored. Indeed, Nowell-Smith (1954) distinguishes between instruction, advice, exhortation and command. Advice may be conveyed in strong terms ('My advice to you, young man, is to get a job immediately') or in very tentative terms ('I would advise you to consider carefully the options before you act'). Much everyday advice is offered in the form of 'If I were you, I would . . .'. Beginning trainee counsellors are sometimes apt to respond to the problems presented by their peers with impulsive 'Why don't you . . .?' or 'Have you thought about . . .?' questions. A good part of counselling training seems to be constituted by the elimination of such naive problem-solving responses and their replacement with more sophisticated, and hopefully more effective, interventions.

There are occasions on which we all need instructions or advice. If I ask for travel directions from someone who is familiar with routes from London to Oxford, I appreciate getting straightforward advice ('The most direct route is x, but y is often better because there's less traffic, nicer scenery, etc.'). This is information which includes implicit advice. On occasions like this, I would find it quite inappropriate to be interrogated on why I want to go to Oxford, or to have my question reflected back to me. However, even in this fairly straightforward example, we can see how advice might backfire. If I take the advice to use route y and my journey takes much longer than I had expected, I may very well blame my adviser. More seriously, I may be advised, for example, to plead guilty in a court of law to an offence I have not committed, in order to get it over with quickly, pay a small fine and keep publicity to a minimum. When this backfires and I receive a more serious sentence and greater publicity than I had been led to expect, then I will feel justifiably displeased with the advice I followed. Daily life may be filled with more trivial examples of asking for advice on what to wear, what to eat and buy.

In the UK, Citizens' Advice Bureaux are so called largely on the basis of *information* conveyed to clients on legal, financial, housing and related issues. Such information has been gathered according to demand, is as accurate as possible and is conveyed as the best information available. Apprising someone of the information most pertinent to their particular concern is not the same as telling them that they must or ought to act on it. In the matter of personal debt, for example, there are recognised procedures for dealing systematically with it. An adviser can pass on this information and instruct clients how to implement it if they wish to. Investigating the possible psychological reasons for someone getting into debt or resisting getting out of it is another matter.

Contemporary mainstream counselling, in most of its forms, distinguishes itself from advice-giving. One of the clearest examples of this is that in some student welfare services there are designated 'student advisers' and 'student counsellors'. The former deal with finances, accommodation, immigration law, and other matters, and the latter with personal, psychological issues. Many welfare-oriented organisations with limited resources do not make this distinction and staff designated as counsellors, welfare officers and staff support workers perform counselling, advisory, advocacy and other functions interchangeably.

Another distinction, however, is that between telling clients what they should do, and facilitating their own efforts to arrive at their own decisions. When Horney (1950) exposed the 'tyranny of the should' and Rogers (1951) promoted the individual's 'organismic valuing process', 'internal locus of evaluation' and individual autonomy generally, classical counselling ideology was born. Western society, in an era and mood of post-war anti-authoritarian, anti-fascistic feeling, was perhaps ripe for such an individualistic, permissive ideology. So enduring has this feeling been, that even decades later a great deal of counselling is understood or caricatured as being mainly non-directive. Many clients and potential clients have heard and believe that 'counsellors do not tell you what to do'. Many counsellors-in-training, especially during their first exposure to clients in placements, appear to bend over backwards to avoid even infinitesimal instances of influencing or advising clients. However uncertain of what counselling *is*, many people are now sure of what counselling *isn't* − advice-giving! It should be noted that this understanding of counselling or of being helped is not, however, universal, since people from many cultures value and expect advice and even authoritative commands, and are confused by the non-directive assumptions of much of western psychology.

One of the earliest writers to claim a clear distinction between coun- selling and advice was Rollo May (1992). Following Freud, May rejected, in his original text in the 1930s, the role of the mentor in counselling and therapy. May argued that advice-giving 'violates the autonomy of personality' and is 'always superficial'. The task of counselling, as of psychotherapy, was viewed by May as the transformation of the personality. It is important to note, however, that May condoned the appropriate use of suggestion, including laying down 'all the constructive alternatives before the counselee'. Rigorous Freudians, according to Smith (1990), strenuously avoid suggestion at all, in part because they would then be colluding with their patients' seeing them as idealized parental figures. Less rigorous non-Freudians, however, 'often without realising it . . . convince the patient through seduction or intimidation to make the desired changes' (Smith, 1990: 27). This begs the question of whether psychoanalysis is truly any less seductive or intimidating than other therapies, but this is not the place to pursue it. It is interesting that Aveline (1992) cautions against the countertransference tendency to want to give 'uncalled-for advice as a means of appearing all-wise'; one can also, surely, fall into a kind of countertransference neutrality, cleverness with interpret- ations or any other way of appearing wise. Most counselling training probably still broadly promotes a non-advisory or even anti-advisory attitude. However, the more pragmatic schools of counselling, particularly the cognitive-behavioural, may be inclined to view the judicious use of commonsense or technical advice as harmless, permissible and often beneficial.

The dangers of giving advice include the following: that it may be incorrect or unwise, and may backfire; that it may constitute a form of collusion (reinforcing the client's false belief in his own helplessness or confusion); that it fails to note, unearth and work with the psycho-dynamics underlying requests for advice; and that it cheats the client of a valuable opportunity of discovering his or her own potent decision-making resources. While these may be valid objections, the dangers of withholding advice must also be considered. It would be foolish, if not unethical, to withhold crucial information or advice when the client is extremely vulnerable or confused, or when she is not likely to know certain things, or arrive at important conclusions, without assistance. In a study of clients receiving 'marriage guidance counselling' (Patten and Walker, 1990) it was found that over 90 per cent of those interviewed believed they would be helped if they were given the counsellor's opinion of their problems, their marriage and of marriage in general. It is integral to certain approaches to counselling to use written techniques, homework assignments and general encouragement of risk-taking, behaviour monitoring and behaviour change, and in these cases suggestion, advice and persuasion may be unavoidable aspects of such approaches. Directiveness on the part of practitioners within these approaches may be mitigated by what personal construct therapists call the 'invitational mode' and cognitive therapists call 'collaborative empiricism'.

Finally, it has been pointed out that no counselling can be entirely free of the counsellor's influence. If I employ a form of wording like 'You might want to consider the advantages of doing x' (as opposed to doing y), this may represent a form of concealed or subtle advice. If I tell the client 'I don't want to withhold my opinion sadistically, but I think it's more valuable if you find your own solution', then I am subtly advising the client that self-made choices are invariably better than others (which may not always be the case). If I resolve never to say 'should' or 'ought', as most counselling trainers advocate, I may resort to other, apparently correct phraseology. Counselling trainees might do well to stop and think what is being conveyed by trainers who advocate avoidance of the 'should' word. 'You should always refrain from telling clients what they should do' – isn't this in some way the paradoxical or nonsensical message being conveyed?

In rational emotive behaviour therapy, for example, therapists tend to say 'If you want to achieve your goals, then you had better do x'. This form of wording supposedly avoids the tyranny of the should, since it advocates that the client has a better chance of achieving his or her goals by taking certain decisions, or by adopting certain thoughts, rather than others; it involves no judgement. However, such wording may easily become covert advice-giving. The same is true in transactional analysis, where, for example, parental injunctions are often tracked down and weeded out, supposedly to be replaced by the client's own freely chosen 'Adult' self-statements. In practice, it is difficult to say whether the original parental injunctions are not simply replaced covertly by a new set of supposedly therapeutic injunctions. In order to avoid falling into the trap of inadvertent influencing, writers such as Ivey et al. (1980) advocate realistic and beneficial acceptance on the part of therapists that they do exert influence and are wise to be aware of and to utilise their power on the client's behalf. Frank (1963) is clear that persuasion and influence generally is a central feature of counselling. The humanistic therapist Jourard (1971: 141) happily acknowledged that his therapeutic repertoire included 'giving advice, lecturing, laughing, becoming angry, interpreting, telling my fantasies, asking questions – in short, doing whatever occurs to me during the therapeutic session in response to the other person'.

Friendship

Affinity, love, liking, intimacy, mutual attraction and acceptance are some of the concepts associated with friendship. We are familiar with the discrimination between real friends and casual acquaintances or fair-weather friends. Friendship implies enduring acceptance, safety and loyalty. A real friend will come to your aid if you need her. A real friend will not talk about you behind your back. She will understand you and your problems. But your counsellor is not your friend. Counsellors make clear 'boundaries between the counselling relationship and any other kind of relationship' (BAC, 1992). Traditionally, counsellors and psychothera-pists do not offer their services to close personal friends, although Freud certainly did so, and the psychotherapist Arnold Lazarus admits to doing so, for example (Dryden, 1991). Freud wrote to Jung, for example: 'Eitington is the only one I can talk to here; we take walks in the evening and I analyse him just in passing' (McGuire, 1991: 164). Today, the blurring of boundaries between friendship and counselling would compromise or damage both kinds of relationship, it is said. This would be particularly true of psychodynamic counselling, in which a rather unnatural relationship is a therapeutic prerequisite, in order to allow for transference phenomena to arise and to be dealt with cleanly and effectively.

The core conditions of person-centred counselling in particular, and of counselling generally, are said to be acceptance, genuineness and empathy. The terms 'non-possessive warmth' and even 'love' are also sometimes used. On the face of it, these conditions would seem to be present in much friendship too. I accept my friend as he is, I sometimes tell him how I feel about him, and I often know what he is experiencing. At least, good friendships may contain high levels of the core conditions. Friendships may be therapeutic, they are certainly sustaining, but they are not 'counselling' – or are they? The poet Alexander Pope refers in *Imitations of Horace* to a Mr Fortescue, who 'wert my guide, philosopher and friend'. I personally know an experienced counsellor who has a long-standing friendship with another experienced counsellor, and who turns to his friend for his own personal therapy and supervision; this is, of course, against the hallowed rules of the profession, but seems to have no ill effects in this case. I suspect that in fact such unofficial arrangements are not at all uncommon. A theological writer on spiritual direction uses the term 'soul friend' of the spiritual guide or director. Critics of psycho-therapy, like Szasz and Eysenck, suggest that therapy is not ultimately distinct from relationships like friendship at all, and that any success it may have is probably indistinguishable from the support and advice derived from good friendships. A newspaper article carried the story of a woman who had had an unsatisfactory experience in counselling. On abandoning her counselling, she had subsequently decided to invite a good friend out to dinner at certain intervals; in return for paying for the meal, she arranged for her friend to listen and respond helpfully to her problems. Apparently this was a satisfactory arrangement. This example overcomes the objection that friendship cannot be disciplined in the way counselling is.

Counselling is distinguished from befriending, which is an activity often undertaken by volunteers working with charitable organisations. Be-frienders may either staff drop-in centres, arrange scheduled meetings or visit people's homes. Often the clients are the bereaved, mentally ill, lonely, or disadvantaged in other ways. The Samaritans describe their work as befriending, and sometimes as listening therapy or befriending therapy, rather than counselling. They aim to be supportive in a dedicated manner. Similarly, in the field of HIV and AIDS, there is a well-established system of 'buddying', or the assignment of a supportive friend to someone who has HIV positive status, often on a longterm basis. In Alcoholics Anonymous, too, there are 'sponsors', or fellow 'recovering alcoholics' who offer a form of committed support. (There is a debate in the world of alcoholism counselling as to whether a professional counsellor who is *not* a recovering alcoholic can be truly empathic and helpful.) None of these activities or relationships is considered to be counselling, although all of them are valuably therapeutic. According to BAC, befriending differs from counselling in that it is usually not an explicitly agreed, contractual relationship and does not usually require in-depth training (BAC, 1987).

Friendships and friendship-like relationships probably help more people with their problems in living than do formal counselling and psycho-therapy. On the other hand, even many people with supportive friends and relatives seek out counsellors. Sometimes this is because they 'don't want to be a burden' on friends; often people believe, for example, that their friends will not want to hear about their depression (but a counsellor is paid to hear about it). Psychotherapy has, of course, been called 'the purchase of friendship', and also 'professionalised neighbourliness'. Now, friends probably do not possess the experience and training of counsellors and may often feel at a loss for what to say to a depressed friend. They *may* be too 'involved', too lacking in impartiality, and so on, to be able to help effectively. This may be one of the main reasons why the 'stranger value' of the paid (or unpaid) counsellor is necessary and effective. However, as Hymer (1988) has suggested, people may often confide in cab drivers for this reason, rather than in friends *or* counsellors. It is easy to forget, also, that counsellors *act as if* – at least during the counselling session – they have no personal problems or distractions of their own, and they are, of course, rewarded in some way for maintaining this 'act'. They may also inadvertently model to clients a mythically all-composed, concerned, attentive ideal.

McLennan (1991) compared students who received informal help from academic staff, friends and family members with those who received formal counselling from professionals. Those receiving formal help reported their experience as more private and impactful, but not necessarily as more effective. McLennan speculates that even minimal training for informal helpers might usefully close the slender gap perceived between formal and informal helpers. Another reason for the need for counselling from professional strangers is the fact that we live in such a busy, mobile, alienated society. Many of us have few real or geographically accessible friends or relatives; who then can we readily talk to when a need arises? Although I have seen no research on the subject, I suspect that a large proportion of lengthy and long-distance telephone calls in fact contain a good deal of friendly support and co-counselling of sorts. The advertising efforts of telephone companies, urging us to pick up the phone and contact old friends or cheer up lonely relatives, recognise this. As McLeod (1993) notes, probably more people use telephone counselling helplines than face-to-face counselling. The extent of informal telephone counselling may perhaps never be measured.

Along with the loss of friends goes the phenomenon of failing to make good friends. For various reasons many people, particularly in urban areas, fail to secure initimate friendships and even fail to learn how to make friends. Lazarus (1989) regards 'friendship training' (resembling social skills and assertiveness training) as an important and frequently necessary therapeutic intervention. It may be that counsellors have in many instances functionally replaced close friends, and also that counsellors can teach some clients how to seek and secure friendships. The other side of this coin is that counsellors may have much to learn from studies of friendship. Within social psychology, for example, research into the development and dynamics of friendship processes may conceivably be able to teach counsellors and therapists to improve ways of forming and maintaining therapeutic alliances with clients, or may even stimulate radical innovations with regard to how counselling might be structured differently (Blieszner and Adams, 1992). In the field of socio-linguistics, researchers have examined in detail the kinds of conversations conducted between friends (Tannen, 1984). This kind of study is likely to alert counsellors to the enormous complexity of differing conversational styles, and the need to resist perceiving communicative differences invariably in terms of psychopathology.

Co-counselling

Co-counselling differs from formal one-to-one, mainstream counselling and also from befriending and friendship. Today there are many variants of co-counselling, but the originator was Harvey Jackins who, in a series of publications (e.g. Jackins, 1978) vividly described his rationale and method of re-evaluation co-counselling. According to Jackins, human intelligence has been obscured by irrationality, which itself results from various 'disintegrative trends' which include the organismic recording of distress patterns and their socially contagious nature. 'Corrective processes' include systematic emotional discharge of the distress and its conscious re-evaluation. Jackins' theory is too complex to represent adequately here, but it is fair to say that it is not open to modification by other therapeutic approaches. Jackins' work tends to read like an extended religious statement and includes uncompromising views on and commitments to cosmic and political issues. Re-evaluation co-counselling is taught practically in classes and students thereafter counsel each other according to well-defined, largely cathartic methods. Jackins believes that 'perhaps 90 per cent of good counseling is simply *paying attention to the client*' (Jackins, 1978: 177; emphasis in original). This does not mean that 'anyone can do it' but that attention that is expectant, 'delighting-in', insistent and persistent, is itself enormously powerful.

A major challenge of co-counselling (in this and other forms, for example, the 'cooperative peer counselling' of Southgate and Randall, 1978) is that it avoids the economic and ideological problems of professional counselling. It promotes the value of co-counselling communities rather than that of hierarchically organised professional counselling. In addition, and perhaps most significantly, people now realise that it is possible to arrange to give and get psychological help from peers, colleagues and friends. Co-counselling, in other words, has come to mean (as well as re-evaluation co-counselling) simply the egalitarian agreement between two people to counsel each other, without an intermediary, without needing to pay or to submit to any organisational requirements or assessments. In this sense, co-counselling is simply the one-to-one equivalent of self-help groups. However, unlike self-help groups, co-counselling appears not to be a thriving phenomenon. This is no doubt partly due to the difficulty of organising an emotionally charged one-to-one activity; it may be due partly to the timidity of would-be co-counsellors, who do not have, or imagine they have insufficient, appropriate skills and knowledge.

More likely, I think, it is due to individuals' wishes and possibly need to put themselves into supposedly stronger, wiser hands. This wish combines with the natural tendency of the helping professions to convey an image of themselves and their expertise that is reassuring and impressive, and that implicitly undermines the will of individuals to go it alone. It is worth remembering, however, that the BAC understanding of counselling hinges crucially on the 'user and the recipient explicitly agreeing to enter into a counselling relationship', at which point 'counselling' takes place, and not merely the 'use of counselling skills' (BAC, 1992). Does this mean that whenever any two people agree to counsel each other, they are counsellors? Any two people wishing to help each other by means of reciprocal, disciplined talking-and-listening, might refer to what they are doing as counselling, and might find that they can meet many of the criteria set out in the Codes of Ethics of various counselling and psychotherapy bodies. Perhaps where they would fail the test would be mainly in the areas of training and supervision requirements. Of course, most people whose essential concern was actually to help each other, would probably not be overly interested in external validation of that help. In principle, many professionals avow a commitment to 'giving psychology [and also, presumably, psychological counselling] away' – that is to say, democratizing it – but in practice, as Sampson (1993) argues, they invariably protect their privileged knowledge and undermine folk psychology and variants of co-counselling.

Counselling skills

Most people probably agree that the kinds of skills which form the basis of practical counselling training are not wholly distinguishable from the kinds of interpersonal and communication skills used in many other occupations and everyday settings. These skills may be said to include attentive listening, accurate understanding, an ability to understand the viewpoint of another person as if from their own perspective, an ability to articulate what one has heard and understood and to know how to paraphrase and to summarize another's concerns expressed through conversation, an ability to engage emotionally with others, and so on. None of these skills is exclusive to counselling as a profession. Counselling is based to a large extent on pre-existing interpersonal, verbal skills, in the same way that advanced athletic performance is based on pre-existing mobility skills. Counselling may focus on, refine, challenge and deepen ordinary communication skills, but it differs from the ability to fly an aircraft, for example, in that flying is something most people do not do at all in the course of their everyday lives.

In recognition of this definitional and occupational problem, BAC has wrestled with these issues and adopted a position on the distinction between counselling and counselling skills. Bond (1989) demonstrates the difficulties involved in distinguishing counselling skills from general communication or interpersonal skills. Some commentators believe that counselling skills are unarguably of a higher order of purposeful communication than ordinary conversational skills. An example often given is that in ordinary conversation speakers listen rather casually, superficially, inattentively and selectively, and respond rather politely, automatically, or self-interestedly. So, is counselling perhaps simply an attempt at better conversational skills? Some approaches to counselling, particularly the person-centred, place such enormous emphasis on the therapeutic power of certain interpersonal attitudes and skills, that it is almost impossible to distinguish in this case between counselling and the use of counselling skills. Indeed, the use of the term 'person-centred' was adopted precisely so that the ideology and skills of 'client-centred' counselling could more readily be applied not only to counselling clients but also to facilitating the personal and organisational growth of students, managers and trainees in a wide variety of settings.

As Bond points out, counselling may be distinguished from counselling skills in its additional requirements for theoretical understanding and ethical and professional boundaries and accountability. Anyone may, in the course of their work or relationships generally, use certain counselling skills on occasion, but they are unlikely to be informed by any coherent theoretical rationale or ethical responsibility. Indeed, in certain circumstances, interpersonal skills can be used which are identical to counselling skills but which have quite different objectives from those of counselling. A salesman, for example, may very well spend time with a client or customer consciously developing rapport, apparently empathising with his client's concerns, but with an ultimate aim of winning the client over and making a sale rather than enhancing the client's autonomy (the concept of 'empathy selling' in business literature testifies to this). However, it is far less clear what the differences are between counselling skills as used by teachers, managers, nurses and other benevolent professionals, and counselling skills as used by counsellors-as-such. We might argue that counsellors have a *therapeutic* brief, as opposed to an educational or management brief, for example. This begs the question, however, of the essential distinctions between *these* activities. Rogers (1980), for example, increasingly regarded his work as facilitating a 'way of being' across professions and communities rather than as a narrowly defined therapeutic profession.

There are many problematic anomalies involved in the question of counselling skills. If counselling cannot be satisfactorily defined, as Howard (1992) has argued, then how can the skills of counselling be satisfactorily defined? One way out of, or around this problem is to use terms like 'helping' and 'helping skills'. Egan (1990), in his 'skilled helper' model, applies these terms to a variety of situations. Egan uses the term 'change agent skills' in reference to the way his model can be used by counsellors, psychotherapists, teachers, managers and others. It is possible for Egan to adopt this position because his own model rests heavily on communication skills combined with social learning theory and a 'bias towards action'. Egan shows little interest in general theories of human functioning and psychopathology, and is, rather, a pragmatist. This raises the thorny issue of whether, in fact, there is consensus about counselling skills between schools of counselling and therapy. It seems that in practice, the orientation which guides your work as a counsellor dictates to a large extent which counselling skills you use more, and which less. Many, if not most, counsellors are taught not to ask questions, or to ask questions very sparingly, yet approaches such as rational emotive behaviour therapy and personal construct therapy rely quite heavily on questioning. As another example, empathic acceptance, understanding and its communication to the client is widely regarded (but especially by person-centred counsellors) as vital to good counselling, yet many rational emotive behaviour therapists warn of the dangers of assuming that clients need high levels of counsellor-offered acceptance and empathy, because clients may learn to depend on this rather than work to create their own self-acceptant attitudes.

It would seem to be beyond debate that counsellors-in-training should ('had better'?; 'would do well to consider how they might'?) gain competency in certain defined counselling skills. If counselling skills are the *sine qua non* of competent counselling, there can be no argument. However, some research comparing the outcomes of counselling provided by trained and untrained counsellors (Durlak, 1979; Hattie et al., 1984) suggests that we may overestimate the value or impact of such training. The untrained paraprofessionals in these studies apparently achieved equal or superior results. Furthermore, if we take seriously the much-cited research concerning the apparently negligible differences between theoretical orientations according to compared outcomes (Luborsky et al., 1975), then we might logically ask what grounds we have at all for confidence in teaching any particular kinds of communication skills. Perhaps we need greater justification for what is being done, and greater openness and debate on these matters. Discovery, rather than dogmatism or blindly accepted tradition, would seem to be the appropriate ethos for counselling training.

I do not dispute that counselling skills may differ significantly from everyday conversational skills or practices. One can readily observe certain differences between the often naive helping strategies of many beginner counsellors, and those who are trained. People can learn to offer subtler, deeper, more accurate and more consistently helpful responses. Beier and Young (1980) in fact argue that counselling trainees need to learn 'to be asocial' deliberately and to offer conversationally atypical responses. However, I believe that some individuals probably learn such responses without formal training, and some certainly pick them up much more instinctively than others. Unfortunately, too, some counsellors probably lose their instinctive abilities as they take on the persona of the 'trained counsellor'. I also suspect that there is a largely undiscussed issue of social class and speech patterns buried covertly within counselling skills training. This is addressed more fully in Chapter 8, but here I wish to point to the likeness between counselling skills and middle class social skills.

In a book called *Advanced Speaking Skills* (Harmer and Arnold, 1978), for example, a programme for improved communication skills includes micro-training in dealing with greetings and introductions, moods, invitations, suggestions, criticisms and complaints, opinions, clarification, changing the subject, making a point more accurate, making sure that you have understood correctly, advice, extensive listening, and so on. The purpose of the book is to develop oral communicative ability. To what extent does this differ from counselling skills? Are counselling skills, perhaps, 'other-centred' and (middle class) social skills in some sense self-centred? This is not the place to enter into such a debate in depth, but it is not incidental that a majority of counsellors are indeed well-educated, articulate middle class people. I do not believe, either, that enough consideration is given to the value to clients of their learning simply to *articulate* their feelings, problems and possible solutions. Indeed, it has been suggested that what clients get out of counselling and therapy very often is simply a new way of talking about themselves. Do counselling skills, perhaps, inadvertently model to clients the middle class value of re-phrasing and thereby re-construing problems in living? Some comfort can be derived, for instance, from telling yourself and others that you have a cash-flow problem rather than that you are broke. Newton (1994) traces many of the ways in which contemporary 'stress discourse' is similarly internalised, as we learn to embrace management-speak and perhaps suppress our own instinctive doubts and feelings.

As a bridge between counselling skills and the overlap between teaching and counselling, consider the following extract from a letter written by Jung to Freud in 1909:

> It is amazing how our work is spreading among the primary school teachers here. A young teacher was with me today, asking for advice: for months he has been treating his severely hysterical wife with good results and extraordinary understanding; he is also treating one of his pupils who suffers from a phobia. The scalpel is being cold-bloodedly wrested out of the doctors' hand. (McGuire, 1991: 158)

Jung was referring specifically to the use of psychoanalytic skills by a presumably untrained or self-trained teacher, and moreover to the successful use of these skills. Almost 90 years later, most psychoanalysts and counsellors would protest at such claims and at the abuse of professional boundaries!

Teaching and coaching

'The counsellor's role is to facilitate the client's work in ways which respect the client's values, personal resources and capacity for self-determination' (BAC, 1992). Many counsellors prefer to see themselves as facilitating the work or process of clients who are struggling to liberate or realise something which is already present or germinating within them. Counselling is distinguished from advising, as we have seen, because it does not impose solutions on clients. Similarly, counselling is not teaching. Or is it? Rarely is it didactic teaching, perhaps, but counselling resembles that understanding of education which values the 'leading out' from the person of their own potential, their own pre-existing aspirations, knowledge and coping resources, for example. Client-centred counselling was largely developed in an educational context and a great deal of Carl Rogers' work was devoted to student-centred learning. Thorne (1990) refers to person-centred therapy as a 'process which is in many ways an education for living'. Counselling is not, of course, education in the sense of covering a curriculum set by others, memorising traditional knowledge and preparing for examinations. But how different is counselling from personal, social and moral education?

Counsellors working from certain models often explicitly teach their clients new ways of looking at matters, frequently in the form of psychological concepts and schemas. Transactional analysis, reality therapy, cognitive-analytic therapy, rational emotive behaviour therapy, cognitive, multimodal and behaviour therapy, for example, all contain relatively simple maps of human functioning and better functioning. Counsellors often teach these, either as an end in themselves or as a specific aid in overcoming particular problems. Teaching useful psychological concepts implies a certain attitude, perhaps something like, 'You may not be aware of this way of assessing and working on your own concerns and I'd like to outline it so that you can make an informed decision about whether we can use it profitably in counselling together, or indeed whether you can use it on your own'. This is an explicit, non-mystical approach to counselling which, it can be argued, offers greater ethical respect to clients than approaches which proceed without any explanation or choice. In effect it is saying that 'here is something many (though not all) people have found useful and this is how it works'. Such 'teaching materials' can be used prior to counselling, in combination with it, or indeed instead of it. Familiarity with the basic Parent–Adult–Child model of TA, progressive relaxation techniques or the ABC sequence of rational emotive behaviour therapy, for example, may be either useful or essential in some counselling contracts. Social skills and assertiveness training, which are essentially behavioural methods, are taught to clients, and behaviour therapists often talk about coaching their clients in new behavioural skills.

Approaches to counselling which make the relationship between client and counsellor central either eschew the notion of teaching altogether or regard the client's learning as implicit, and as something which must happen autonomously. Put simply, it is as if the very act of explicitly teaching the client something robs him or her of the opportunity of discovering it for themselves. In these approaches, based on faith in the client's self-discovery, and given sufficient time, the focus is on unearthing obstacles to resourcefulness. It is also assumed that people learn naturally what they need to know for their own development. As Lazarus (1989) has argued, people lose their way in life or become dysfunctional in many different ways, not only through unresolved intrapsychic conflicts or traumas. Many have learned faulty or unhelpful ways of thinking, feeling and acting, and it is possible that such erroneous learning, or even complete deficits in certain areas of learning, may only be made up for by being taught. Lazarus insists that 'teaching, coaching, training, modeling, shaping, and directing are necessary. No amount of empathy, genuineness, or unpossessive caring is likely to fill the hiatuses.' The counter-argument to this is that many people have been bombarded in their childhood with unhelpful and even traumatic teaching which has mentally scarred them, and the last thing they need is yet more imposed ideas from an 'external locus'; self-knowledge comes from within, the argument runs. Unfortunately such an argument cannot proceed very far without admitting that the (usually psychodynamic or person-centred) counsellor implicitly coaxes this self-knowledge into awareness. Words and concepts like coaxing and facilitating, or providing the conditions for growth, cannot ultimately escape educational connotations.

The term 'coaching' may be avoided by many counsellors because it echoes somewhat parental expectations and rather external attitudes associated with discipline. Yet there is very little difference between a client saying 'I want you to help/counsel/facilitate me in my goal of becoming more self-aware and assertive', and a client who says 'I want you to coach me'. The subjective association of the word 'coach' for some may be aligned with 'push' and 'discipline'. Even so, these concepts are not so different from aspects of the concepts of contracting, confrontation, frame management and so on. In every case, the counsellor or therapist (or coach) provides a framework, rationale, expertise, environment and expectancy.

Rusk (1991) refers to the therapeutic work he conducts as 'guided self-change' and to himself as a consultant. He sees himself as a 'coach of change' who is interested in helping to restore balance in people's lives rather than being a professional connoiseur of 'symptoms of emotional or mental illness'. Rusk is critical not only of medically derived models of therapy, but also of humanistic models which forget the realities of client autonomy and resourcefulness to which they pay lip-service. As a coach, consultant or guide, he acts in a demythologised manner, appearing more as a fallible, if informed and committed, friend than as someone in an unnaturally professionalized role. He urges those seeking help that 'If you'd rather be coached and educated than treated, then you are opting for the model of guided self-change' (Rusk, 1991: 146). Sessions are held in a variety of settings and all the trappings of professional phoniness are avoided. Allowing yourself to be known as a coach implies that you have grappled, and continue to grapple with the central problems of being human and humbly seeking wisdom, however well qualified you may apparently be.

As I argue in Chapter 8, counselling has an unavoidable social dimension. Counsellors and therapists, by virtue of their training and their unique access to the privately disclosed suffering of large numbers of citizens, are aware of the kinds of things that go wrong for people in childrearing, in formal education and in society generally. Counselling has an inevitable educational function, helping clients to reconsider and re-learn in highly personalized ways, coping attitudes and skills. A great deal of psychoanalytically informed counselling and therapy has an implicit mission to provide corrective emotional education. Writers such as Nelson-Jones (1988) emphasise the role of the psychoeducational in counselling, often referring to it as 'life skills training'. Many humanistic counsellors (for example, Reich and Goodman) have informed or endorsed forms of alternative or 'free' schooling, in line with a person-centred ideology. What is perhaps a conundrum is why so many counsellors are attracted to working as counsellors, often helping to shut the stable door after the horse has bolted, rather than as teachers, where the damage might be partly prevented. Freud's view on this was that educative, preventive therapy with children was likely to be undone by the influence of neurotic parents and that it was therefore better to psychoanalyse parents in the hope that their therapeutic gains would somehow rub off on their children. My main point here, however, is that it is very hard genuinely to separate the therapeutic from the educational.

Consciousness-raising

Consciousness-raising is in a sense educational, but is often associated with specific, often political or spiritual activities. Under this heading I include a great deal of psychological groupwork and group therapy, women's and men's groups, anti-racist groups and groups and movements which promote transcendental or paranormal experiences. Consciousness-raising is not necessarily a group phenomenon, but tends to be associated with groups more than with dyadic situations. It is closely linked with the rise of the human potential movement in the USA, that is to say with sensitivity training, encounter, est, Arica, feminism, black consciousness, men's consciousness, and so on. I have seen marathon encounter groups referred to as 'group counselling'. It is not a homogeneous movement but represents a belief in the possibility of heightened awareness of certain personal, spiritual and political issues by means of committed learning and exposure in groups large and small.

Most consciousness-raising is clearly different from most individual counselling in that it is not tailored to the unique problems and needs of individuals. Consciousness-raising groups usually have certain radical and rather unchangeable agendas. Clearly, however, many of the aims of both counselling and consciousness-raising groups overlap. Re-evaluation counselling may be said to embrace both individual and group aims. Women and men whose primary aims for self-change are related to an evaluation and personal overhaul of sexist attitudes in themselves may opt for such group experiences instead of or in combination with individual counselling or therapy. Some groups dedicated to personal and social transformation, however, pose a challenge to the identity and potency of individual therapy.

Est, for example, which is a large group experience promising both personal and social transformation, exists outside the mainstream counselling profession altogether. Est, or Erhard Seminars Training, currently known as 'The Forum', was the brainchild of Werner Erhard who, having himself explored scientology, Zen Buddhism, Dale Carnegie positive thinking, psychocybernetics and other change processes, reportedly experienced a radical transformation in his personality. He subsequently put together the est training package, which incorporated a disciplined large group setting (upwards of 250 participants), philosophical presentations, participants' public sharing of their problems, and various exercises oriented towards gaining altered states of consciousness. 'Mind traps' such as resentment, regret and righteousness are pointed out by the trainers. Est contains or replicates aspects of Gestalt therapy, public confession and other powerful psychodramatic phenomena which often produce momentary peak experiences. It has a rationale for continuing training in personal transformation. It also has a programme of social action. In his biography of Erhard, Bartley (1978) refers to certain partial likenesses between est and the work of Carl Rogers and Abraham Maslow. Est promotes the self-experiencing of acceptance, truth and responsibility. The challenge that est presents to the 'straight' psychological (and theological and philosophical) establishment is that it appears to move easily and with integrity across these disciplines and their central concepts, claiming to embody rather than simply contemplating them. The problem with est is that it is seen by many as a gimmicky, flash-in-the-pan project, authored by a charismatic former salesman, which can do as much harm as good. Harrison (1990: 128) remarks that est has caused concern because of 'the number of participants who have been unable to cope with the extremely rigorous, high pressure methods used'.

This is not the place for a detailed consideration of est or other projects which resemble it. It is worth considering, however, that there are some likenesses between est and scientology, Alcoholics Anonymous and other 'life-transforming' systems. Those hostile to est and similar approaches suggest that it breaks down psychological defences by the use of privation, public confession and crowd pressure, and that it may be considered a cult (Harrison, 1990). Rarely are systems of individual therapy or counselling considered cults, but they have sometimes received similar criticisms of brainwashing, privation and aggressive defence-breaking (Sargant, 1957). Where most counselling differs undeniably from est and its likes is in its gradualism. Although not all counsellors always work cautiously, a majority respect the need of individual clients to work at their own pace and according to their own agenda. Innovative approaches to counselling such as neuro-linguistic programming (NLP – another process which was created out of a variety of motivational, hypnotic, cybernetic and other theories) create both fascination and concern within the counselling profession. NLP aims to help people transform themselves, to accelerate the learning process, to provide creative tools for therapeutic as well as educational, organisational and other change. Like est, NLP has the flavour of a 'quickie' therapy which is unashamedly commercialised and often addressed more to the already successful than the desperate and disadvantaged. Many consciousness-raising projects have both revolutionary and damaging potential, and most are far less subject to regulation than counselling. But the same could be said of evangelical religion, of course.

Charismatic and fortuitous encounter

By the term 'charismatic encounter' I mean those meetings between people which, fortuitous or not, prove to be powerful, timely, transformative events. I have (and I imagine most people have had) the occasional experience of meeting someone unexpectedly, in conversation with whom I have felt changed, subtly or dramatically, transiently or enduringly. Sometimes such meetings are with decidedly significant, charismatic individuals, but sometimes they are simply with a kindred spirit, someone who feels as you feel, and whose affirmation of your views or feelings has a profound effect on you. Sometimes these meetings are entirely fortuitous, sometimes they are sought. The role of serendipity in general and life-changing encounters in particular has not gone altogether unnoticed by psychologists (Bandura, 1982) and certainly not by novelists (see, for example, John Fowles's *The Magus* and Luke Rhinehart's *The Dice Man* and *The Search for The Dice Man*). Usually these are meetings in the flesh, but it is also meaningful to speak of meeting a like mind through the medium of a book or other work of art. Christians might speak too, of course, of having a personal, life-transforming encounter with Christ.

The significance of such encounters for the subject of counselling is that they can have great impact, sometimes in a very short time, and sometimes in a manner that transcends the impact of months or years of counselling. Most counsellors will perhaps admit that immediate and profound rapport with a client is relatively rare. Clients and counsellors may like, admire and even sometimes fall in love with each other. They may also work hard to dispel or interpret the veils of illusion, transference and counter-transference which keep them from an optimal therapeutic alliance. I believe it sometimes happens by chance that a counsellor and client meet each other for whom the anticipated roles of helper and helped do not, and cannot, materialise. When this is realized by both parties, counselling may either terminate, or proceed with intermittent intrusions from this domain of the 'I and Thou'. Clarkson (1990) counts this kind of relationship as one among many which can and do manifest within psychotherapy: 'it is very likely that those ordinary relationships which human beings have experienced as particularly healing over the ages have been characterized by the qualities of the I–You relationship'.

I am not concerned here with the so-called 'real relationship' or 'existential bond' within counselling, however, but with those encounters and relationships which, outside of counselling or psychotherapy, have a healing impact. They may do so because you happen to meet someone at the right time who tells you something about yourself or about life that no one else has told you. It may be that you meet someone acknowledged or not to be a charismatic, enlightened figure, whose very presence agitates, excites or moves you profoundly. It may be that you meet someone who feels about life exactly as you do, which leads you to have the transformative, mirror-like experience of feeling completely affirmed, accepted and understood (by someone who is not trying, as part of their job, to make you feel this way). You may meet someone who says something quite simple, but timely and truthful, which impacts profoundly on you. I recall the first person, a youth worker, who suggested to me that perhaps I was as persecutory towards my mother as I believed she was towards me. The possibility of such catalytic reframing had entirely escaped me until that moment!

It was Martin Buber who, perhaps more than anyone else in our time, drew attention to the potential for abuse, healing and even radical transformation within the interpersonal relationship. Buber's (1937) *I and Thou* has had an enormous influence on the world of therapy, especially for a work that is not primarily psychological in kind, and whose author was sceptical that any therapy or counselling could offer a genuinely full, human encounter (see Kirschenbaum and Henderson, 1990). For Buber, the I–Thou encounter paralleled encounter with God, and is associated with presence and grace rather than with intention, prescription and non-egalitarian helping relationships. This kind of encounter has nothing to do with the therapeutic use of 'immediacy' or the self-conscious development of genuineness. Buber refers to the importance of 'the between' and 'the primally simple fact of encounter'. None of this is predictable or exploitable, even for benevolent ends. When it is healing, it is so by grace rather than by design.

There are, of course, reciprocal critiques of such views. Counsellors cannot usually wait for the healing advent of grace, for example, but must get on with the task of counselling. It is possible, according to Bollas (1986), that fascination with such transforming encounters, interpersonally, aesthetically and spiritually, indicates an unconscious search that may have begun in the earliest days and weeks of life. Bollas suggests that the comings and goings of the mother register acutely with the infant, and can lead to a phenomenon he refers to as a search for the transformational object. Buber's interpersonal mysticism could be said to fall into such an analysis. Indeed, Buber's own mother deserted the family when he was three years old, and Buber had to learn the reality of the situation from a 12-year-old girl who told him that his mother was never returning. As he admitted, 'all that I have learned in the course of my life about genuine meeting had its origin in that hour on the balcony' (Friedman, 1982: 5).

There is an assumption among many psychotherapists and counsellors that the therapeutic process necessarily takes time, that is, a considerable length of time. Unfortunately, there is relatively little research into time factors and actual, atomistic change, but the growing interest in brief forms of counselling and therapy has helped to unearth some pertinent indications. The timing of receiving therapy may be a crucial factor in its success. Single-session therapy (Talmon, 1990) relies for its impact partly on the belief in and identification of decisive moments in life. Perhaps, just as Buber's early experience of loss produced sudden and enduring effects, so therapeutic encounters in adult life may similarly produce rapid and enduring change. For Krishnamurti and Bohm (1985) change is not a process occurring over time, but an immediate result of choiceless, unflinching self-confrontation with and acceptance of truth. Counsellors and therapists are, on the whole, sceptical about sudden and dramatic personal transformations, which fly in the face of most developmental theories. Certainly it is true that many such experiences are spurious, shaky and even potentially dangerous, but equally, history testifies to many dramatic breakthroughs in the lives and work of leading figures in religion and science, for example, that have stood the test of time.

Self-analysis and self-help

There was no one before Freud to whom he could turn for analysis of his own unconscious conflicts; Janov, discovering primal therapy, had to experience and understand his own 'primal pain' without expert help from primal therapists. It is allowed to many founders, because they are considered to be geniuses, to forego formal therapy. Unlike ordinary neurotic mortals, they are often thought to have some mysterious faculty whereby their own dream analysis or primalling can be legitimately self-facilitated. Thereafter, the entire process must be carefully studied, tabulated and trained into non-genius practitioners in depth over a period of some years. It is interesting to consider that validated self-discovery and dramatic psychic breakthroughs, often within a short period of time, are quite common at the time a new therapeutic theory and method is born. It is thereafter invariably considered impossible or imprudent for any trainee to make serious self-discoveries or to make innovative therapeutic breakthroughs themselves: the founding geniuses demand obedience!

Today, almost all psychotherapy and counselling training demands that trainees undergo a period of personal analysis, therapy or counselling. The period varies but the premise – that every trainee must be exposed to some sort of psychological overhaul performed by an approved practitioner – is fairly universal. Some flexibility with regard to group therapy or different therapeutic orientations may be allowed, but one method of personal analysis or personal growth is entirely ruled out of court. This is, of course, self-analysis or self-counselling. (The term 'self-therapy' is sometimes used but 'self-counselling' is rarely used, perhaps because counselling necessarily denotes an activity in which one person counsels another.) It is strange that the subject of self-discovery – as I like to call the whole business of self-analysis/therapy/counselling – should receive such scant attention and respect from the professional therapeutic community. When you consider that autonomy is perhaps the most sacred concept in counselling, it is indeed odd that little interest is shown in 'autonomous training' (that is, training oneself). Counsellors applying for BAC accreditation (and, I am sure, for other forms of licence to practise) must demonstrate that they have undergone some kind of personal therapy over a certain period; they do not have to demonstrate exactly what, if indeed anything, they have learned from the experience. If one were to state on such applications 'I have spent a great deal of time meditating on my everyday relationships and conflicts', I doubt very much that this would be given much credibility. This is regrettable since there is much to be learned from genuine and deep communion with oneself, and the whole subject of solitude and self-discovery deserves far greater attention (Storr, 1988).

Spiritual self-discovery and moral guidance in the many forms of mysticism and classical wisdom found within major philosophical schools and religions may be said to pre-date psychological self-discovery by thousands of years. Artemidorus, for example, wrote *The Interpretation of Dreams* in the second century AD, partly as a manual for the self-interpretation of dreams. The *I Ching*, thought to have been written about 1,000 years BC, has offered inspiration and guidance to shamans and ordinary people, as well as sages like Confucius, throughout the ages. Twentieth-century self-help literature and self-help movements have been anticipated by the literature of mystical and spiritual guidance and by perennial reactions against established religions. Respect for self-discovery in modern psychological literature is most evident, however, in the concept of self-analysis advanced by Karen Horney and carried on in many guises since her work. Certain of the less elitist therapeutic writers, such as Adler, Horney and Fromm, and more recently Ellis, Harris, Dwyer, Dryden and others, appear enthusiastic about promoting therapeutic ideas beyond the confines of the consulting room. Self-help literature varies enormously, of course, in how popular and diluted or scholarly and modest it may be, but undoubtedly it has a widespread, tremendous impact. For some people, reading such books is sufficient help in itself; sometimes a particular book may effect profound changes in individuals; sometimes these books are extremely useful in conjunction with counselling. A notable example of self-discovery facilitated by therapeutic literature is the 'intensive journal program' of Ira Progoff (1975), which is based on an integration of depth-psychological, creative and spiritual concepts. Craighead et al. (1984) present a summary of the evolution of self-help, its varieties and results according to research.

The psychologist Dorothy Rowe, author of many such works, urges people to consider self-discovery and selfhelp *instead* of therapy. In a letter (The *Independent on Sunday*, 26.4.92) she lamented the 'disgraceful scene' of the current field of therapy. In the letter she wrote: 'perhaps the solution is not to turn to the professionals for help but to help ourselves by learning how to understand ourselves. Many of my readers tell me that they have done just this, and that, by reading widely and talking to lots of different people, they have changed not just themselves but their nearest and dearest.' Included in Mozak's outline of Adlerian psychotherapy (Mozak, 1989) are the comments that 'although the definition of psycho-therapy customarily refers to what transpires within the consulting room, a broader view of psychotherapy would include the fact that life in itself may be and is often psychotherapeutic' and that 'many fortunate people, trained in courage and social interest, do it for themselves without therapeutic assistance'. Such views are echoed vigorously by Wood (1984) who argues for a 'moral therapy' based on personal courage and determi-nation, which would entail shunning the inherently responsibility-post-poning nature of most counselling and therapy. The phenomenon of 'flight into therapy' has not been well documented, but Maeder (1989) gives some account of how many psychotherapists have sought escape from the rigours of ordinary life by becoming mental health professionals.

Krishnamurti, similarly, urges people to avoid gurus (not only spiritual, but also psychological gurus) and to learn directly from their own everyday experience. It is not only the so-called geniuses, masters, founders and enlightened ones who are capable of seeing deeply into their own psyches and into the nature of being; rather, it is anyone and everyone. Furthermore, one of the main reasons why people commonly fail to take their own powers of introspection and self-change seriously is that they are enslaved to the illusion that someone else knows better. This critique of hetero-therapy (healing, insight and action provided by others) does not offer a recipe for simplistic or guaranteed auto-therapy (healing, insight and action from within) but rather a spur to seek self-knowledge by self-discovery. Hetero-therapy may even compound whatever mistakes the person is already making by taking them further away from self-trust, covertly teaching them to value counsellors' words and assumptions more than their own. Many models of counselling recommend the facilitation of the client's self-experiencing, but few regard the facilitator as potentially superfluous or even dangerous. Symington (1986) speaks of the 'external ritual' of psychoanalysis as 'the agent which helps self-analysis to occur' but does not seriously examine the possibility of bypassing the ritual altogether. Such possibilities belong exclusively to the likes of founders and anomalies like Fairbairn who, as Symington reiterates, became a psychoanalyst on the strength of his own self-analysis, rigorous thinking and 'considerable independence of mind'.

There are many permutations on the theme of self-help, supported self-help and guided self-change. Many counsellors practise a form of brief pragmatic counselling which incorporates homework assignments for clients, the use of bibliotherapy (purposefully recommended self-help or theoretical texts), emphasis on increasing self-responsibility, self-efficacy and anticipation of living better without dependence on counselling (Dryden and Feltham, 1992a). Many people who might not dream of going for personal counselling are often quite prepared to consult astrologers and 'agony aunts' and to derive some comfort from newspaper astrology and problem pages. According to Marjorie Proops, one of Britain's best-known agony aunts, many of her correspondents appear to have insurmountable problems which can be categorised as either self-created or completely unavoidable. Apparently many writers of letters to problem pages, although they may not get the answers they hope for, derive comfort from the mere act of disclosing their concerns in writing, and having them acknowledged (Proops, personal communication, 1992). What counsellors may learn from this is that people experiencing problems in living obviously construe what is likely to be helpful to them quite differently, and their help-seeking choices probably depend on factors of class and culture as much as on anything else.

The phenomenon of self-help groups is of great significance. Although these represent a form of help from outside oneself, they are generally of a collaborative, mutual-aid nature. Any expertise found in selfhelp groups stems from the fellow-suffering of other members. Alcoholics, drug addicts, people with mental health problems, single parents, carers of difficult children, bereaved people, and many others with common concerns meet together to share their experiences and to offer each other help. This help may take the form of advice, practical assistance, companionship, solidarity or peer-counselling. The greatest strength of such groups lies in shared experience, members deriving solace and support from both getting and giving succour. Misery loves company, as the saying goes. It is sometimes forgotten that many, if not most, candidates for counselling and psychotherapy training gain their initial interest in therapy from their own suffering, searching and personal therapy. Indeed it is not entirely unfair to suggest that many receivers of therapy graduate to training as therapists and, along the way, vicariously and unconsciously attempt to 'cure' themselves completely (Guy, 1987; Maeder, 1989). Logically, then, in some sense training institutes may be considered a variety of implicit self-help group. Officially, this is not the case – such people are screened out – but unofficially and unconsciously, it is probably another story altogether. Certainly many therapy and counselling trainees report that they learn a tremendous amount about *themselves* from their training.

The caring and helping professions

Counselling may be regarded as a caring profession among others, although some commentators might baulk at the connotation of 'caring for' clients in therapy. Care can have paternalistic connotations. Most people, however, probably accept that counselling belongs in some sense with social work, probation, nursing, psychiatric nursing, welfare work, pastoral work and paramedical occupations such as occupational therapy. It is notable that most of these professions are staffed by a majority of women and have relatively low status and pay. Supportive, nurturant occupations may be seen, rightly or wrongly, as logical extensions of the traditional roles and expectations of many women. Most of these jobs include a counselling element, and certainly frequent use of counselling skills. Caring professions are often considered vocations, one of the proofs for which is the relatively low level of remuneration attached to them: you have to like or love people, love spending a lot of time with them, looking after them, being patient with their suffering or deficits, to want to work in such professions.

Sometimes referred to as the 'core professions' (Pedder, 1989), these activities may be viewed by some as valuably supportive but in some way as professionally insufficient or transitional. It is no accident that Pedder and others have considered the core professions to be a possible necessary preliminary experience to psychotherapy training. The supportive skills required in the core professions are viewed by such commentators as of a lesser order of therapeutic skills than the in-depth, uncovering, working-through skills of the (analytic) psychotherapist. While the official line is always, of course, that caring professionals are doing a marvellous job, the unspoken belief is often that such jobs involve inferior skills. Also too seldom openly addressed is the significant difference between the typical client of caring professionals, who is often from the lower social classes, and the average client of psychotherapists (who used to be known as the YAVIS, or young, attractive, verbal, intelligent and successful person). This sort of distinction may have broken down somewhat in recent years, but it still holds broadly true that social workers, for example, deal with multiply disadvantaged, less articulate clients and psychotherapists deal with motivated, articulate and often economically comfortable clients (Landsman, 1982).

Counselling fits into this picture somewhere in between. As pressure mounts on social workers and probation officers, for example, to manage their cases rather than to do much casework with them, so these workers may reminisce or look to counselling as an occupational escape, or a step up (or back) into doing real, direct, face-to-face work with people. Counselling has in recent years acquired a certain glamour. Soon after the first wave of AIDS cases were emerging in Britain, a newspaper report carried an article in which a community care worker wryly observed that nobody wanted to do the much-needed messy, domestic jobs in this field;

instead, everyone wanted to be a counsellor. Along with this newly found glamour and respect for counselling goes its tenuous professionalization. As I have shown, counselling is now being defined separately from the mere use of counselling skills.

But counselling is also held out as not being casework. Social work or casework is sometimes said to have a different value base from that of counselling, having an agenda for clients of psychosocial change and usually being bound by agency policies which may overshadow the autonomy of practitioners and clients alike. For social workers, regular supervision is not mandatory. I know a probation officer whose application for accredited counsellor status was unsuccessful partly on the grounds that her clinical experience was considered to be casework and not counselling, although she perceived her work to be psychodynamic counselling. Consider, however, the following definition of social work (apparently originated from within the British Association of Social Workers, and reported in the *Guardian*, 12.3.93):

> Social work is the purposeful and ethical application of personal skills in interpersonal relationships directed towards enhancing the personal and social functioning of an individual, family group or neighbourhood . . .

You might not often hear of neighbourhood counselling, but otherwise this definition sounds remarkably similar to official definitions of counselling.

In an article written by a probation officer on post-traumatic stress disorder (Clare, 1992), a distinction is made between critical incident stress debriefing and counselling; the writer warns that 'those leading the debriefing must resist slipping, or being drawn, into a counselling mode'. Professional distinctions are examined further in the next chapter, but here it is salient to note that the caring professions have historically jockeyed for power, and this is reflected in nomenclature and salaries. Bessell (1971) documented the split between social work interviewing and counselling, for example, and noted the fact that at that time in the UK the middle classes were beginning to turn to marriage guidance counselling, while poorer citizens made use of probation officers.

Let us look, however, at one of the essential, universal activities of counsellors and psychotherapists. What therapists have in common with caring professionals and primary caregivers – mothers, fathers and parental substitutes – is that they offer, or try to offer, emotional support, containment and understanding. The very roots of words such as 'psychotherapy' and 'clinical' point to attendance, waiting-on and bedside care. Counsellors and therapists aim to provide therapeutic acceptance, constancy and psychological 'feeding'. The analyst Lomas (1987), writing on psychotherapy as 'a second attempt at parenting', acknowledges the variety of methods used, which include commonsense, listening, comforting, understanding, encouraging and criticising. Analysts have spoken of the 'maternal reverie' and the 'nursing triad'. A great deal of counselling includes an element, at least, of reparenting. The Cathexis school of transactional analysis has developed specialized clinical applications of reparenting, particularly for severely disturbed psychotic clients. Other models offer varieties of reparenting, such as that represented by the concept of the corrective emotional experience. Even the less obviously nurturant models like cognitive therapy provide a form of warm, one-to-one help which is not dissonant with an image of caring reparenting.

Perhaps one provocative way of thinking about connections between counselling, psychotherapy and the caring professions is to suggest that they are all forms of mothering. Sayers' (1991) view is not so far from this, in fact. Psychoanalysis has been referred to by Helene Deutsch as 'par excellence a profession for women' and certainly in the UK the vast majority of counsellors, like nurses, are women. Aveline (1992) notes that women possess the ideal therapist qualities of empathic concern, respectfulness, realistic hopefulness, self-awareness, reliability and strength to a far greater degree than men. As members of different altruistic occupational families, caring professionals themselves might be considered to be distinguished by their caring for different kinds of problem children, or clients. Low-paid carers tend to work with the unruly, poor or resourceless, and affluent carers with fairly comfortable clients. The distinction is reflected in the term 'supportive psychotherapy' which has connotations of warm, maternal acceptance (and less prestigious skills), as contrasted with the kind of therapy which is seen as doing serious, 'depth' and 'uncovering' work. An irony not to be missed here is that psychiatrists and psychotherapists, the better paid and respected within the caring professions, as depicted in one American study (Maeder, 1989) may often be far from ideal parents to their own children.

Psychotherapy

The origins of this term are disputed. It may have been first used by J.C. Reil in 1803 in an article entitled *Rhapsodies in the Application of Psychic Methods in the Treatment of Mental Disturbances* (Clare and Thompson, 1981). According to Efran and Clarfield (1992: 211) the word 'psychotherapy' was 'coined around 1889 simply by combining the words for mind (*psyche*) and treatment (*therapeia*). In the dualistic thinking of the day, it seemed apparent that if there were treatments for the body, there also should be some for the mind.' As we have seen, the term 'counselling' with its modern connotation of therapeutically oriented counselling, appeared in about the 1930s. Efran and Clarfield echo the observations of Szasz (1988) and Howard (1992) when they say that the term 'psychotherapy' (or 'counselling') 'can be applied to almost anything clients and therapists decide to do together, provided it isn't against the law'. London (1986) endorses this view, suggesting that the 'cornucopia of treatments' known as psychoanalysis, sex therapy, pastoral counselling, guidance, assertiveness training, stress management, transcendental meditation and even est are all forms of psychotherapy.

Psychotherapy is, of course, talking therapy, or treatment, and as such it is, at the very least, intimately related to counselling. Psychotherapy and counselling certainly share many of the same critics and many other features too, but there are also alleged differences which we cannot overlook. It is necessary to devote considerable attention to the relationship between these talking therapies, partly because so many people are genuinely confused about the debate, and partly because this very confusion promises to yield interesting clues to the substance of our question 'What is counselling?'

Brown and Pedder (1979: ix) suggest that psychotherapy is:

> essentially a conversation which involves listening to and talking with those in trouble with the aim of helping them understand and resolve their predicament.

Corsini (1989: 1) states that:

> psychotherapy is a formal process of interaction between two parties, each party usually consisting of one person but with the possibility that there may be two or more people in each party, for the purpose of amelioration of distress in one of the two parties relative to any of the following areas of disability or malfunction: cognitive functions (disorders of thinking); affective functions (suffering or emotional discomforts); or behavioral functions (inadequacy of behaviour), with the therapist having some theory of personality's origins, development, maintenance and change along with some method of treatment logically related to the theory and professional and legal approval to act as a therapist.

Aveline (1992: 11) tells us that:

> the unique feature of psychotherapy is the structured professional relationship between the therapist and one or more patients . . . who meet in a relationship which is genuine, equal in feeling but asymmetrical in disclosure, and which is directed towards assisting the patient in making changes in personal functioning.

Bloch (1982: 24) suggests that:

> psychotherapy is an interpersonal process in which a socially sanctioned healer meets with a person who seeks out help because of incapacitating distress or an inability to function adequately.

Bloch points out that 'psychotherapies' is a more accurate term than 'psychotherapy' because of the large number of different forms it takes. He also distinguishes between psychotherapies in terms of their goals of treatment. Thus, there is crisis intervention, supportive psychotherapy, symptom-oriented psychotherapy and insight-oriented psychotherapy. He also emphasises the centrality of the 'therapist–patient relationship' which is 'different from other forms of relationship such as marriage or friendship in important and fundamental ways'.

Kramer (1989), in a chapter asking 'What is psychotherapy?', approves of Wolberg's definition (see below) but goes on to question how this 'ambiguous profession' can really be satisfactorily defined. He cites the case of a psychiatrist who undertook research with a group of women experiencing problems with premenstrual syndrome. Kramer claims that the women had chatted with each other while waiting to see the psychiatrist, and that she had asked them about their symptoms and given them practical advice, information and encouragement. She had intended no psychotherapy, yet 80 per cent of these women reported a recovery from their symptoms. Kramer also cites a case in which the self-psychologist Michael Basch reported using pragmatically empathic responses to an irate cab driver. Basch's intent had apparently been simply to mollify the driver (presumably in the middle of dense traffic), yet he learned later that this man had derived great benefit from the conversation. Was this psychotherapy? Kramer argues that 'psychotherapy is an art. Except that it is often bumbling and mundane' (1989: 217).

A few further quotations will perhaps confirm the definition. 'Psychotherapy is the psychological, as opposed to physical or chemical, approach to the treatment of psychological disorder involving primarily verbal interaction between two or more individuals' (Wolberg, 1977). Psychotherapy is distinguished from ordinary conversation in that the therapist invariably takes his or her patient seriously, listens in an unusually concentrated way, withholds personal reactions or responds asocially, in 'unexpected, surprising ways' (Kiesler and Denburg, 1993). According to Herman (1987) psychotherapy involves 'a skill both in listening and in replying, of infinite complexity and dazzling sophistication'. Samuels et al. (1986) consider (Jung's conception of) psychotherapy to be 'a dialectical process between two psychic systems reacting and responding to one another'. J.D. Salinger's character Holden Caulfield, in the novel *The Catcher in the Rye*, asks a friend, whose father is a psychoanalyst, what he would do to him if he were to consult him. 'He wouldn't do a goddam thing to you. He'd simply talk to you, and you'd talk to him, for God's sake. For one thing, he'd help you to recognize the patterns of your mind,' Caulfield is told. Adam Phillips (1993), celebrated author of *On Kissing, Tickling and Being Bored*, and a psychotherapist, declares that psychoanalysis is essentially an improvisation, an interesting conversation, the aim of which is 'not to cure people but to show them that there is nothing wrong with them' (Phillips, 1993: 21). Bettelheim tells us that 'introspection is what psychoanalysis is all about' (1989: 19), so we may say that the talking therapies generally are a form of accompanied or guided introspection. Most succinctly, psychotherapy is 'remedial discourse' (Heaton, 1993).

So far, could anyone detect any clear difference between counselling and psychotherapy? Certainly no unsuspecting client-to-be would learn much from these phrases. But I have kept the polemics and details back. I have not so far alluded to forms of psychotherapy which derive from non-psychoanalytic sources. (Debates between schools of counselling and psychotherapy are referred to in Chapter 5.) In the UK, a great deal of tension exists between those psychoanalytically trained therapists who wish jealously to protect and limit the identity of psychotherapy to the talking treatment of the psyche by strictly psychoanalytic means, and more liberal therapists from humanistic, cognitive-behavioural, transpersonal and integrative camps who are willing to entertain myriad claims to the title of psychotherapist. An early comment on this conflict is found in Fromm (1963: 167):

> Free association soon deteriorated . . . Other therapeutic schools reduced the role of the analyst to that of a sympathetic listener, who repeats in a slightly different version the words of the patient, without trying to interpret or to explain. All this is done with the idea that the patient's freedom must not be interfered with. The Freudian idea of free association has become the instrument of many psychologists who call themselves counselors, although the only thing they do not do is counsel.

It is broadly true to say that in North America the conflicts between psychotherapists and counsellors are less pronounced than in the UK, and that the meanings of these terms differ in the UK and the USA. Indeed, Corsini (1989: 2) argues that 'no definition can be made which will include all psychotherapies and exclude all counseling methods'. The debate has also been largely meaningless in Europe, where counselling is far less developed as an activity distinct from psychotherapy than it is in the UK, and where difficulties abound in the translation of the word 'counselling'. The book *Brief Counselling* (Dryden and Feltham, 1992a) has been translated into German, for example, as *Psychologische Kurzberatung und Kurztherapie* (literally, 'short advice and short therapy'). In Holland, psychotherapy is deemed to be what registered psychotherapists do, with other forms of assistance using psychological knowledge known as *begeleiding* (guidance).

In the UK there might be said to be two main views on the alleged differences between counselling and psychotherapy. One is that they are entirely or largely synonymous, and the other that they are largely or utterly distinct. For proponents of person-centred counselling/therapy there is no meaningful distinction. Indeed it is often claimed that 'counselling' is so favoured by the person-centred tradition because Carl Rogers, developing his theories in the 1920s and 1930s in the USA, which legally prevented psychologists from practising as psychotherapists, sidestepped legal restrictions by adopting the term 'counselling'. Counselling came into prominence later in the UK, when psychotherapy, and particularly psychoanalytically oriented psychotherapy, was historically and institutionally well rooted. I believe that many of the professed differences between counselling and psychotherapy stem from purely historical and ideological factors and prejudices, but I will now outline the argument as currently understood.

First, from the perspective of psychotherapists, these are some of the perceived differences.

1 Psychotherapy is an in-depth, time-consuming, personality-transforming exercise.
2 Psychotherapy is based on a lengthy, in-depth training which demands of trainees extensive personal analysis, several times a week, over a period of many years.
3 Psychotherapy does not seek for superficial changes in the patient's life, and instead of symptomatic treatment aims for profound self-understanding arrived at by painstaking 'working-through' of unconscious conflicts.
4 Psychotherapy is based on a well-founded knowledge of the dynamics of unconscious processes, and advocates that no enduring personal change is possible without rigorous analysis of the unconscious, usually through work with and in the transference.
5 Psychotherapy has a sound grasp of developmental, including pre-verbal, stages and the psychopathology attaching to these, and consequently is equipped to deal with serious psychological disturbances which are rooted in early infancy.

The following are some of the perceived differences from the point of view of counsellors.

1 Counselling respects the self-knowledge and self-determination of the client and does not pre-suppose that counsellors have privileged access to, or the right to interpret, clients' complex inner lives.
2 Counselling acknowledges that clients' goals are to be respected and that if these indicate a demand for apparent 'symptom-removal' in a short period of time, this cannot be justly regarded as an illegitimate or ineffective aim.
3 Counselling is a non-medical enterprise which values the power of non-judgemental, attentive listening and an ethic of enabling and empowering for people from all walks of life.
4 Counselling is a skilful but not elitist activity.
5 Counselling acknowledges the complexity of individuals, the diversity of theories of human behaviour, and the value of a pragmatic as well as an idealistic attitude.

This is putting the case politely. The alleged differences may be clearer if described in the actual, derogatory terms sometimes used in casual conversation by counsellors and psychotherapists themselves. An anti-counselling psychotherapist might be heard to opine that counselling is a well-meaning, amateurish, superficial activity undertaken by unvetted, barely trained lay people, which varies from an inane head-nodding and reflecting process to a haphazard mixture of advice-giving, 'wild analysis' and shallow symptom-removal. By contrast, psychotherapy would be advanced as a scientifically based profession whose practitioners are carefully selected, who receive years of personal analysis and intensive supervision, and who may competently diagnose, contain, interpret and thoroughly examine most aspects of the unconscious conflicts of their patients. An anti-psychotherapy counsellor might describe psychotherapy as a pseudo-scientific activity which labels people, gives them no choice of treatment, pathologises them, encourages or forces them to spend inordinate amounts of time and money in unaccountable and often ineffective therapy with a pseudo-expert whose services are usually so expensive or unobtainable as to make psychotherapy an elitist nonsense. By contrast, counselling is a modest, respectful, client-centred, egalitarian activity which offers choice to people and which realistically offers accessible, affordable help to them in settings with which they are familiar.

In order to examine closely such alleged differences, I cite now some organisations' definitions and descriptions. The British Association of Psychotherapists (BAP), through their Council Member for Public Relations, Jill Curtis, (personal communication, 1992) defines a psychotherapist as someone who:

> has been trained to work in a specific way with people – a process of exploration undertaken by two people – therapist and patient. During this exploration, the patient relates thoughts, associations, feelings, memories and dreams. The therapist clarifies and makes links between the conscious and unconscious, present and past experiences. This can take time, and there are no short cuts.

Obviously this refers to a particular form of psychotherapy, namely the psychoanalytically derived form. There are many kinds of psychological therapy which aim to help people without, for example, dealing with dreams or even memories, and which aim to produce results in a short time. These cannot be disbarred from calling themselves psychotherapy. They cannot all even be dismissed as non-psychoanalytic therapy, since there are many varieties of brief psychoanalytic psychotherapy. However, we have to accept that this is one organisation's view of what is and what is not psychotherapy. In their leaflet *What is Psychotherapy?* (BAP, 1992), psychotherapy is defined less exclusively as 'a form of treatment for those who are experiencing difficulties within themselves or in relationships with others. It has been called the "talking cure" because the method employed is verbal communication rather than the use of other means, such as drugs'. The description goes on to say who can be helped by psychotherapy – 'those troubled by feelings of depression, emptiness, futility and incapacitating fears, extreme mood swings or uncontrollable rage . . . those who experience dissatisfaction in their sexual, interpersonal, work and social relationships or those who are unable to make relationships'. (This description must cover a large section of the population!) Like counselling, such psychotherapy is a talking therapy which claims to be able to help a wide spectrum of people, given an indefinite period of time.

BAP is a relatively long-established institution (1951) with an understandably conservative position. Let us look at the presumably more liberal statement from the Association of Humanistic Psychology Practitioners (AHPP) in Britain. AHPP (1991) define a counsellor as:

someone trained to deal with immediate problems and crises which arise, such as bereavement, a broken relationship, a difficult marriage, a specific illness like cancer or AIDS, problems with children, etc. Many counsellors also deal with long-term problems. Counselling can also be done on a couple, family or group basis. Some counsellors use active techniques and give specific advice.

In the same document, a psychotherapist is defined as:

someone with a specialised, professional and broad-based training and the ability to work in depth with clients, sometimes for two or three sessions a week and often over an extended period of time, with people who may have complex problems.

This latter definition goes on to specify the length and quality of training, personal therapy and supervision required of AHPP approved psychotherapists. It also mentions that a knowledge of transference, countertransference and psychopathology is necessary. Now, I think it is obvious that even a humanistic agency such as AHPP seeks to make a supposedly qualitative distinction between counselling and psychotherapy. Counsellors work with certain 'specific problems' while psychotherapists work with 'complex problems'. Counsellors tend to do crisis (patch-up?) work, while psychotherapists work 'in-depth' and 'over an extended period of time'. This sort of wording reinforces the view that counsellors are lesser-trained problem-solvers in comparison with their extensively trained peers in the psychotherapy world who competently grapple with profound and complex intrapsychic issues. The acclaimed differences emerge: counselling is OK (runs the between-the-lines message) but psychotherapy is the real thing. To paraphrase a television beverage commercial or two, psychotherapy reaches the parts of the psyche other similar talking therapies can't reach; while psychotherapy might look and taste almost exactly like counselling, you can't beat the real thing. If this seems a cheap analogy, remember that counselling and psychotherapy *are* businesses whose training institutes have personnel and reputations to protect and promote, and part of any business is the promotion of its unique selling point. The early 1990s have witnessed, for example, advertising and legal battles by Coca Cola against rival soft drinks manufacturers.

Currently in the UK anyone without fear of prosecution may call himself or herself a counsellor or psychotherapist. Some training courses bear the title of Master's in Psychotherapy and Counselling as if the two activities are one. Indeed, certain courses now bear titles such as MA in Therapeutic Counselling, the terms 'therapeutic counselling' and 'psychological counselling' sometimes being used to identify counselling as essentially a psychotherapeutic activity. All counselling courses include psychotherapy texts in their reading lists. Many counselling publications (for example, the Sage *Counselling in Action* series) are written from a perspective of the interchangeability of these terms. The British Association for Counselling acknowledges that no final distinction can be made between the two activities.

Quilliam and Grove-Stephensen (1990: 22) in their consumer guide to counselling claim that:

> we spoke to counsellors who said they regarded themselves as therapists; we spoke to therapists who said they were counsellors . . . In the course of our research we collected a catalogue of completely contradictory definitions of the two words. However, when we asked a number of professionals why *they* chose the label they did, off the record quite a number admitted that it was a marketing strategy: 'counselling' sounds safer, 'therapy' sounds more daring.

Brown and Pedder (1979) adapt a model of psychotherapy containing four levels, which run from support and counselling, psychodynamically informed helping interactions and full 'dynamic psychotherapy' centring on the therapeutic relationship, through to behavioural psychotherapy. Counselling as such is regarded as belonging to an 'outer level' where 'ventilation of feelings and discussion of current problems enable a client to make and carry out appropriate decisions'. Furthermore, 'Rogerian therapists [counsellors] . . . do not explore at such depths as more analytic therapists'. Clearly the view held here is that counselling and psychotherapy reflect surface and depth respectively, even though both activities may be considered levels of *psychotherapy*. Jung made a similar distinction when he spoke of minor and major psychotherapy (see Samuels et al., 1986). It is amusing to realise that just as Brown and Pedder regard client-centred counselling as supportive and facilitative, but not exploratory, so many commentators today criticize person-centred therapy/counselling as being *too* exploratory, but not active enough. It should also be remembered that proponents of approaches like primal therapy are critical of the psychodynamic approaches precisely because the latter are considered anything *but* deep. This is a major criticism fired at psychoanalysis by Alice Miller, for example, who is the best known ex-psychoanalyst turned sympathiser with primally oriented therapy.

Mahrer (personal communication, 1992) comments that 'counselling and psychotherapy are distinguishable for those who find it professionally and politically important to distinguish one from the other. In terms of theory, practice, and training, I regard the two terms as essentially overlapping'. I personally trained as a counsellor. Many of my course texts were books on psychotherapy by psychotherapists. I have been a client in several different kinds of psychotherapy. I have seen clients for single (one-off) sessions, some for a few weeks or months, and others for two or three years. I have had many friends and colleagues who are psychotherapists. I have participated in group supervision sessions with both counsellors and therapists. Apart from differences in jargon and style, with their implicit underlying beliefs, I detect no essential difference between the work of counsellors and psychotherapists.

Thorne (1992) reviews the alleged differences, and notes that such tensions and battles existed for Rogers many years ago when he established the right of the Counseling Center at the University of Chicago to bear that name in spite of fierce protests from the Department of

Psychiatry. Thorne examines current literature purporting to define these terms and finds many of the above-mentioned alleged differences. He also addresses the claim that counselling and psychotherapy *overlap* but dismisses this argument on the grounds that this implies a continuum whose underlying meaning is never explained. What is usually implied by the overlappers, however, is that counselling is to be found at the shallow end, psychotherapy at the deep. Thorne concludes that clients generally know that one and the same activity is being practised under different banners. More importantly, he cautions that the 'quest for differences is both fruitless and dangerous'.

A counsellor colleague told me the following true story. A man who had attended clinical sessions with a psychoanalyst for many years, at a later stage in his life consulted a counsellor, for the sake of geographical convenience. After some experience of her way of working he asked her, quite reasonably, 'Why do you call yourself a counsellor when you do the same thing as my analyst did?' Since the counsellor was not even a psychodynamically trained counsellor (which would have helped to explain the likeness) we must ask why two apparently quite distinct activities appeared identical. Was the analyst a poor one, or the counsellor an exceptionally good one? Was the client wrong, or lacking in discrimination, or transferentially flattering/seducing the counsellor? Is this anecdote an anomaly? Or could it be that many talking therapists, whatever they may think or say they do, whatever their training, in fact often behave rather similarly in the consulting room?

This anecdote receives ironic endorsement from the analyst Symington (1986: 331) who says, 'At the end of a long analysis a patient said to me that he had not heard me say anything which he could not have heard from his mates at the local pub.'

Freud's celebrated Wolf-Man, however, was quite clear that a distinct difference existed. Many years after seeing Freud, following the death of his wife he had received help from the psychoanalyst Ruth Brunswick. This was much appreciated, but in the Wolf-Man's words, 'One could hardly call that a real analysis; it was more of a *Trost* (comfort, consolation)' (Gardiner, 1973: 341).

The difference between 'simple counseling' within a family therapy format and family therapy 'proper' is described by Richter (1974: 189), with reference to a particular case:

> This family was seen at long intervals only and their conflicts were not analytically worked through with the help of interpretations and explanations. The doctor limited himself to listening, to making supportive comments and, much more rarely, interpretations. Moreover, at a number of points he actively intervened with practical help.

Richter suggests that these factors, especially the leaning towards support rather than 'analytical working through', 'indicate a form of activity on the part of the doctor that is most accurately termed "counseling".' We might speculate that there are times in psychotherapy or family therapy when the work could be called counselling, and times in counselling when the work might be referred to as psychotherapy. We might also bear in mind the adage that 'all counselling is family counselling' (that is, the client's family is always implicated). This would perhaps take us, however, even further into ultimately fruitless semantic territory.

Clarkson (1994) believes that it is important to maintain the differences between counselling and psychotherapy. In her view, counselling is more often short-term work, with less seriously disturbed clients; it focuses on 'evolutionary change' rather than revolutionary change, and 'counsellors oil the wheels of someone's experience so that they manage to function better (1994: 9)'. Psychotherapists 'deal with more serious problems; . . . clients are seen frequently; . . . repetitive patterns of behaviour are identified, worked on and cleared. . . . Psychotherapists will usually have a wider range and greater flexibility in their working methods than counsellors or psychoanalysts' (1994: 12). This is claiming that there are not only real differences, but in many or most respects psychotherapy is superior to, or more comprehensive than, counselling. For Bugental (1992) too, psychotherapy is a 'life-changing' enterprise. A transcript of a clinical session recorded by Bugental has a client saying 'What will it be like to talk to a *psychotherapist*? I don't like that word; it scares me. Maybe I should be just seeing a *counselor*' (1992: 24; emphasis in original).

The claim that psychotherapy can be and is applied to more serious conditions than is the case for counselling has often been refuted. The clinical psychologist Johnstone (1989), for example, suggests that NHS psychotherapists are overly steeped in psychoanalytic theory, help only the most articulate, rewarding, middle class clients and have difficulty understanding and adapting to clients who are not middle class. Johnstone (1989: xi) also provides a curiously mixed definition of the terms under consideration:

> *Psychotherapist* is a general term for anyone of whatever profession who practises psychotherapy, the process of helping someone to understand and overcome their problems by encouraging them to talk through them in regular sessions, either on a one-to-one basis, or as a couple, or a family, or in a group. The term 'counselling' describes the same process, perhaps carried out in a more low-key way. (1989: xi)

Although almost anyone can practise psychotherapy, counselling is still a low-key version of it!

Naylor-Smith (1994) attempts to answer the question about the differences between counselling and psychotherapy, but from a psycho-analytically oriented psychotherapist's biased position. He is in no doubt that a spectrum exists and that counselling and psychotherapy show up on this in very different intensities.

> The exploring of the unconscious involves great skill. A practitioner has to become used to listening to communications at many different levels. This is especially true of understanding the transference. Our own therapy makes us

sensitive to the atmosphere in the room. . . . It is surely a good rule that we should not work with clients on a more frequent basis to that we have ourselves experienced in our own therapy. (1994: 286)

Psychotherapy is identified as intensive work (dealing with transference, phantasy, dependence, regression and so on) carried on during two, three or more sessions a week. Unless you have undergone a process of this relentlessness and frequency yourself, what you practise is unlikely to be (competent) psychotherapy. In this version of defining characteristics, psychoanalytic constructs and conventions self-servingly distance psychotherapy from counselling. Presumably counsellors who protest that they are aware of, and do work competently with, transference and other unconscious processes within their counselling, must be deluding themselves!

John Rowan (personal communication, 1993) regards counselling and psychotherapy as essentially overlapping but points out that counselling suffers from the fact that its courses are generally shorter (anything from a few weeks to three years, part-time), while courses in psychotherapy are never less than one year and usually three or more years, part-time. This lends added prestige to psychotherapy training. Of course, most (psychoanalytically oriented) psychotherapy training demands that trainees undertake therapy themselves, sometimes three times a week for several years. This factor also lends greater prestige to psychotherapy, since counselling courses rarely expect trainees to receive a comparable amount of personal therapy. However, one would have to compare actual hours of training to determine whether typical psychotherapy training is really longer or more substantial than, for example, BAC recognised counselling courses. Masson (1988: 293) claims that his own part-time psychoanalytic training took eight years, but could probably have been condensed into just a few hours of pertinent reading. He suggests that the real reason for a protracted training period is the indoctrination of therapists, or producing professionals who will have a great stake in remaining loyal. Since there is no research which shows any proven connection between receiving personal therapy as a trainee and offering more effective therapy as a therapist, this factor is not conclusive evidence anyway for the superiority of psychotherapy over counselling.

One might compare the typical content of psychoanalytically oriented psychotherapy and counselling courses in Britain. The former will probably contain a personal therapy requirement, participation in an experiential group, infant observation, seminars on theory and techniques, working with training patients and supervision. Theory centres on personality structure, mental processes and psychotherapeutic technique. Depending on the precise theoretical orientation, the writings of Freud, Klein, Jung and others will be studied. A psychiatric placement may be required. A typical substantial counselling course includes a core theory and comparable theories of personality development and therapeutic interventions, professional ethics, social contexts of counselling, personal development work, a practical placement and supervision. In addition, detailed and closely observed counselling skills training (often involving much role play or 'use of self') is usually an intrinsic part of any counselling course. My impression is that some psychotherapy training is strong on requirements for personal therapy and theory but weak on micro-skills training, while some counselling training is weak on require-ments for personal therapy, perhaps. It should also be noted that whereas for counsellors regular clinical supervision for the entire professional lifetime is mandatory, for psychotherapists and analysts this is not always the case.

This comparison could be stretched much further by throwing behav-ioural psychotherapy into the equation; representatives of this approach have objected that there is no real agreement on what constitutes an effective training in psychotherapy, and that this could only be measured ultimately by reference to improvements in clients' conditions (Sieghart, 1978). I cannot, in conclusion, see many substantial differences between psychotherapy and counselling training. Perhaps, since psychotherapy training is generally longer, it is likely to attract those who can afford the higher fees involved, and to reflect the values and personalities of this group. It has been claimed that prestigious training courses in Jungian analysis can cost well in excess of $100,000 and a commitment of at least six years (Noll, 1994).

Esterson (1988), like Halmos (1965), proposes that the term 'counselling' be used in place of all other terms referring to interpersonal helping. Esterson complains that the profusion of professional titles is an expression of practitioners' own confusion about what they are doing. He rejects the medical model and what he regards as the pretences of psychotherapists, and calls for honest brokers, perhaps to be known as existential counsellors, who should 'have no particular axe to grind, ready to admit being out of their depth and working on the principle that if one cannot help, one should not hinder' (Esterson, 1988: 166). Esterson has rejected, for himself, the titles of psychotherapist, family therapist, psychiatrist and so on, in favour of the connotations of guide, teacher and fellow-traveller, associated with counselling.

I believe all the above factors point to something deeply shaky at the heart of counselling and therapy that begs for essential analysis. The apparent name game under question ('What is counselling and what psychotherapy?') is sometimes justified as important in terms of protecting the public: potential consumers should know what they are getting, who is well trained and who is not, who is competent to rummage around in your unconscious and who is not. Rhetoric about protecting the public may be concealing both a very real ignorance and confusion among therapists and a culpable resistance to examining the semantic and institutional mess the field is often said to be in. Another issue, which may be termed the proprietary problem, is: who possesses the right to define counselling and psychotherapy and to dictate what goes on under those names? BAC

acknowledge that the word 'counselling' cannot be owned by the organization. Some psychotherapy organizations, as we have seen, seem rather
more possessive.

Talking therapists show great zeal when examining the minutiae of
clients' psyches and of their own theories, yet great apathy or coyness
when asked to examine the minutiae of their own professional semantics
and power plays. If it is hard to defend the idea that psychotherapy is a
more skilful activity than counselling, requiring far greater self-awareness
and lengthier training, then perhaps there is a reason for this difficulty. If
the critics of talking therapy are right when they say that its success
depends more on interpersonal bonds and non-specific relationship factors
than on theoretical approach or training, why is this idea so furiously
denied, suppressed or neglected? I believe that the popular success of
counselling in recent years highlights the embarrassing probability that
'lay' people with only a certain amount of training quite possibly often can
achieve results similar to those achieved by others who have had expensive
and extensive, supposedly specialized training. Some people with minimal
training may harm their clients, but Masson (1988) and others have argued
that often even the best trained and most revered therapists harm clients.

If the terms were clear and honest, there would exist no objection to
different activities being called counselling and psychotherapy, or any
other names. Having been asked to teach counselling to a group of
psychotherapy trainees, I have had the first-hand experience of wrestling
with the differences in practice. While I found that many of these trainees
were schooled in the idea that the client's deep and inevitably time-
consuming 'process' was almost sacred, I also found them very open to
considering the ethical and economic importance of working collabora-
tively with clients on what clients themselves want and what they (or the
agencies helping them) can afford. I have found few people disputing the
idea that many clients and counselling agencies cannot support indefinite
intrapsychic exploration. Limitations of time and money mean that the
discoveries and methods of brief therapy and counselling must be
experimented with and applied conscientiously. Sensitivity to the individual differences and needs of clients means that thoughtful counsellors
and therapists will want to adapt what they offer. As one writer on
therapy has commented, perhaps it is not ethical, when asked by someone
with little money wanting to buy a hat, to sell him a suit, since he cannot
afford it and does not want it (Goldberg, 1977). Yet the more stubbornly
we cling to our preferred therapeutic definitions, the more we place
ourselves in the position of the salesman who always knows best.

I will end this look at psychotherapy with a brief reference to brief
therapy. I have noted that there are many varieties of brief psychotherapy
even within the psychodynamic tradition, and many more outside it. It
seems to me that when we begin to allow terms like brief psychotherapy
and long-term counselling, with each of these disguising a multitude of
differing theoretical orientations, then we are implicitly confessing that the

field of the talking therapies is complex beyond linguistic redemption. Some forms of time-limited psychotherapy last 12 weeks, for example, while some counselling in practice lasts many years. Perhaps in the future, when we have more understanding and integrity, we will represent the field of therapy far more fairly and accurately to consumers.

It seems that the differentiation industry is growing rather than shrinking. The British Psychological Society (BPS) has introduced its Diploma in Counselling Psychology. Counselling psychology is different from mere counselling in that its practitioners must hold a psychology degree or equivalent and must use applied psychology in their counselling work. BPS (1993) acknowledges that 'counselling activity' takes place in many settings, but emphasizes that:

> It should be clearly defined as *counselling* by its scope, method, duration and intensity and not as social work, education, befriending or an activity which, by its setting, client expectation and organizational culture is perceived to be something else.

I hope that this tour of counselling's cousins helps to expose many of the overlaps, myths and actual distinctions between counselling and related activities and relationships. It may raise more problems than solutions, but if these are thought-provoking problems which can help to clarify and demystify the field, then I commend them to the attention of practitioners and consumers alike.

This is not an exhaustive list or analysis of such problems and never could be, since the range of human relationships and systems of personal knowledge is so immense. I have not looked at precise distinctions between counselling and psychiatry, and complementary medicine. I have not looked at the links between talking therapy and incidental therapeutic activities (many people obviously find therapy of sorts in their work, in the arts and religion). Neither have I looked at commonsense, folklore and wisdom. It is worth mentioning here that commonsense (a consensual, practical approach to life's problems) is regarded by many commentators as the basis of all effective psychological help. Alfred Adler was not ashamed to note the importance he attached to it. Reality therapy contains and dispenses a great deal of commonsense. Farrell (1981) admitted that psychoanalysis had a case to answer in respect of commonsense and its criticisms. The psychologist Stuart Sutherland (1992), as I have mentioned earlier, approves of cognitive therapies, but ranks even these as a form of glorified commonsense. Obviously commonsense often does not supply the answers or help that many suffering people seek, particularly when it is thrust at them in an unsympathetic manner. But equally, therapists and counsellors who lose sight of commonsense (or common wisdom, awareness of practical considerations, or necessary humility) altogether, are likely to become arrogant or dangerous practitioners.

4

The Emergence of
Contemporary Counselling

Any social theory of human social relations that stubbornly refuses to
see humans as evolved animals will come to grief.

Paul Gilbert (1989)

Although counselling in its modern form is certainly distinguishable from
other current and historical forms of healing and helping, it cannot be
understood as an entirely novel human process. The need for systems of
caring and talking therapies cannot be understood separately from a
consideration of human nature itself, including the universal and perennial
problems of suffering and psychopathology. This rather large area has
been the subject of a study by Gilbert (1989) which is based on an
evolutionary perspective. With the evolution of nursing – the phenomenon
of vulnerable and dependent human infants needing extended protection
and feeding – human beings achieved a quantum leap towards qualitative
existence and recognition as valued individuals. It has been argued that
human survival came to depend on increasingly complex modes of social
interaction and regulation, and that this adaptation has had not only vast
benefits but also great costs (Campbell, 1974: Freud, 1930). Social
cooperation has yielded rich and complex cultures spanning millennia and
characterised by the development of advanced language and technology.
Civilisation may also be simultaneously equated, however, with the suppression of healthy instincts, the use of language for self-deception and
deception of others, and ideological conflict between large groups leading
to war and genocide. Needless to say, these latter phenomena are reflected
in individual and social pathology.

Gilbert points out that throughout human evolution, the dependence of
infants on mediators (parents) has fostered an enduring propensity
towards care-eliciting and care-giving behaviour. Co-operative behaviour,
from the hunting and grooming of primitive human beings to the creative
teamwork of business colleagues, has enormous survival value, and
reciprocal altruism is a readily understandable behaviour. Along with this,
hedonic behaviour (associated with dependency and pleasure-seeking) and
agonic behaviour (associated with fight/flight responses) have developed.
Diverse observers have claimed that the struggles and successes of human
evolution (phylogenesis) have been internalised and are apparent in the
individual development (ontogenesis) of each human being from birth

onwards. It is not within the scope of this book to trace particular behaviour patterns, either phylogenetically or ontogenetically. What I do wish to raise, and remind readers of, is the long history and omnipresence of the human irony: we need each other, and yet 'hell is other people'; love-making and war-making (love and hate on the individual and global plane) are dramatically different sides of the same coin; we crave intimacy and yet we need space.

Such tensions are pervasive and are by no means absent from the hearts and minds of twentieth-century helping professionals and their institutions. We may constantly grapple with such ambiguities, yet arguably we are ever-prone to individual and collective self-deception with regard to how successful we have been in accepting and rising above these tensions. It has been noted that, as twentieth-century commentators on the therapeutic enterprise, we suffer inevitably from both ethnic chauvinism and temporal chauvinism, belittling or humouring the therapeutic efforts and rituals of our colleagues who are culturally and historically distant from us (Grossinger, 1982).

Care-eliciting and care-giving behaviour is universal but takes myriad, informal and professional, forms. In our own western therapeutic world, tensions abound between the many schools of therapy and their views on psychopathology and treatment. Individual caring professionals and their institutions, apparently dedicated to the relief of human suffering, *also* dedicate a great deal of effort to warring between themselves (Saltzman and Norcross, 1990). It is of some interest to speculate that the evolution of certain gender differences – the female as concerned primarily with attachment to and nurturance of the young, the male with separation from and later practical education of the not so young – has perhaps replicated itself respectively in the more nurturing (for example person-centred and psychodynamic) and coaching styles of counselling (for example behaviour therapy, reality therapy). Notable in this context, too, is the still persistent conflict between the affectively-biased and the cognitively-biased therapies.

These remarks are intended to underline some of what we do not fully know about ourselves as evolved animals and to commend an attitude of enquiring humility. As 'wounded healers', counsellors are probably not only as emotionally impaired as other human beings, but also as epistemologically impaired (see Chapter 7). It is easy for us to believe in our own ethnocentric theoretical orientations if we do not look at and ask questions about other times and places in which verbal and non-verbal therapy for human suffering was (and is) developed and applied (Kiev, 1964). Grossinger (1982) paints a picture of the earth as both hosting sickness and providing the means for its remedy in a wide diversity of ways, including allopathic and homeopathic medicine, talking therapies and somatic therapies. Indeed, sociological interpretations of health and illness increasingly point to problems in the conceptual relativity of health and illness. It is against this background of evolutionary and historical factors that we must consider the rise of the modern talking therapies. It may be, after all, that our therapies are essentially forms of or rationalis-ations for needed primitive psychological grooming, nursing and crooning (perhaps the simple 'Mmmm, mmmm' is more significant and powerful than we realise).

Some historical antecedents

The primitive study, understanding and remedying of sickness may be dated from the Palaeolithic era. The wearing of charms and amulets to ward off evil or unluckly spirits is one of the earliest signs of an awareness of anxiety and an attempt to address it. Aesculapius, claimed to be either a Greek god of medicine or an Egyptian magician (c.2900 BC), was believed to visit and cure sick people in their sleep. Early Greek hospitals provided for patients to receive this cure through the auspices of priest-physicians. Weatherhead (1952) regards this practice as the earliest known form of healing suggestion. In fact, according to Weatherhead, superstition, religious healing and ritual provided the roots of what we know as psychotherapy today:

> Astrologers, sorcerers, magicians, in Egypt, Babylonia, Judea, Chaldea, Arabia, Greece and Rome, believed in the efficacy of charms and incantations, of strange concoctions and in religious rites, and at this stage it is impossible to separate spiritual and physical healing. Indeed, it is not wholly possible even now. Here, in this strange medley of superstition and magic, were the origins both of religious healing and psychotherapy. (Weatherhead, 1952: 30)

Hippocrates, in the fourth century BC, is generally credited with ushering in a post-Aesculapian medicine by shunning the notion of supernatural causes. He discriminated between various forms of insanity and suggested that there were appropriately different forms of treatment. At this time Greeks and Romans began classifying those considered insane and devised elaborate treatment plans, which included exercise, music, diet and occupation, as well as the administering of emetics, purging and blood-letting. Interestingly, Celsius, writing in the first century AD, refers to Hippocrates as the person 'who first separated medicine from philosophy'. These trends – the distinctions and similarities between religious, philo-sophical, and scientific systems of understanding and healing – are discussed in other chapters. The Old Testament, for example, is replete with examples of physical and mental sickness, its diagnosis as invariably related to sin and punishment and its cure dependent on priestly or divine intervention.

Ellenberger (1970) traces some of the ancestry of dynamic psycho-therapy. He notes certain kinds of 'primitive therapy', including incuba-tion, which involved spending time in a cave experiencing apparitions or dreams; these would form part of a larger ceremonial interpretation and healing process. (The Japanese Morita therapy (Reynolds, 1980) and aspects of isolation techniques used in primal therapy, may reflect these incubation practices.) Ellenberger argues that primitive forms of hypnosis, telepathy and placebo treatment can be found or inferred from evidence. He refers, too, to 'rational therapies' or empirical applications of herbalism and prescribed, healthy changes in lifestyle found in primitive cultures from Liberia to Lapland. 'Philosophical psychotherapy' is the name given by Ellenberger to systems of thought and mental training such as yoga and Zen Buddhism, from the East. In the West, the various schools of philosophy (Pythagoreans, Platonists, Stoics, Epicureans) were more than intellectual schools; they also represented disciplined ways of living. A notable example is that of Galen, whose methods of self-control employed Stoical principles and who recommended alliance with a personal mentor. In Galen's *On The Errors of the Soul* intellectual and emotional sources of error are distinguished. Ellenberger suggests that our contemporary tendency to form divergent schools of therapy has a strong likeness to the diversity of Greek schools of philosophy.

In about 500 BC Aeschylus had referred to *iatroi logoi*, or 'healing words', as the equipment of the philosopher as physician of the soul. Foucault (1988) maps the concerns of Zeno, Epicurus, Epictetus, Seneca, Marcus Aurelius and others for the care of, and attention to the self. 'Spend your whole life learning how to live' was an aphorism approved of by Seneca and which, according to Foucault, 'asked people to transform their existence into a kind of permanent exercise' (Foucault, 1988: 49). Our contemporary interest in personal growth and self-improvement resonates with this. Retreating within oneself, seeking advice on conduct and general principles for living were vital questions for Seneca and others who, often from mid-life onwards, took up the study of philosophy in earnest. Special morning or evening times might be devoted to introspection, enabling one 'to commune with oneself, to recollect one's bygone days, to place the whole of one's life before one's eyes, to get to know oneself' (Foucault, 1988: 50). As well as this turning in on oneself, importance was attached to consultation with others. Early Greek philosophical schools encouraged the practice of tutoring, mentoring and spiritual direction. Some Romans employed philosophers to give advice and comfort, and sometimes such personal consultations were regarded as part of the function of friendship and social obligation. In addition to providing 'soul service', Epictetus stressed the significance of what we might now call holistic medical attention.

Some of the insights of the social historian Zeldin (1994) are suggestive. The ancient Egyptians, he reports, had their own variety of medical specialists and a belief that patients needed to talk and craved the attention of the doctor even more than seeking a medical cure. Considering Socrates the first conversationalist, Zeldin argues that actions have historically spoken louder than words and that speech has often been regarded as vain or foolish. Philosophy and democracy however encouraged dialogue and the expression of personal views. Storr (1988) suggests that the concept of individuality did not emerge much before 1200 AD and took several centuries to develop. Self-portraiture and autobiography did not really emerge until about the fourteenth century. The birth of salons from about the time of the Renaissance encouraged certain people to express themselves elegantly, although when greater sincerity was sought, they may have turned to letter writing. Our own age is increasingly dominated by technological communication of even intimate concerns (witness the advent of computer-assisted therapy and counselling by e-mail). What will future historians have to say about intimate communication in the late twentieth century?

Developments in psychiatry

In Europe from the Dark Ages to the late medieval period (c.475–1500 AD) people considered insane were often believed to be visionaries, but equally attracted fear and vilification for their supposed surplus of sin and their involvement with witchcraft, demonic possession and other super-natural forces. In thirteenth-century England, the concept of demonic possession began to give way to that of madness. In 1247 the Priory of St Mary of Bethlem in the city of London, was founded for the care of the insane. By the fourteenth century a large measure of official compassion was evident in the idea and practice of housing those who had 'lost their wits' until their 'reason was restored'. Along with this faith in the healing powers of nature or time often went, however, a public perception of the afflicted as vagrants and dangerous lunatics. Various laws passed between the fourteenth and seventeenth centuries focused on locking up insane relatives and on powers of seclusion generally. Simultaneously, a certain fear and respect was evident in the belief that the insane possessed special or supernatural insights.

Throughout the eighteenth century, statutory and philanthropic protec-tion of the insane was accompanied by abuse and malpractice, including beatings and chaining. Greater compassion and optimism, as well as practical welfare provision, continued to grow slowly. At the end of the eighteenth century certain pioneers (for example, the Frenchman Pinel) banned cruelty in hospitals and commended 'good-humoured resource-fulness' in staff. Pinel also devised the classification of mania, melancholia, dementia and idiotism. Insanity began to be accepted as a legal defence. In the early nineteenth century, enlightened reformers talked and wrote about the 'moral management' of the insane by attendants who were often former patients or members of religious communities. Szasz (1988) attributes to Johann Heinroth (1773–1843) the birth of modern psychiatry and psychotherapy. At about this same time, the beginnings of occu-pational therapy were in evidence.

Samuel Tuke established The Retreat at York in 1792 with a regime of tolerance and understanding that might have evolved further had the language to explain his ideals been available. Tuke also promoted the idea that patients were responsible for their actions. The understanding and treatment of people considered insane became relatively compassionate at the same time that psychiatric nursing was evolving. Thomas Digby, said to be the father of psychiatric nursing, managed the first purpose-built asylum in Australia in 1836 and showed that experienced attendants achieved at least as much success as medical practitioners. At this time, too, the job titles of attendant, keeper and nurse became interchangeable and mental nursing was commended as a worthwhile career for women. Patients were being classified as pauper lunatics or as private patients. Formal training of attendants began in England, Scotland and Australia in the late nineteenth century. It was recognised that mental nursing differed from general nursing in requiring different skills of judgement and observation. In the late nineteenth century the physician Kraepelin pioneered the classification of psychiatric disorders. At the turn of the century, research into mental illness was being funded and in 1911 the Diploma in Psychological Medicine was initiated in several universities, thus lifting the status of psychiatry generally. Promising developments in the treatment of shellshock, and also tertiary syphilis, also introduced a note of optimism into psychiatry. At about the time that Freud moved to England (1938) group therapy began to be practised by mental nurses. Respect for psychiatry grew at the time of the second world war, and the idea of mental health services and advocacy for the mentally ill also grew. In the 1940s group therapy and therapeutic communities based on psychoanalytic principles expanded.

Psychiatry has spawned and suffered a succession of theories and practices and has seen the ebb and flow of its reputation. The advent of electro-convulsive therapy (from the late eighteenth century onwards) and psycho-surgery (from the 1890s) stimulated first hope, then hostility. Psychotropic medication was from the 1950s the main breakthrough in the management of mental illness, but research into the causes of serious mental health problems remains inconclusive. In spite of the hope engendered by the anti-psychiatric movement begun by Laing, Cooper and others in the 1960s, there is little realistic prospect of the talking therapies making a major impact on schizophrenia, manic-depressive illness and other intractable psychiatric conditions. People suffering from these conditions, however, need considerable psychological support and often being listened and talked to are major helpful factors. Melanie Klein, Winnicott, R.D. Laing and others may have added to our understanding of or useful speculation about the causes of psychosis and schizoid states, but no one has discovered any consistently successful talking treatment for such problems. The general humanistic ethos of the psychotherapies probably has been responsible for liberalizing psychiatry and for helping to restore greater dignity to people with serious mental illnesses. It may have also encouraged experiments into community support and treatment.

One particularly important area in which the talking therapies, including behaviour therapy, appear more humane and effective than a biomedical approach is the treatment of the so-called neuroses, or mild to moderate depression, anxiety and other problems in living. Non-medical counselling proves to be both popular and reasonably effective in helping many people who might otherwise have been abandoned to the perils of the minor tranquillisers, for example. The Royal College of Psychiatrists in its 1992 Annual Report cites the evidence of a MORI attitude survey, which showed that while 30 per cent of the public doubted the helpfulness of antidepressant medication, 85 per cent considered that counselling would be an effective treatment for depression. Indeed, users of psychiatric services repeatedly demonstrate in surveys their wish for and faith in counselling. At the same time, a great deal of stigma is thought still to attach to the subject of serious depression and it may be that many people avoid reporting such conditions to medical or psychiatric staff for fear of being labelled and being coerced into unwanted treatments.

Developments in psychology

Capretta (1967) traces the elements of psychology from primitive animism, early Greek philosophy and natural science. Scientific thought begun by Aristotle was developed by others, including the Alexandrians Herophilus and Erasistratus, who contributed some of the first knowledge of the nervous system. Attempts to analyze consciousness by introspection date from the time of the Greeks and early Christians, especially Augustine. Philosophers across the centuries wrestled with the mind–body problem, with the concepts of commonsense, intuition, hedonism and perception, among others. Craniologists and phrenologists studied and attempted to account for individual differences and psychological functioning in terms of physical bumps and hollows in the cranium. Anatomical and physiological research has become extremely sophisticated in what remains a search for definitive locations within the brain of the many cognitive and affective functions. Physiological psychology, philosophical psychology and experimental psychology remain strong forces within the discipline of psychology, although the philosophical strand has suffered from the relative dominance of the natural science paradigm. No one can put a precise date on the birth of psychology, but the first journal of psychology, *Mind*, appeared in 1876, founded by Alexander Bain.

Clinical psychology may be said to date from the early Greeks, and particularly from Hippocrates and his view of the humours (blood, phlegm, black and yellow bile) and their role in the onset of illnesses. After Hippocrates and Galen, Aurelianus developed further understanding of mental disease and advocated relatively enlightened methods of treatment, including discussion. Paracelsus in the sixteenth century, and later Mesmer in the eighteenth century, focused attention on the power of magnetism. Exactly what is considered clinical psychology and what dynamic psychiatry, or its precursors, is open to debate.

Mesmerism dates from 1774, when Franz Mesmer, a German doctor, discovered that he could heal various illnesses by means of his own 'animal magnetism' combined with the use of actual magnets. Mesmer had a number of apparently spectacular successes, but also failures. He treated individuals but also conducted large group sessions using physical apparatus. He was regarded by many as having extraordinary powers, including the ability to influence people physically from a distance. Part of his method, often, was to induce a state of crisis in those he treated. This was based on a belief that certain fluids fill the universe and join people, and that in crisis their balance can be therapeutically changed. Another aspect of Mesmer's power was the induction of therapeutic crises in others by harmonica playing; a crisis room was prepared for those so affected, as many were. A royal commission in 1784 found no evidence of any magnetic fluid and concluded that imagination was responsible for any therapeutic phenomena associated with Mesmerism. Ellenberger (1970) believes Mesmer to resemble a magician more than a psychotherapist. However, consider the following comment on Mesmer's work: 'To make healing possible, he must first establish a rapport, that is a kind of "tuning", with his patient. Healing occurs through crises – manifestations of latent diseases produced artifically by the magnetiser so that he may control them' (Ellenberger, 1970: 69). This statement could also be made of aspects of psychoanalysis and other contemporary therapies.

Puységur extended Mesmer's methods by inducing a 'strange kind of sleep', resembling somnambulism. A crisis would be followed by a certain lucidity and an ability to self-diagnose and overcome one's own sickness or problem. This 'magnetic sleep' was later to be known as hypnotism. Puységur asserted that the essence of the healing principle in animal magnetism was simply to 'believe and want', thus casting a new psychological light on the process. The development of hypnosis continued with Bernheim, considered by some to be the most prominent psychotherapist before Freud. Indeed, Bernheim stressed the power of conscious suggestion, and gradually used this method – which came to be known as psychotherapeutics – more than hypnotism. It was Charcot who helped to achieve real credibility for hypnotism by charting its phases, studying and curing hysterical paralyses, and attempting to put these into some sort of neurological framework. He also showed an interest in faith healing. On the one hand, he apparently enabled people to walk who had been paralysed for years, and on the other he was regarded as a charlatan by Mesmerists, neurologists and others.

It has been speculated that Charcot's charisma, and the subsequent unwillingness of his staff to doubt him, coupled with the phenomena of expectation, conformity and even instances of outright fraud, accounted for at least some of his ostensible success. Today, hypnosis and hypnotherapy are regarded as legitimate clinical methods by some, as spurious by others. The latter half of the nineteenth century also saw the continuation of fortune-telling, mirror-gazing, crystal ball-gazing and spiritism. A line of direct influence can be traced from Mesmer himself to Mesmerism in the United States, as practised and developed by Phineas Quimby, who in turn treated Mary Baker Eddy, the founder of Christian Science. Freud, of course, had studied with Bernheim and Charcot and imbibed many of the European and American enthusiasms of the late nineteenth century, including some of the psychology of William James (Brown, 1961). Psychoanalytic developments receive attention in the following chapter.

The British Psychological Society was founded in 1901. British clinical psychology as a profession dates from the 1950s and had to contend with a well-established psychiatric profession and also with psychoanalysis. The Maudsley Hospital and the Tavistock Clinic were the centres of much of this new development and conflict. Hans Eysenck, following observations in North America, established clinical psychology training at the Institute of Psychiatry. Eysenck, certainly, was responsible for severe criticisms of all psychoanalytic traditions from the 1950s. Pilgrim and Treacher (1992) show that clinical psychology evolved from reliance on psychometrics through to behaviour therapy, and then to eclecticism. They argue, too, that the ethos of managerialism has superseded all others. Clinical psychologists were to be regarded as scientist practitioners, steering clear of the unproven, and perhaps unprovable, tenets of both psychoanalysis and humanistic therapy. As NHS professionals, they have less power than psychiatrists but more statutory power than psychotherapists or counsellors. Many clinical psychologists are ready to describe their clinical work as either counselling or psychotherapy and most probably practise somewhat eclectically (using behaviour therapy, cognitive-behaviour therapy, personal construct therapy, psychodynamic and person-centred methods). While this profession, comprising only about 2,500 members in the UK, often claims to offer superior treatment, especially in cases of severe mental distress – such as phobias, obsessive-compulsive disorders, eating disorders and so on – many counsellors and psychotherapists who are not psychologists provide very similar services.

Social background of the emergence of psychotherapy

Thomas's (1971) account of astrology, witchcraft, magical healing, divination and prophecy in sixteenth and seventeenth century England charts the relative decline of these activities against the strength of the Christian religion. Human life in these times was insecure, life expectancy was quite short and people were concerned with illness and ill fortune generally. Magical explanations and practices existed alongside official religious ones. Indeed, at the beginning of the sixteenth century it seems likely that there were as many wizards as members of the clergy. Popular magicians were known as 'cunning men', 'wise women', 'charmers' and 'sorcerers'. These helpers sometimes charged quite high fees and people would be prepared to walk 20 or 30 miles to see them. Traditional folk medicine combined commonsense remedies, often derived from practical nursing and midwifery experience, with knowledge of the healing properties of plants and other natural elements.

Belief in demons, the Devil, possession, curses, poltergeists, ghosts and fairies, was commonplace (as it still is in certain cultures). Astrologers and almanacs were regularly consulted as a means of allaying anxiety. But much of the strength of these beliefs declined towards the end of the eighteenth century, assisted by the Church's campaign against them. Advances in medical understanding and the introduction of insurance also helped to undermine the need for lucky charms and soothsayers. However, this subculture of belief in parallel explanatory worlds still exists, as the so-called New Age phenomenon in the late twentieth century attests. Thomas ventures to guess that 'about a quarter of the population . . . holds a view of the universe which can most properly be designated as magical' (1971: 667). Magical beliefs serve to 'ritualise man's optimism' and 'magic is dominant when control of the environment is weak' (Thomas, 1971: 648). It is tempting to think that those who had, and have, less socio-economic power, are prime candidates for belief in magic and the supernatural, but contemporary examples of affluent followers of, for example, Bhagwan Shree Rajneesh, or participation in various modern cults, challenges such an explanation.

Sennett (1986) attempted to identify historically the time when a meaningful public life gave way to the dominance of privacy and intimacy. Part of his analysis centres on English coffee-houses in the early eighteenth century, where conversation flowed, information was exchanged and an egalitarian ethos prevailed. Theatre-going also invited lively public conversation. Men's clubs were created in large part for privacy, although their very exclusiveness soon produced boredom. Parks were built and allowed for brief open encounters between anyone. At about the same time as this flux in the balance between public and private life, the notion of 'the right to be happy' began to take hold, supported by a switch from the Renaissance belief in physical 'humours' to the concept of 'natural sympathies'. The family began to assume a new importance. Gradually childhood came to be regarded as a quite separate realm from adulthood. Sennett suggests that by the nineteenth century, such was the pressure for the 'regulation of appearances' and 'fear of involuntary disclosure of emotion' (1986: 323) that hysterical disorders became inevitable. For London (1986), psychoanalysis was the timely cure for the Victorian 'age of repression'.

The very tension between private self and public reality invited the kinds of symptoms Freud was to grapple with. For Sennett, the narcissistic inwardness of twentieth-century human beings and loss of civilised participation in public life has led to a tyranny of intimacy. 'Masses of people are concerned with their single life-histories and particular emotions as never before; this concern has proved to be a trap rather than a liberation' (1986: 5). Even some contemporary psychotherapists have begun to suspect such a problematic shift (Hillman and Ventura, 1992). Sociologist Nikolas Rose (1989) offers an account of how psychology has been used in Britain during this century to help the war effort, the aftermath of war, the shaping of our educational system and the underpinning of a vast psychotherapeutic enterprise. Perhaps without awareness of the process, we have been swept up by a norm of autonomy which is mediated by psychological experts and special therapeutic language.

Pilgrim (1990) in a concise account of the context of early British psychotherapy places particular emphasis on the moral therapy of Tuke and others in the nineteenth century, since this was an attempt to offer kindness and consideration instead of physical treatment. Medical practitioners in the early twentieth century were in the main hostile to psychoanalysis but attention shifted, after the First World War, away from the treatment of madness to that of shell shock and other forms of breakdown among 'normal' people. Interest in psychotherapy – talking treatment – began to find a niche, often being applied to military problems and tried in experimental group settings. Gradually a vying for legitimacy between psychoanalysis and behaviour therapy came about. Psychoanalysis and its derivatives held some partial sway within the NHS but grew in the private sector where behaviour therapy has traditionally had little influence.

A focal point in the professionalisation of the talking therapies in Britain was the government report on scientology (Foster, 1971) which galvanised groups of psychotherapists into action, resulting in an official report on the need for the statutory regulation of psychotherapists (Sieghart, 1978). Scientology represented (and still represents) an interesting case of a movement which has claimed to offer methods of personal salvation, including a regressive, auditing process resembling a form of psychotherapy, as well as seeking the status of a church. Its detractors, of course, insist that it is a pernicious cult. Scientology throws into sharp focus the question of how one may discriminate between genuine and benign psychotherapies and fraudulent and/or dangerous lookalikes. Hubbard's *Dianetics: The Modern Science of Mental Health* was published in the USA five years after the end of the Second World War, and made a substantial appeal (Hubbard, 1950). It talks explicitly about 'therapy' and many of its concepts echo or copy psychotherapeutic terminology. It was obviously in the professional interests of both psychoanalytic and behavioural therapists to seek to distance themselves from scientology, both for scientific and economic reasons. In an age when official religion has declined and psychotherapy has boomed, scientologists have shrewdly kept the door open to belonging in both camps.

Zeldin (1994) asserts that conversation has always been, and still is, impeded by class differences, especially but not only in Britain. Gender too is a significant factor and Zeldin cites the views of American sociolinguistics scholar Deborah Tannen, who says that women gossip and indulge in the exchange of secrets and problems in order to overcome isolation, while men are not generally good listeners, tending instead to be pragmatic problem-solvers. Zeldin suggests that conversation differs sharply from confession and its secular variants because it requires equality. He also makes the interesting claim that while human beings have always sought escape from their personal troubles, most resort to pleasure-seeking, avoidance or suffering in silence. In one contemporary study cited by Zeldin, only 8 per cent had sought counselling; only 2 per cent had ever participated in political protest. Zeldin's scattered historical and current examples demonstrate that dialogue and help-seeking practices have their fashions and we can perhaps only guess whether our current wish to huddle together in pairs and small groups for counselling represents real progress or a transient fashion.

A note on non-western therapies

A vast subject in itself, comparative and transcultural therapy must be taken into account in any analysis of western talking therapies. All that can be done here is to refer to a few instances of therapies in other cultures and times. Kiev (1964) presents examples of folk psychiatry from around the world, including Alaskan shamanism, indigenous Yoruba psychiatry, withcraft in Cochiti therapy and psychotherapies among North American Indians, aboriginal Australians and the Kenya Luo. Kiev argues that certain therapeutic phenomena such as ritual, suggestion, emotional arousal, elicitation of hope, expectancy, the presence of a sanctioned healer and designated healing setting, are universal. This has been endorsed by Frank (1963). The Vodun priest (or *hungan*) of Haiti, for example, utilises client expectancy and anxiety, and his own standing in the community. Certain West Indian withcraft practices known as *obeah* involve catharsis induced by the practitioner, who is paid to deal directly with the perceived destructive elements within the sufferer. Belief in evil spirits, known by a multiplicity of names, pervades folk psychologies.

The originally Siberian term 'shaman' refers to charismatic healers who may become possessed during trance states and undergo their own cleansing sickness experience. A shaman is 'one who knows', who gains insight and healing power from life experience. Awe induction is often part of the shaman's craft. Shamanism is one of the exotic practices now to be found in humanistic therapy circles in the west, and the idea of the wounded healer has now become a commonplace. Our own psychological explanations and language for suffering and its remedies usually exclude reference to awe and evil spirits but make free use of metaphors derived from Greek myths, strange neologisms and impressive sounding scientific terms, often alluding to unobservable psychic states. Certain traditions of psychological healing (for example, psychoanalysis and other 'intellectual' therapeutic methods) have gained at least some academic and professional credibility in the west, but shamanism, as well as many other affectively-biased and subjectivity-loaded humanistic therapies, have largely remained in the non-academic sphere.

According to Kakar (1984) the kind of introspection required by psychoanalysis and other talking therapies is historically alien to Indian culture. Kakar regards psychoanalysis as belonging to a western tradition that can be traced to ancient Greek philosophical thought, whereas the healing traditions of India relate to sacred categories of thought where the Self is not an autobiographical entity but a transcendental reality. Kakar's own study of Indian healing suggests that theories of possession by demons and spirits still feature prominently. Even in Muslim societies where the Koran forbids magical practices, *sayanas* (wise or cunning people) are sought after for their ability to call up and vanquish demons. Many healers rely on 'soul knowledge' which may entail knowing how to be a 'conduit to Allah'. Years of healing practice can lead to certain gurus possessing 'soul force' or a quality of potent detachment. Kakar makes an interesting distinction between patients and supplicants, the former having psychological problems, the latter seeking better fortunes in life and better health. He also suggests that dissociation may be 'the single most widespread psychotherapeutic technique in the world today' (1984: 105). Special breathing techniques, re-birthing, dance and music which effect altered states of consciousness are all dissociation techniques.

Kiev warned in 1964 that certain western talking therapies could – and obviously should not – be imposed unthinkingly on other cultures, although they might be used complementarily. The 1990s show that sensitivity of this kind has still to be improved, but increased attention to cultural factors by medical anthropologists is now in evidence. Just as Kakar (1984) noted a leaning among some Indians towards western-style therapies in order to become comfortable with their own individuality, so we can observe the quantum growth in the west, from the 1960s, of interest in Zen, yoga, meditation, Carlos Castaneda, Bhagwan Shree Rajneesh, alternative medicines, and so on. Kakar speculates that the unconscious of the western individual may be more collective in nature than we have realised, which may help to explain the phenomenon of the western seeker.

Belfrage's (1981) wry account of a pilgrimage to India to learn from Bhagwan refers to a friend who, after 'an endless psychoanalysis', had studied academic psychology, trained as a psychotherapist, yet still felt unfulfilled: 'Is Bhagwan what she needs?' (Belfrage, 1981: 24). Included on the menu of therapeutic and spiritual activities available at Bhagwan's Poona ashram were chaotic breathing, a vipassana intensive, structural integration, Tai Chi Ch'uan, Zazen, primal therapy, massage, hypno-therapy, Sufi dancing and Tathata. This was a time when the cross-fertilisation of oriental therapies and western human potential experiments was at its height. The Indian writer Gita Mehta (1990) is aware of the danger of searching for false exotic solutions to life's problems and has commented that:

> If the white man lives in a madhouse of abstractions, then we live in a madhouse of distractions. But we give our distractions philosophical names, such as Bhakti Yoga, the meditation of adoration, Hatha Yoga, the meditation of physical endurance. . . . Our meditations and our spiritual techniques have degenerated into payola systems. . . . like the practical jokes being perpetrated daily in the ashrams of India. (1990: 193)

Contemporary New Age developments include a large measure of non-western and archaic ingredients, however. An article in the humanistic magazine *Cahoots*, for example (Lambrias, 1994) discusses the process of Soul Retrieval, a neo-shamanic voyage of self-discovery. The illustrative client, who had been raped years earlier, reports being enormously helped by her Soul Retrieval Guide who facilitates an imaginal journey involving an Animal Helper, a Spirit Guide (called Merlin) and a River of Life. The client reports that she can 'see all my chakras', that there are many healing colours available to her, and she wonders who her 'dowsing guide' is on this journey. She summarises the journey as wonderful and helpful. The Soul Retrieval Guide in question is able to call on his powers of hypnotherapy, past lives healing, Spirit rescue, Earth Bound releases, and so on. Whatever one makes of this, it is a fact that many people practise in such ways and many claim to be helped. Reaction against the western medical model of treatment has spawned the anti-psychiatry movement and a turning towards alternative medicines including homeopathy, born in the early nineteenth century, whose proponents often claim effective treatments for psychological ills, and originally Chinese healing methods such as acupuncture, again, a treatment method that is applied as much to psychological as to physical ills.

One of the questions deserving attention is why different therapies emerge and thrive in different places, cultures and times. Along with this question might go the question of whether therapies are more localised than we realise, and whether they are sometimes applied unhelpfully beyond their time and place. Meier (1967: 33) has been one of the few therapists to suggest that 'sanctity is bound up with locality' and that there may be a meaningful 'geography of the human psyche'. Psychoanalysis was born in nineteenth-century Vienna and expanded rapidly to the UK and the USA. Certain commentators believe that it is now declining in popularity in the USA as socio-economic and scientific factors throw unfavourable light on it. Humanistic therapy grew out of American – particularly Californian – soil, reflecting certain cultural conditions which are not found in considerably poorer countries (Pilgrim, 1992). In the UK, person-centred and psychodynamic therapies remain dominant, reflecting perhaps a certain liberal tradition and fascination with depth explanations. Family therapy flourishes in Italy, where the nuclear family has long been of central importance. Jungian therapy, although growing in influence throughout the world, remains most influential in affluent cultures such as

Switzerland. Morita therapy and other meditational therapies retain a strong place in Japan, but are largely unknown in Britain and the rest of Europe. The factors underlying successful import and export of talking therapies have been surprisingly little studied.

Counselling is born

Counselling (or perhaps here we should use the American spelling 'counseling') may be dated from the early 1900s, according to Weinrach (1992) and Whiteley (1984). In its modern, distinctive form as a psychologically informed, disciplined activity, it is clearly an American-inspired phenomenon. While psychoanalysis and psychotherapy have strong European roots, most adaptations of psychotherapeutic theory and practice, including the development of counselling, have come from American soil. Obviously this is no accident and greater understanding of this fact would be helpful in understanding exactly what counselling is.

Whiteley (1984) tells us that vocational guidance was the source of counselling as a profession. Frank Parsons and others in Boston, USA, offered vocational guidance to young people at a time when educational and careers opportunities began to flourish. Indeed, Parsons probably established the first counselling centre in Boston in 1908 and is still referred to for the significance of the dimension of social action associated with his work (Bond, 1993). In 1913 the National Vocational Guidance Association was founded in order to help match individual preferences with available jobs and to effect rapid social improvements. Psychometric testing also began to get under way at about this time, with the advent of the First World War, and the ability to identify individual differences and aptitudes meshed well with the vocational guidance movement. The aftermath of the war demanded resources for rehabilitation counselling. Whiteley suggests that the mental hygiene movement of the early 1900s, associated with Beers and others who focused attention on mental breakdown and its treatment, was an integral part of the formation of counselling psychology. Rollo May (1992) wrote what is thought to be the first book on (psychotherapeutic) counselling in the 1930s.

Special mention is made by Whiteley and many other commentators of Carl Rogers, whose artful avoidance of conflict with the psychiatric profession led him to name his activities counselling instead of psychotherapy, and whose early work with maladjusted children led him to formulate non-directive counselling. Rogers's published views on counselling and psychotherapy, suggesting that they could be conducted by non-medical practitioners, helped to throw open the doors for rapid expansion of the counselling psychology movement in the USA.

The American Psychological Association (APA) rapidly expanded in the 1940s and 1950s, and its Division 17, originally the Division of Personnel Psychologists, became the Division of Counseling Psychology in 1953.

From about this time the APA has suffered from various controversies over the definitions of counselling, counselling psychology and clinical psychology.

The American Association for Counseling and Development (now the American Counseling Association) came into being following the joint convention of the National Vocational Guidance Association, the American College Personnel Association, the National Association of Guidance and Counselor Trainers and the Student Personnel Association, in 1952. These groups became divisions within AACD and were joined successively by groups representing counsellor education and supervision, career development, schools counselling, rehabilitation counselling, employment counselling, multicultural counselling and development, religious and values issues, group work, addictions and offender counselling, mental health counselling, military education and counselling, marriage and family counselling and college counselling. The American School Counselor Association (ASCA) is the largest division, followed by the American Mental Health Counselors' Association (AMHCA). AACD (now ACA) membership grew from 6,089 in 1953 to over 58,000 in 1991.

Special mention should be made of German-born but British Hans Hoxter, who in 1950 founded the International Association of Educational and Vocational Guidance which eventually became the International Round Table for the Advancement of Counselling (IRTAC). IRTAC now has the distinction of being a non-governmental organisation recognised by the United Nations to speak for counselling. Inspired by both psychoanalysis and the American counselling movement, Hoxter established links between American counsellor educators and British universities, arranging for visiting Fulbright fellows to help set up and teach on the first counselling courses in the UK at Keele and Reading in the 1960s. Naturally, the influence of Rogers and of student-oriented counselling generally was paramount in these developments. The British counselling scene may be fairly said to have been enormously influenced by this American input. Some would say that counselling in the UK is, indeed, an American import.

The British Association for Counselling (BAC) grew out of the Standing Conference for the Advancement of Counselling (SCAC), itself founded in 1971. From the mid-1970s discussions were held which led to the official formation of BAC. The National Association of Young People's Counselling and Advisory Services (NAYPCAS) had its inaugural meeting in 1975, before BAC came into being. Bill Kyle, a Methodist minister, had first proposed an organization for pastoral counselling in 1965, which became the reality of the Westminster Pastoral Foundation in London in 1969. The Dympna Centre was founded by the Roman Catholic priest Louis Marteau in 1971. Student counsellors were already working in schools and colleges in Britain in the late 1960s and early 1970s and the Association for Student Counselling was one of the earliest established associations of its kind in the UK. The early 1970s also saw in the UK the formation of the National Institute for Careers Education and Counselling (NICEC).

As in the USA, then, in the UK counselling had its origins primarily in a concern for the welfare of students and young people. The well-worn adage that whatever happens in the USA happens 10 or 20 years later in Britain, appears to be true of the development of counselling. In 1977 BAC had 600 members. By 1993 this had risen to approximately 10,000 and by 1995 to 13,000. Like ACA, BAC has its divisions, which include the Association for Student Counselling, the Association for Pastoral Care and Counselling, Association for Counselling at Work, Counselling in Medical Settings, Counselling in Education, Race and Cultural Education in Counselling and the Personal/Sexual/Relationships/Family division.

Like ACA, BAC has experienced ongoing debates about the meaning of counselling, its distinctiveness from other similar activities and the means of professionalizing it. In 1974, a writer in SCAC's *Counselling News* (Deitch, 1974) suggested that the differences between counselling and social work were mainly historical: 'social work dates from the latter half of the 19th century and is based on helping the poor and needy. Therefore it has become mainly the resource of the working class. Counselling is a relatively new concept with no standard body of knowledge, which causes confusion and conflict among its practitioners.' As the report made by Russell et al. (1992) shows, attempts to address this confusion are continuing. It is notable that within BAC membership different opinions exist among those who consider counselling and psychotherapy to be identical and those who consider them to be quite distinct. It has been mooted within BAC that the organization might consider changing its name to the British Association for Counselling and Psychotherapy, but there seems currently to be insufficient appetite for such changes to be implemented.

The growth of psychotherapy had been taking place earlier than, but also alongside that of counselling. Although the London Psycho-analytical Society was established by Ernest Jones in 1913 and the Tavistock Clinic was set up in 1920, psychotherapy as a profession really began to become firmly established in the UK from the 1930s, with the arrival of Sigmund Freud and Anna Freud, and later with that of Melanie Klein and others. In the 1950s a number of psychoanalytic institutes developed, sometimes splintering into others with different theoretical leanings. The Association of Psychotherapists (now the British Association of Psychotherapists) was formed in 1951. It was seen as a coming together of Freudian and Jungian psychotherapists, a forum for case discussions and conferences and a starting point for psychotherapeutic training. It was not regarded as necessary for psychotherapists to be medically qualified, although there had been major disagreements about the question of lay analysts. It came to be recognised by some that psychoanalysis profited from evolving separately from clinical psychology and psychiatry, and even that it was conveniently regarded by some as a movement of harmless eccentrics.

Many psychotherapy training bodies still retain the status of outsiders, that is as independent institutions with no direct affiliation with health or academic bodies.

Voluntary and mutual aid associations

Alcoholics Anonymous was founded in 1935 by the New York stock-broker William Wilson and Ohio surgeon Robert Holbrook Smith (later known in AA as Bill W. and Dr Bob). Wilson had had a religious experience which seemed to free him from his own destructive enslavement to alcohol, and he and Smith agreed to help each stay sober by using spiritual principles. Both men were involved with the Oxford Group, an evangelical Christian movement of the 1930s. They based their explanation for their own recovery from alcoholism on the recognition that they had been 'powerless over alcohol', their 'lives had become unmanageable' and that 'a Power greater than ourselves could restore us to sanity'. These precepts became the now-famous 12 steps of AA, which lead all those following them through a sequence of total abstinence, soulsearching, confession and active helping of fellow sufferers. AA mushroomed from that point to the international organization it is today. AA estimates that it has over 88,000 groups worldwide, with over two million members in 134 countries. Although it cooperates with helping professionals, it is essentially a self-help movement (indeed, a fellowship) based on non-psychological principles and not belonging within mainstream counselling psychology. Its critics decry its allegedly pseudo-scientific approach, its reliance on spiritual principles, folklore and peer pressure. Nevertheless, vast numbers of people apparently attest to its benefits and it has expanded into similar fellowships for drug addicts, gamblers, 'shopaholics' and many other groups of people with compulsive behaviour.

The British organization Relate, formerly the National Marriage Guidance Council, was established in 1938. It grew from the work of Dr Herbert Gray, a clergyman, who was concerned at the rising divorce rate, felt impelled to research the issues and, together with colleagues, to begin to educate people. In 1943 a London office was opened which offered counselling. Its service was rapidly demanded and its centres expanded. It now has about 500 centres offering couple counselling, sex therapy, divorce counselling, conciliation, education and training. A voluntary agency whose service is in great demand, Relate struggles to keep down apparently unavoidable waiting lists. Relate is staffed largely by trained but volunteer counsellors. Unlike the Samaritans, whose ongoing commitment is to befriending, Relate seeks to increase its professionalization by upgrading its training standards. It also conducts ongoing research into marriage and relationship breakdown and acts as a lobby for marriage and family life.

The Samaritans was established in 1953 by the English clergyman Chad

Varah. Varah (1985) was puzzled by the statistics on suicide which included the reports that three people killed themselves in London every day and that the majority had visited their doctor within three weeks of their death. He speculated that they did not need, or could not benefit from, medical or psychiatric help, but might respond to some other form of help. He conceptualized suicide as an emergency and a service for suicidal people as an emergency service. An energetic and extremely gifted man, Varah had been involved in sexual counselling since 1935, but visualized this new service as being staffed by non-specialist volunteers. By his own persistence and creativity he launched The Samaritans first in London, then nationally, and it is now a worldwide organization. The Samaritans offers confidential telephone and personal befriending or 'listening therapy'. Their aim is 'to be available at any hour of the day or night to befriend those passing through personal crises and in imminent danger of taking their own lives'. Samaritan volunteers are carefully chosen and trained but the organization is dedicated to remaining non-professional (not unprofessional). Its overriding aim is the reduction of suicides.

Personal social services

The personal social services in the UK (Sutton, 1989b) evolved from the many nineteenth-century philanthropic organizations, originally church-based, which addressed the needs of the most poor and vulnerable in society. In the twentieth century the state has gradually taken over responsibility for much of this work. A seminal text in social work (Biestek, 1957) offered the central principles of individualization (respect for each client's uniqueness); purposeful expression of feelings; controlled emotional involvement on the part of the social worker/caseworker; acceptance and non-judgementalism; client self-determination; and confidentiality. Biestek, a Jesuit priest, drew from psychoanalytic and theological sources. In another text on casework, Heywood (1967: 43) gives the following succinct account of the development of social work principles:

> Caseworkers are heir to four streams of tradition: first, that of active philan-thropy, compassionately concerned about the inarticulate minorities; secondly, that of men's democratic struggle for the right to self-assertion, self-fulfilment and self-responsibility; thirdly, the assertion of the feeling part of man, first overtly stressed by the romantic writers and painters at the beginning, significantly, of the machine age, and later underlined by the theory of Freud and of the analysts; and, fourthly, the inductive thinking of the social scientists.

Heywood goes on to outline the conditions of acceptance, open com-munication, trust and confidentiality. She argues for a casework method based on eliciting facts, searching for a pattern, formulating a tentative psycho-social diagnosis, a plan of acton tailored to the individual client and a process of helping the client to put the plan into action. Those familiar with the work of Egan (1990) and with the more reality-oriented, problem-solving styles of counselling, will readily see the similarities. Where much contemporary counselling appears to depart from social work is that, although counsellors may engage in some form of psychological diagnosis, they are far less likely to diagnose or address clients' social problems. They are also not primarily bound by agency policies but by professional ethics and client agendas.

As Sutton (1989b) points out, the development of social work has been very much influenced by Freudian theory and remains so, but has also taken in some of the concepts of humanistic psychology, particularly client-centred tenets. Where counselling and counselling skills are taught on social work courses, the client-centred or person-centred approach is likely to be given prominence, often along with a certain amount of psychodynamic theory. Social workers are frequently involved in discussing issues with their clients (for example, child abuse) which impinge on certain statutory obligations and for this reason, as I have mentioned earlier, many counsellors are wary of too close an identification of counselling with social work. But as Sutton and others have argued, counselling and social work interviewing are intimately related.

Sutton (1989b: 112) writes that 'a worker discussing welfare rights entitlement who sees the distress on a client's face would swiftly move from "interviewing" to "counselling" and back again, as time and circumstances permitted'. The current BAC view on this appears to be that such counselling is more properly called the use of counselling skills than counselling. The term 'social work counselling' is, however, also used (Scott and Freeman, 1992). It should be mentioned that many social workers refer to their face-to-face work with clients as counselling and in some cases as psychotherapy. The Group for the Advancement of Psychodynamics and Psychotherapy in Social Work (GAPPS), which is a member of the United Kingdom Council for Psychotherapy (UKCP) advocates that much casework be considered psychotherapy:

> In most social work agencies there is a place for actual psychotherapy for a small number of clients, and in such settings as child guidance clinics and psychiatric departments the social workers are in effect often expected to carry out psychotherapy. (Temperley and Himmel, 1986: 14)

Professions in conflict

While some in Britain may prefer to regard the established professions of psychiatry and clinical psychology, and the still emerging professions of psychotherapy and counselling, as being in a state of harmonious interplay, this would be a difficult claim to justify. Consumers of these services are probably confused about the differences. Rusk (1991: 151) advises consumers in an American context that professional titles cannot be trusted and that 'an MFC (Marriage and Family Counselor) is likely to be more flexible and less dogmatic than a psychiatric MD or institute-certified psychoanalyst'. Practitioners themselves may seek common ground but are quite likely to press for the uniqueness or superiority of their own profession. A medically qualified psychiatrist who spends some of his or her time providing talking therapy will not argue that lay counsellors can provide comparable services but is likely to argue that he or she is offering a superior service. The *Diagnostic and Statistical Manual*, now in its fourth edition, serves the purpose, for example, of demonstrating the ability of (mainly American) psychiatrists and psychologists to assess, identify and specifically treat a wide range of psychological malfunctions. Counsellors are unlikely to refer to such works, and some psychotherapists admit to using them only because their terminology impresses and is required by health insurance companies. Psychiatrists sometimes offer 'psychiatric debriefing' to survivors of traumas such as being held hostage. The same activity provided by a counsellor is referred to simply as counselling or debriefing. I have seen the term 'psychiatric counselling' in use (*Guardian*, 17.1.95), presumably referring to counselling by community psychiatric nurses.

London (1986: 136) believes that 'the main fight has been between psychiatrists and psychologists; the former seek monopoly control, the latter a bigger slice of the economic pie'. I have personally heard psychologists referring to counsellors as 'soft' (that is, less rigorous than themselves) and counsellors dismissing psychologists as scientistic, unsupervised, and ignorant about the importance of the therapeutic relationship. Counsellors regularly decry the 'medical model' as supposedly used by all psychiatrists, and psychiatrists are not slow to cast doubt on the competency of counsellors (Persaud, 1993). But fights and debates there have been from the very beginning of psychoanalysis. Freud was always in favour of allowing, indeed encouraging lay analysts, or analysts who were not necessarily medically trained. He resisted what he saw as the tendency of American psychiatry to annex psychoanalysis, regarding it as a discipline in its own right, somewhere between medicine and ministry. Carl Rogers, as we have seen, did battle with the psychiatric establishment. But many psychoanalysts too have been anxious to preserve the superiority of their discipline over the supposedly inferior discipline of psychotherapy and, in the UK, disagreements within the United Kingdom Standing Conference for Psychotherapy eventually split it into the United Kingdom Council for Psychotherapy and the British Confederation of Psychotherapists, the latter representing those who insist on analytic purity, more frequent sessions of training analysis for trainees, and so on.

All such fights and splits are always represented as concerns for standards of practice and protection of the public, but sceptics have long dismissed these claims as bogus: the real issues, they say, are about protecting the guilds of practitioners themselves, their reputations and their livelihoods. Pilgrim and Treacher (1992) have spelled out many of the issues at stake in these turf wars, especially as they impinge on the profession of clinical psychology. All talking therapies probably help somewhat, according to these authors, but clinical psychologists, like others, exaggerate their distinctiveness and effectiveness. The public is 'encouraged to believe that clinical psychologists really *are* experts in human misery, instead of practitioners who have a partial, confused or uncertain understanding of their fellows and a fairly modest set of current proposals for the amelioration of their distress' (Pilgrim and Treacher, 1992: 195).

Consumers face, then, a bewildering array of different theoretical models of therapy, but in addition these are practised by confusingly similar or overlapping professions; as well as psychiatry, psychoanalysis and psycho-therapy, one must consider counselling, psychiatric nursing, social work and other allied professions and lay helping activities. Each has its tradition, figureheads and certification procedures and most attempt to demonstrate some degree of superiority with regard to others. There is nothing new in this, of course. Religions and philosophical schools have jostled for credibility and converts over the ages. Religion has attempted to eradicate magic (Thomas, 1971) and science has sought to displace religion. Malan (1979: 6) cites the case of the early Franciscans who paradoxically began to attract great wealth and status, including a 'holier than thou' reputation, thus causing friction among competing religious orders and academic authorities. Such phenomena can be seen easily with hindsight, but faced with our own contemporary competing professional claims we seem rather less sure about who can and cannot command our belief as bona fide talking therapists.

Professionalisation

Freud faced early on the question of what kind of profession psycho-analysis might be. In 1926 his junior colleague Theodor Reik was taken to task by the Austrian authorities for practising as a psychoanalyst when he was not medically qualified. Freud defended Reik and the principle of allowing lay (non-doctor) analysts (Freud, [1927] 1978). He argued artfully that since analysts used no medicines but only talked and exchanged information, they could not very well be forbidden to do this. Freud even alluded to Christian Science in his argument, stating that although he disapproved of it, it could not be forbidden because nobody could be certain of 'the right path to salvation' and nobody had the right to dictate where personal salvation might be sought. On the one hand, Freud strongly asserted that analysts were not a 'chance collection of riff-raff, but people of academic education, doctors of philosophy, educationists, together with a few women of great experience in life and outstanding personality' (Freud, [1927] 1978: 79). On the other hand, he also envisaged the possibility of a large scale training programme, perhaps converting social workers into lay analysts who would resemble a kind of Salvation Army ([1927] 1978: 85).

Amateur or lay counselling has been conducted for decades, and indeed with pride, in various voluntary organisations. Much counselling was offered by social workers, child care workers, doctors and almoners before any separate body of counsellors emerged. Part of a talk entitled 'What is counselling?' given by John Wallis in 1955 to the National Marriage Guidance Council was reported in the following terms:

> Counselling, in short, is not just a matter of technique or psychology; it rests on a sensitive and intelligent understanding of the terms on which we all live, learnt mainly from the Counsellor's own experience. He must treat his client as he would himself wish to be treated. He will find no short cut, no secret of success; he will never be fully 'qualified'. He must not expect miracles, still less presume to work them. By using his heart as well as his head, by listening with reverence to the 'inner voice', which is the third part in each consultation, he may achieve his objective and guide those who consult him to discover their own solution.

This wording conveys perhaps how closely counselling was associated with Christianity. It was often regarded as an altruistic service and its efficacy as dependent on 'heart' and reverence. At this stage it would presumably have been unthinkable and undesirable that counselling would one day become a profession in its own right. Even in a recent text on counselling in the voluntary sector (Tyndall, 1993), there are hints of misgivings about the tendency towards professionalisation. Tyndall recalls that the Catholic Marriage Advisory Council's counsellors were dubbed 'formal friends' as late as 1980. He also makes the point that counsellors in voluntary organisations are much more likely to do home visits than are so-called professional counsellors. The person-centred, psychodynamic and Egan models of counselling are still much more in evidence in voluntary settings than are the newer models. It is unlikely that there will be much decrease in demand for counselling from voluntary organisations, if only on economic grounds. Counselling that is not wholly professionalised will therefore probably continue for some time to come, even through tensions generated by increasing attention to counsellor accreditation.

From about the time counselling was taking hold in Britain in the 1960s, the Foster Report recommended that legislation be introduced for the control of psychotherapy (Foster, 1971). Ten years later a Bill to the House of Commons along these lines failed. In 1982 BAC organised a working party to discuss the Foster and Sieghart Reports, and regular meetings known as the Rugby Psychotherapy Conference were held until 1989. This was transformed into the United Kingdom Standing Conference for Psychotherapy in 1989 and into the United Kingdom Council for Psychotherapy (UKCP) in 1993. The UKCP has over 70 member organisations representing the majority of psychotherapy training organisations. BAC is not one of these, but is known as a 'friend of the Council'. The UKCP publishes a National Register of Psychotherapists, corresponds

with Government departments and has links with the European Association for Psychotherapy.

The British Psychological Society (BPS) also responded to the Foster
and Sieghart Reports. According to Pilgrim and Treacher (1992) this
created problems within BPS, with its Division of Clinical Psychology
arguing in 1979 that BPS urgently needed a register of applied psychologists. Since then chartering for psychologists has been instituted, as it has
also for counselling psychologists. BPS members had rapidly become
aware of competition. 'If, as was the case, and still is, anybody could put a
plaque on their door saying 'Psychotherapist', there was the spectre of a
motley collection of self-styled therapists with no training in psychology or
medicine competing for mental health clients' (Pilgrim and Teacher, 1992:
148). BPS, like the UKCP, presents its credentialling processes as primarily
in the interests of protecting the public. Increasing competition among
mental health professionals and anticipated regulatory pressures stemming
from Britain's closer ties with Europe since 1992, are however seen as the
real motivators for professionalisation by many critics. According to an
article in The *Sunday Times* (26.9.93), the UK has something in the order
of 30,000 paid counsellors/therapists, an additional 270,000 volunteer
counsellors, and an estimated 2.5 million people who use counselling skills
as an integral part of their employment.

The British Association for Counselling first introduced its counsellor
accreditation scheme in 1983. Its aims include the protection of clients, the
education of the public and clarifying and raising standards of training
and practice. It is a voluntary procedure (although applicants must pay a
not inconsiderable fee to apply), involving demonstrations on paper that
one has completed a certain number of hours of training in counselling
theory and skills. Applicants submit case studies, evidence of a certain
number of clients seen over so many years, evidence of personal and
professional development, and the testimonial of a supervisor. It has been
highly contentious, since many very experienced and able counsellors
either cannot, or choose not to meet its requirements. Although its
purpose has never been to suggest that the accredited are superior in
competency to the unaccredited, the scheme has had exactly this effect.
Newspaper advertisements for counsellors now usually ask that applicants
be either BAC accredited or eligible for accreditation, so it has become
something of a *sine qua non* for those seeking employment as counsellors.
BAC also has schemes for the recognition of supervisors and of training
courses. Again these are voluntary, but somewhat costly, and like individual accreditation must be renewed every few years. The requirements
for all these schemes have added prestige to counselling as an emerging
profession but are also criticised from many angles.

The calculated professionalisation of the talking therapies is clearly
contentious. Humanistic therapists Brown and Mowbray (1990) complained that increased regulation would lead to 'a deterioration in the
prevailing ambience of openness and choice'. Defending the human

potential model of growth, they argue that it is about holistic education and development and should not be associated with the medical model and the kinds of licensing or accreditation produced by it. They quote Will Schutz: 'Licensing does not protect the public. Licensing does not exclude incompetents. Licensing does not encourage innovation. It stultifies' (Brown and Mowbray, 1990: 35). An empowering alternative recommended by Brown and Mowbray is that of full disclosure on the part of practitioners of their training, qualifications, experience, competency, philosophy, and so on. Individual clients might sue if necessary, if they felt that incompetence or dishonesty was involved, but this system would give power back to both practitioners and clients, rather than to the state or to therapeutic bureaucracies. A footnote to this article by Miriam Dror, an American therapist, complains that the American licensing system is 'humiliating, irrelevant, non-seeing' and 'entirely controlled by the insurance agencies'. At the time of writing, the provisionally named Independent Therapists' Network (ITN) is taking up just these issues by attempting to form an alternative to BAC and UKCP, in which self and peer accreditation is to be championed, bureaucracy is challenged and the right of small groups of therapists to define and police their own work is defended.

Even Carl Rogers (1980: 244) was sceptical about licensing:

> I have seen the moves towards certification and licensure, the attempts to exclude charlatans, from a vantage point of many years, and it is my considered judgement that they fail in their aim. . . . There are as many *certified* charlatans and exploiters of people as there are uncertified.

Rogers seems to concur with the view that an atmosphere of licensure is stultifying, and suggests that there can perhaps never be any way of certifying competence in any field of human relations. (Incidentally, it has been suggested but is seldom acknowledged or discussed publicly that there may conceivably be a very small number of charlatans or abusive counsellors or therapists, an equally small number of brilliant or highly gifted counsellors, separated by a vast army of merely good enough practitioners.) In spite of all this, great hopes exist that refinements in accreditation procedures, in the likelihood of a new national register of counsellors, and in National Vocational Qualifications applied to counsellors, will lead to reliable measurement of counselling competencies (Russell and Dexter, 1993). A case can indeed be made for the analysis of the key skills of counselling, but this is still not a universally favoured direction. What is undeniable is the steady growth of demand for counselling, of counsellor training programmes and even of senior academic appointments in counselling and psychotherapy which surely mark confidence in the stature of the talking therapies as a legitimate field of knowledge. Whether they constitute an 'impossible profession' or not, and even if there is continual tension between professional and lay claims, the talking therapies are a phenomenon to be reckoned with.

5

Models of Counselling

Quot homines tot sententiae
(As many opinions as there are men)

A detailed examination of the surfeit of schools and theories, of practices
and practitioners that compete with each other conceptually and
economically, shows vagaries which, taken all at once, make unclear
what it is that psychotherapists do, or to whom, or why.

(London, 1986: xv)

Estimates vary as to the number of different theoretical approaches to
counselling and psychotherapy but the figure of 300 is often agreed as
representative. Textbooks aiming to represent the field usually find it
necessary to include between 10 and 20 mainstream approaches. The
United Kingdom Council for Psychotherapy has eight groupings: analytical psychology; behavioural and cognitive psychotherapy; experiential
constructivist therapies; family, marital and sexual therapy; humanistic
and integrative psychotherapy; hypnotherapy; psychoanalytic and psychodynamic psychotherapy; and psychoanalytically-based therapy with
children. In this chapter I propose to look at how this state of affairs
has come about, whether it is inevitable and healthy, or unhealthy, and
what it means for the question 'What is counselling?'.

Within the smorgasbord of therapies (one cannot easily say 'coun-
sellings'!), our question becomes 'What is psychodynamic counselling or
therapy?', 'What is person-centred counselling or therapy?' and so on.
How much does each approach have in common with others? Do the
practitioners of one approach even agree that what is done under the
banner of another approach is counselling or psychotherapy at all? The
question of the differences between counselling and psychotherapy
dwindles to nothingness beside the question of the divisions between
schools of therapy. Experts in each of the following approaches may well
object that I have misunderstood or caricatured them. A real problem for
anyone trying to provide an overview of this field is that its practitioners
are often fiercely wedded to a chosen approach and deny the validity of
outsiders' criticisms. This is a little like declaring that you cannot
legitimately criticise scientology, Christian Science or classical psychoanalysis unless you have first been a fully initiated member of that
particular approach.

Psychoanalysis and its variants

It is remarkable to consider the very short time span in which psycho-analysis developed into an internationally recognised intellectual pursuit and clinical practice. Freud's early forays into neurology, hypnosis and cathartic therapy had been surpassed by about 1886 by the new methods of free association and interpretation of the unwitting expressions of unconscious material. Dramatic early cures and intense interest by Freud's circle of followers, and the necessary exit of Jewish analysts from Nazi Germany to England and America, ensured that by the time of Freud's death in 1939, psychoanalysis was a major intellectual force.

Freud subscribed to a belief in psychic determinism and saw himself as a scientist in pursuit of the truth. He worked through various theories of human development and mental illness and many today defend psycho-analysis by describing it as a constantly evolving discipline. Detailed exposition of Freudian theory is beyond the scope of this book and is familiar in broad outline to most counsellors and therapists, as well as (if often in distorted form) to the general public. Human beings have certain innate drives and complexes which are tested in the developmental stages of infancy. Awareness of sexuality and its forbidden nature plays a central part in Freudian theory. The mind, consisting of conscious and un-conscious functions and energies – most notably the id, ego and superego – is engaged in constant conflict, attempting to defend against its deep turmoil while at the same time seeking to resolve its miseries. Psycho-analysts have charted the many defence mechanisms employed in this battle and have shown how dreams, jokes, slips of the tongue and other phenomena reveal clues to unconscious conflict.

Freud promoted the term 'talking cure' (which was originated by Breuer's client 'Anna O', or Bertha Pappenheim), but much of psycho-analysis and its derivative therapies is characterised by silence or near-silence on the part of the therapist. Classical analysis is less a conversation than an asocial forum for the the patient's free association of ideas, images, memories and so on. Since the 'answers' are all within the patient, the analyst refrains from influencing him or her, and provides only very sparse, delicate and finely timed comments. A large element of psychoanalysis is the transference, or the patient's unconsciously distorted perceptions of and emotional claims on the analyst, who will inevitably be seen and treated as significant people from the patient's past. The analyst allows and perhaps subtly encourages transference to occur and assists the patient gradually to gain more realistic insights and perceptions. Anyone who spends several hours each week in the company of another person who listens intently but refuses to engage in distracting conversation, is likely to be thrown back on the contents of their own mind. It has been said that psychoanalysis resembles a situation of social and sensory deprivation. In psychoanalysis nothing is regarded as trivial or insignificant. (A parallel is to be found here in certain Christian traditions which regard nothing as morally insignificant.) One of the popular conceptions of psychoanalysis is that it makes everything appear to be deeper or more complicated than it actually is, or that analysts are people who can see a thousand hidden things in the most casual of mundane remarks.

Psychoanalytic treatment aims to foster insight and greater self-awareness: if I am less driven by unconscious forces to act against my best self-interest, I will automatically, albeit gradually, become freer generally. Because a thorough familiarity with the wiles and grip of the unconscious is so fundamental to practising as an analyst, every analyst must undergo a lengthy psychoanalysis of their own. Self-knowledge equips one to relate to others with reduced distortions in one's attending to and understanding, providing sensitisation to the exquisite nuances of intrapsychic and interpersonal manoeuvres. Psychoanalysis has also affirmed a belief in the conversion of psychic conflicts into physical manifestations, including psychosomatic illness, and has been partly responsible for spreading the view that a great deal of illness results from repressed unconscious material. A common example is 'He gets headaches because (among other things) he suppresses his anger at his mother'.

Before moving on to look at variants of psychoanalysis, a word about language is in order. Jacobs (1994) has described some of the distinctions between psychoanalysis, psychoanalytic psychotherapy and psychodynamic counselling. Freud originally used the terms 'psychical analysis' and 'psychological analysis', and 'psychoanalysis' probably made its debut in 1896. The purity of Freudian psychoanalysis has been an issue since its earliest days, and many still claim that psychoanalytic and psychodynamic therapies are dilutions or distortions of the true model. Very similar anxieties and proprietary struggles have been in evidence in Christianity over the past 2000 years, of course.

Classical analysts still retain the tradition of referring to the person who is subject to analysis as the analysand or patient, the term 'client' being viewed with distaste. This reflects, perhaps, the scientific aspirations of Freud and the concept of the receiver of analysis as sick, as a research subject, or as a supplicant. Indeed, many classical analysts still have their patients lie on couches. Psychoanalytic terminology also reflects concerns with expertise and depth. In spite of Freud's argument that non-medical practitioners could practise as analysts, psychoanalysis remains a rather elite profession. Since an Oedipus complex and similar inner phenomena cannot be directly observed, but only inferred, psychoanalysis requires a certain suspension of disbelief or criticism.

Jung's break with Freud decisively established analytical psychology (or Jungian psychotherapy) and Adler's departure spawned individual psychology. Freud's stress on infantile sexuality was one of the grounds for these departures and a perceived need to honour the spiritual and societal aspects of life another. Those linked with Freud are sometimes referred to as 'depth psychologists' or as 'insight therapists' which accurately marks them out from behaviour therapists, who are interested in the observable. Depth can refer to the extent to which a person's true feelings, thoughts and motives are hidden, and also to how far back in an individual's past problems stem from. The metaphor of depth is also open to numerous questions and criticisms of its reality. We can imagine deep things that do not exist. Most people will accept that there probably are all sorts of hidden, hard to uncover, or forgotten reasons for why we act as we do as adults, but as the history of schisms within psychotherapy attests, consensual accounts of deep or intrapsychic phenomena are not always forthcoming.

Karen Horney split from the Freudian orthodoxy because she was dissatisfied with its results and saw a need for theoretical changes, including greater attention to social and cultural factors. She experienced bitter controversy over her views and was virtually forced out of the New York Psychoanalytic Institute. She is often referred to along with Erich Fromm and Harry Stack Sullivan as belonging to a movement which values the interpersonal, cultural and feminist. Melanie Klein wished to pay greater attention to the actual behaviour of babies and infants and formulated theories which departed from Freud's, thus leading to distinct and separate trainings and traditions in psychoanalysis. Sayers (1991) regards Horney and Klein, as well as Helene Deutsch and Anna Freud, as responsible for a major change in the analytic tradition, away from patriarchal assumptions and individual issues, towards 'the present and interpersonal issues concerning maternal care and its vicissitudes – identification, idealization and envy, deprivation and loss, love and hate, introjection and projection' (Sayers, 1991: 3).

Rifts within Freudianism have sometimes been quite bitter and involved various feuds, excommunications and the founding of new, independent schools. It is difficult to disentangle personal motives and interpersonal incompatibilities from theoretical differences but it seems certain that the rifts involved have been rather more than sincere differences of opinion. Jung said of Adler, for example, 'If Adler ever says anything sensible or worth listening to, I shall take notice of it, even though I don't think much of him as a person' (McGuire, 1991: 282). To Freud, Jung wrote 'Adler and Stekel were taken in by your little tricks and reacted with childish insolence. I shall continue to stand by you publicly while maintaining my own views, but privately shall start telling you in my letters what I really think of you' (McGuire, 1991: 293). Hogenson (1994) has also drawn attention to Jung's perception that Freud, often refusing to admit to his own neurotic behaviour (for example, a probable affair with his sister-in-law, Minna Bernays), protected his reputation by screening out from awareness whatever was inconvenient for his theories.

Just as Freud is known to have carefully nurtured his own position and fame, so others have nurtured theirs. From Jung and Adler, Horney and Klein, to Reich, Perls, Moreno, Berne, Ellis, Beck, Janov and others, fiercely independent therapists have broken with the tradition in which they trained, to establish their own schools. Until relatively recently there has been little sign of therapists and counsellors acting like a scientific community, anxious to pool knowledge and advance understanding. Not only are there many therapeutic systems and institutes resembling, in some sense, religions, but also there are many schisms within each system – and certainly within the psychoanalytic tradition – resembling church denominations. Buirski (1994) has examined some of the differences. What will presumably always distinguish all forms of analytic therapy and counselling from others is the belief that obvious personal problems are invariably underpinned by hidden, powerful forces requiring expert identification, containment, interpretation and working-through. Simply dealing with the 'symptom' will not radically help the client to alter the balance of conscious management and unconscious conflict in his or her life.

Psychodynamic therapy is probably the most prestigious and the most criticised of all therapies. It is said to be elitist and unavailable to any but the most affluent and already well-functioning. It is protracted, often lasting many years. It is, say critics, not particularly effective. It does not necessarily produce desired behaviour change. Its practitioners refuse to entertain serious criticisms. Philosophically, it cannot hold much water. It is a belief system resembling a religion rather than a treatment for psychological ills (Dryden and Feltham, 1992b). It is often predicted that this form of therapy in particular is declining in popularity and credibility (at least in the USA), with the cognitive-behavioural, integrative and eclectic approaches being in the acsendant.

Rightly or wrongly, Freud is considered the father of the talking therapies and psychoanalysis is historically the fount of most contemporary forms of psychotherapy and counselling. Even those approaches owing little or nothing to psychoanalysis often define themselves by reference to Freud's legacy. So what is it about the ideas behind psychoanalytic therapy (two people sitting in a room together) that has had such an impact on the world this century? It is the concept of the unconscious and the claim that it can be understood and mastered, so as to liberate individuals from stubborn, compulsive, self-defeating behaviour, that seems to have stirred hopes. Analysis is tantalising because of its implicit promise: if only those aspects of our mental functioning which cause us to suffer can be uncovered, we will be significantly relieved, happier, full of self-knowledge. If only we can find an analyst who can fully accept and understand us in all our craziness, who will give us a second chance to grow up and flourish, all shall be well. The expertise of the analysed analyst parallels the knowledge and power of the shaman who has undergone intense suffering. The analyst may be regarded as an expert code-breaker of unconscious messages. Furthermore, the psycho-analytic relationship is a special, intense, one-to-one form of communion and psychoanalytic theory has also been applied at a macro level to art, culture, religion, history and contemporary business organisations.

Behaviour therapy and cognitive-behaviour therapy

Behaviour therapy has its roots in experiments with animals in the early 1900s. Thorndike, Watson and Pavlov were early key figures. Not until the 1950s, however, did this research become formalised into therapeutic systems with the work of Skinner, Wolpe, Lazarus, Eysenck, Rachman and others. Unlike psychoanalysis, behaviour therapy has no single, dominant charismatic figure but has developed out of experimental psychology and learning theory principles. Eysenck (1992) in particular has proclaimed the scientific efficacy of behaviour therapy and has decried the theories and applications of psychoanalysis and other therapies as unscientific.

Behaviour therapy is based on what can be observed, studied, measured and reliably changed. At its simplest, it is about the way in which the environment impinges on human beings and how they respond, healthily and unhealthily. Classical behaviourism held that the mind or psyche could not be directly observed or treated and that a science of psychology could only treat behaviour and behavioural problems. This position has shifted for most behavioural practitioners who are now willing to embrace cognitive-behavioural principles, but nevertheless a core insistence on the need to work with quite specific, discreet problems remains. Indeed, behaviour therapy is often said to be highly successful with specific phobias, compulsions and obsessions, when other talking methods fail or seem to have only a moderate impact.

Speculation about possible distant or intrapsychic causes of personal problems is eschewed, as are lengthy conversations, silences and so on. Behaviour therapy is essentially about *doing* something systematically about problems, and is sometimes contrasted with insight therapy by being referred to as action therapy (London, 1986). Whether abruptly or gradually, the client is encouraged to face feared situations or extinguish counterproductive behaviour. Counterproductive habits are identified and altered, desirable but missing behaviours (for example, certain social skills) are taught. Some have suggested that behaviour therapy is close to the spirit of commonsense and that in fact it can be regarded as a form of clinically systematic commonsense. Bellack and Hersen's (1985) *Dictionary of Behavior Therapy Techniques* includes entries on 'dry pants training', 'habit reversal', 'nicotine fading' and so on. It can be construed as a talking therapy to the extent that it relies on cooperation and re-education rather than on drugs or surgery. Also, of course, the various forms of cognitive-behaviour therapy include a great deal of information-gathering, questioning, disputing and other dialogical phenomena. It is noteworthy that Albert Ellis, founder of rational-emotive therapy, recently renamed it rational emotive behaviour therapy to emphasise his belief that clients must take action to overcome their problems, and that talking, thinking and cognitive restructuring alone cannot achieve durable concrete changes.

At the core of cognitive-behaviour therapies (including cognitive therapy, rational emotive behaviour therapy, problem-solving and self-management therapies, and possibly personal construct therapy) is the observation that our thoughts affect our feelings, for good or ill, that thoughts can be identified and changed, and that behaviour can be profitably experimented with in conjunction with thought monitoring. We are not, in other words, slaves to our wretched emotions. Ellis has acknowledged his debt to philosophers such as Epictetus in the formulation of rational emotive behaviour therapy. But the principles of using thought to override or modify undesirable feelings and self-defeating behaviour have been in evidence throughout history. Jane Austen, for example, referred to this kind of practice as 'exertion' and described various methods of remedial self-talk in *Sense and Sensibility*.

Critics of behaviour therapy commonly regard it as shallow, scientistic and incomplete. Some argue that it is not a form of psychotherapy at all because it does not recognise the mind or soul or that it marginalises all aspects of the human being except the measurable and problematic. It appears not to offer any place to free will, since everything can be accounted for in terms of previous causes and the application of somewhat mechanical remedial actions. Psychoanalytic critics suggest that even when behaviour therapy appears to succeed clinically, the behaviour that has been eliminated is likely to resurface elsewhere, perhaps in other symptoms, because its underlying causes have been left unaddressed. Critics from the ranks of humanistic therapy decry the mechanistic ethos of behaviourism, its ownership by oppressive clinical authorities and its hostility towards the values of the human potential movement. Proponents of behaviour therapy ignore the 'whole person' in favour of the conveniently treatable parts of people. For behaviour therapists, there simply is no unconscious – although Lazarus (1989) concedes that there are 'non-conscious' processes – and the relationship between therapist and client is relatively unimportant, and certainly not in itself a healing avenue.

I will look briefly at certain aspects of rational emotive behaviour therapy in order to highlight differences between schools of therapy. REBT is founded on the view that our problems stem not from events themselves but from the ways in which we mediate events, in other words from our irrational thinking. Because we hold certain convictions that life should be fair, comfortable, painless, and so on, and that if it is not we are bound to suffer, we are locked into responding dysfunctionally to events. When we begin to analyse, not the alleged biographical elements behind our problems, but the irrational ways in which we typically interpret events, inwardly demand that they be otherwise and generally upset ourselves, then we can challenge ourselves with more rational ways of thinking and behaving. It is not awful that certain things happen to me, rather it is inconvenient but tolerable; when I begin to modify my responses in this way, my immediate problems take on a different light and

REBT has the potential, so it is argued, to pervasively alter the way we live our lives. The therapeutic procedure entails the disputing of irrational thoughts and experimenting with new ways of behaving, discovering, for example, that it is not the end of the world if I experience embarrassment or failure. The more one accepts the philosophy of REBT, the less one is likely to upset oneself. So REBT is about making a conscious change in the very way we have habitually thought about everyday events, and it does not require the recall of childhood events or a particular kind of relationship with the therapist. Indeed, Ellis has made it plain throughout his voluminous writings that it was because he became disenchanted with traditional psychoanalytic practice that he formulated his own, more efficient therapy focusing on how we perpetuate our problems and how we may, often forcefully, set about changing them.

Obviously, REBT is altogether different from psychoanalysis and there is no way of reconciling the two approaches. Which is right? Which is truer to our experience? Which is more effective? These are the kinds of questions we need to ask when comparing therapies. One of the problems with REBT is, perhaps, that it leaves little room for philosophical analyses which do not have a Stoical bent. REBT is relatively fixed and incapable of lending itself to subtler philosophical expositions. It is more immediately accessible to those who are already 'thinkers' and have some inclination to solve their problems by thinking and taking action. It does not adequately address those who process events in terms of feelings and images, for example (Lazarus, 1989). Like psychoanalysis, it requires belief; you have to accept it and work at it before deciding that it is or is not for you. In addition, REBT appears to be politically somewhat conservative in that it teaches implicitly a philosophy of acceptance. If you learn the trick of not upsetting yourself about events, you are probably less likely to want to change them. Perhaps most worryingly, if you learn not to upset youself about anything at all (see Ellis, 1988), you are quite likely to lose sensitivity towards, or patience with others who *are* readily upset. Clearly, counsellors who espouse an REBT approach are offering their clients something that is completely different from the feelings-oriented humanistic approaches and from the history-and-relationship, psychodynamic approaches. They also offer an interpretation of human reality and aspirations that is quite distinct from these other approaches.

Humanistic therapies

Humanistic therapy and the human potential movement began in the 1940s but really flourished in the 1960s and 1970s, both in America and Britain. The movement is referred to as humanistic not in the atheistic sense, but in contrast to the scientism of behaviour therapies and the sometime aspirationally scientific and possibly over-professionalised schools of psychoanalytic therapy. Since humanistic therapy espouses an innate potential for self-realisation and a generally egalitarian ethos, expert systems do not easily find favour. There are a number of distinct therapies which belong under the humanistic umbrella, including Gestalt, person-centred, primal and other experiential therapies, encounter, psychodrama, co-counselling, bodywork, feminst therapy, men's groups and many experiments in pushing back the frontiers of knowledge about and experience of deep feelings, spirituality and liberation from personal and social oppressions. Humanistic therapy and counselling view the person as whole, not as body and mind in conflict, nor as mind in necessary conflict with itself.

Consider the following description of Gestalt therapy (taken from an advertisement):

> Gestalt therapy is a theory and practice developed to help people release their potential for creative growth, and to help them find their capacity to choose and to change, to enhance their lives and to achieve greater fulfilment. It looks at how we become stuck, blocking our energy and thus our potential, and how to free that energy. It emphasises the creative potential of people, believing we all have the potential for further growth.

The concepts of energy, growth, potential, process, self-actualisation, creativity, authenticity, real self, feelings and peak experience are those which characterise humanistic therapy generally. Human beings are basically good, strong, truthful, curious and self-determining, and what holds them back is anything from traumatic intra-uterine and birth experiences, subtle and gross emotional abuses by parents, teachers and others to oppressive cultural forces including patriarchy, racism and homophobia, intellectualisation and the internalisation of parental and cultural messages which lead to blocks to personal growth. The task of the various humanistic therapies is to provide the climate, relationships and techniques which will facilitate an attack on these negative forces and the unleashing of the energy within. Given the holistic values and mission of this approach, it follows naturally that the methods used include talking, screaming, crying, dancing, singing, chanting, breathing, massage, bodywork and intensive encounter and that a large measure of attention is given to the flow of non-verbal, here and now phenomena.

Fritz Perls, co-founder of Gestalt therapy, regarded humanistic therapy as a third force against psychoanalysis and behaviour therapy. Indeed, he openly pronounced both other forces to be 'crap' (Perls, 1969: 1–2). The growth movement was and is dedicated to individualism, and a particular kind of spontaneous and expressive individualism at that, that is not at ease with the psychoanalytic or behaviourist establishments. Humanistic therapies are generally much more here and now based than psycho-analytic models, and make more active use of the current (therapeutic) relationship. Person-centred therapy, by contrast with many other humanistic models, has to be seen as quite mild; even though it promotes individual autonomy, it seems to accommodate itself happily to student counselling services, for example, and to other 'establishment' settings. It is difficult to see how primal therapy – an approach that encourages people to regress into early, traumatised states of mind-and-body, characterised by dramatic crying, wailing, shouting and convulsion-like movements – would be welcomed into student counselling services, statutory settings or employee counselling services, for example. The extreme end of the humanistic therapies may be regarded as necessarily challenging all external constraints. When people are encouraged to express more and more of what they are actually feeling, in the belief that suppression of such feeling is tantamount to self-betrayal and making oneself sick, then a certain risky, revolutionary quality is unleashed. New lifestyles are likely to follow, as people discover that they can no longer compromise themselves. It is not enough to empty oneself of the suffering from one's personal past, but life must be lived continuously in the spirit of self-actualisation and obstacles must be confronted.

The form of humanistic therapy that has found most favour in Britain is the person-centred approach. It is probably the approach most widely taught on training courses and perhaps a majority of practitioners describe themselves as person-centred or 'basically person-centred'. The core conditions of unconditional positive regard, empathy and genuineness, first promoted by Carl Rogers, are often used as the fundamentals of skill training for counsellors, even on courses that diverge from Rogers' approach. Rogers argued that human beings are self-directed, creative, positive beings who have their own sense of inner self-worth, that these qualities are prevented from flourishing by early adverse life conditions, but they can be nurtured back into health given the right therapeutic conditions (the three core conditions). Because we are the only ones who truly know ourselves and what is right for us, it is the task of counsellors to facilitate our self-discovery and growth and not to interpret things for us or to set agendas or in any way falsify our own experience. The more we find ouselves accepted in therapy, including our most intimate and idiosyncratic feelings, thoughts and values, the more are we likely to accept ourselves, love ourselves and flourish. The more we are empathically understood, the more will we appreciate the precious nuances of our everyday experiences. By finding our true, inner compass, we will know how to deal with our problems.

Person-centred counselling has an in-built anti-authoritarian value system: only the individual knows what he or she needs and no one else has any right to dictate otherwise. It is no doubt due to this that person-centred counselling has been so very influential in Britain since the 1970s. This approach is self-evidently hostile to authoritarian models of therapy such as behaviour therapy, but also somewhat to the idea of therapist expertise and opaqueness inherent in the psychoanalytic tradition. The purist model of person-centred counselling holds that the core conditions are always necessary and are sufficient in themselves to effect therapeutic change. Hence, nothing can be added in the way of radically new techniques or fundamentally new theory, and the central component in person-centred training is the trainee's own openness to inner and interpersonal experience.

Person-centred counselling has an aura of goodness and simplicity which may explain some of its attraction. But it has its critics too. Many argue that it is fine as far as it goes, it provides a good grounding in listening skills, self-awareness and therapeutic alliance, but not much else. When it seems to be effective, this is probably due to the fact that many clients really only need a good listener, but person-centred counselling is not particularly effective with more severely disturbed clients, including those who are very depressed. Davenport (1992) suggests that practitioners who insist on adhering to the person-centred approach regardless of evidence that certain approaches and techniques may be more effective for certain clients risk breaching ethical and legal requirements. The criticism has also been put that this approach is naive in relation to socio-political issues. Practitioners may spend a great deal of time waiting for certain clients to see and understand how they are oppressed, for example, and some clients may never reach any such conclusion, but the person-centred counsellor will always strive to avoid influencing the client, even when to do so might be beneficial. The process can be accused, then, of being at times wilfully time-wasting. Certain critics have challenged even the tenet of the core conditions, arguing that an emphasis on warmth and empathy is likely to influence the client to believe irrationally that he or she cannot survive or thrive without such unconditional empathy. Kegan (1994) and others have challenged the very idea of non-directiveness as an impossibility. A major problem with the person-centred approach, then, at least in its purist form, is that it is arguably not *person*-centred at all, but centred on so-called 'person-centred' dogma.

Rowan (1983) argues that humanistic therapy naturally leads to transpersonal therapy and theory. In other words, an interest in growth in our feelings and experiential potential logically proceeds into spiritual territory. The transpersonal approaches have been dubbed a 'fourth force' psychology, built around the writings and methods of Jung, Assagioli, Grof, Wilber and others, which is concerned with our contact with the spiritual, mystical or cosmic. I do not propose to look at this area in depth (it is partly addressed in Chapter 6) but rather to state simply that along with the previous three broad approaches to counselling, it demonstrates how wide is the territory with which counselling is concerned, from mental illness, through problems in everyday life to aspirations towards religious or mystical experience. Small wonder that Persaud (1993) and others have complained that counselling may have been inappropriately applied well beyond its original and rightful scope. Rowan (1994) in fact suggests that we cannot understand what counselling is at all unless we take into account all possible levels of personal or psychospiritual development, and treatment methods ranging from hospitalisation to mystical practices.

Eclecticism and integrationism

Ever since Eysenck attached the description of 'mish-mash' to eclecticism, the word and concept have been out of favour. It is currently much more fashionable to talk about integration or integrationism, although there are important differences in meaning. Perhaps most mature clinical practitioners find themselves dealing flexibly, and therefore eclectically, with their clients; the same procedure does not fit all clients and one naturally adapts with experience (Goldberg, 1992). On the theoretical front, too, it is difficult to see how counsellors can be wholly satisfied with any narrow school of therapy, when the very diversity and complexity of human beings surely challenges the possibility of ever arriving at a comprehensive theory of what human beings are psychologically, how we become dysfunctional and what will rectify matters.

What has really challenged counsellors in relation to the theories they adhere to is the still widely accepted finding, from psychotherapy outcome research, that in terms of effectiveness there is little if any difference between the different models (Luborsky et al., 1975). Obviously some comfort is afforded counsellors by such research, but it has thrown up the necessary and embarrassing question: if each distinctive theory of therapy describes human problems, their aetiology and remedy, in quite different ways, each is implicitly predicting that its theory and methods are likely to be more demonstrably effective than others. Otherwise, each would in effect be saying no more than 'here is yet another theory which complements the existing field while at the same time adding nothing essential to our understanding of dysfunctional processes or therapeutic potency'. Clearly, founders of new schools of counselling are not saying this. Each claims to offer uniqueness, new insight, greater explanatory adequacy, better results, or at least some slight edge over other approaches. Now, this cannot apparently be squared with existing research evidence; if any methods stood out significantly above the others, something would be proven and clients would begin to get a predictably better service. Methods which were consistently shown to be less effective would gradually fade away, one presumes.

This kind of (meta-analytic) research had to have some impact, and what it appears to have led to is attempts to identify therapeutic factors common to all forms of counselling (that is, relationship, or 'non-specific' factors); to identify specific techniques that may be used beneficially apart from the theories associated with them (eclecticism); and to question whether, or to what extent, different therapeutic theories might be brought together in some form of meta-theory and/or meta-methodology (integrationism). A sincere desire to get at theoretical truths and at better clinical methods underlies much of the new field of eclecticism and integrationism (Norcross and Goldfried, 1992). Not only is the general public somewhat sceptical of the theories of counselling (in so far as these are known and understood) but counsellors themselves are clearly sceptical of many approaches other than their own, Albert Ellis being one of the most outspoken, for example, in his condemnation of the psychoanalytic approaches. Yet all counsellors probably have some sense of the limitations of their school and wish to improve their work. Eclecticism and integrationism (or integrative therapy) therefore have their attractions.

Several problems arise, however. Exactly how can you integrate theories which are diametrically opposed? Although Wachtel (1987) has attempted to present an account of the commonalities between psychoanalysis and behaviour therapy, others argue that these approaches are so far apart in their visions and practices that integration is impossible. It is relatively easy to see how some of the experiential approaches might be fused, or the cognitive and behavioural. Attempts have indeed been made to weld together a combination of Gestalt therapy and transactional analysis; cognitive-analytic therapy is composed of object relations theory, personal construct psychology and elements of cognitive and behaviour therapy. For Lazarus (1989) such attempts are doomed and misdirected. Instead of asking how we can marry certain theories and techniques together, our starting point should be with the assessment of clients' actual needs and therapeutic methodology should aim to use techniques to deliver what clients actually need across the whole spectrum of their functioning. Lazarus' multimodal therapy is one of the few attempts to put together a systematic eclecticism. Lazarus has little time for theoretical empire-building and suggests that we frankly acknowledge the limits of our current knowledge in therapy and counselling. It seems to be the case that although a movement towards integrationism or eclecticism characterises the contemporary field and engenders hope, there is still no hard evidence that these new approaches offer greater effectiveness.

Therapeutic arenas

The complexities do not end here, however. Added to the many competing theories, provided by competing professionals, we must at least briefly allude to the different arrangements or arenas in which counselling takes place. Individual therapy is the most common form of therapy, but it is of course also conducted with couples, families and groups, and each of these modalities has its competing specialised theoretical schools of thought. Sex therapy and child psychotherapy are also often considered to be quite distinct forms of therapy requiring special training and utilising special techniques, but I will not dwell on these here. Individual therapy mirrors the place accorded individualism generally in our society and it may be that our view of linear time and individual cause and effect chains underpins the feeling that individual therapy is truer or more effective than other kinds (Slife, 1993). In fact, as with comparisons of different models of therapy, there is no evidence that individual therapy has superior outcomes to group therapy. Comparison of individual forms of counselling does throw up intriguing questions about the nature of counselling. Who is the client in couple, family and group therapy? Who is the expert? What happens to confidentiality? Who is equipped to understand multidimensional transactions?

The problem of proliferation

The proliferation of models of therapy can be defended by the argument that it represents theoretical richness and mirrors the diversity of humanity. Many have come to believe, however, that it is more of an embarrassment and the push towards integration may have something to do with overcoming this embarrassment. Saltzman and Norcross (1990) represent both the richness of differing clinical inputs and the fascination or embarrassment of clinicians interpreting clients' material in utterly different ways. A fundamental question here is – why has there been such a proliferation and why does it continue? I tend to believe that therapeutic theory resembles theories in religion, politics and philosophy. There is always disagreement and there are usually polar opposite views. Hanging on to a view usually becomes more important than trying to reach a consensus or a significant advance in knowledge. This is where counselling probably falls into the same trap as most other human enterprises; it becomes territorial and fragmented, and an example of 'systemic flaw' (Bohm, 1994). Each theoretician gravitates towards explanations that are to his or her taste, that suit his or her personality (Corsini, 1989). Each sees only part of the whole picture, yet insists that it is the whole. For example, feelings count for everything in primal therapy, thinking counts for everything in cognitive therapy; enduring childhood pain is the total explanation in one theory, while in another it is the tendency to abdicate adult freedom and responsibility that provides the key explanation. Each has much to gain from proprietorial defence of its own position. We might also argue that each has its own particular range of aims: behaviour therapies address highly focused, concrete problems; psychoanalytic therapies seek to assist people to become simply somewhat less miserable than they have been; humanistic and transpersonal therapies are interested in only radical changes.

Why can we not break out of this fragmented pattern? If we were truly dedicated to finding the best possible ways of helping our fellow citizens to solve their problems and live more satisfyingly, would we continue to cling so tenaciously to our prized but limited theories? If we were really dedicated to truth-seeking, would our priority not be to ask why we are a problem-creating species and what we can do about it? Instead of this course, we prefer to generate endless explanations and to reify them. We prefer to protect our professional standing rather than to pose necessary questions that might shake our professional foundations. So, for example, it is the official position of the British Association for Counselling that training courses wishing to become recognised must demonstrate that they are founded on a particular core theoretical model. Most of these orthodox, core theoretical models are not more than a few decades old and many will probably be extinct or relatively disused within a few more decades. Arguably, most of them began life eclectically themselves, partially incorporating, partially rejecting other methods. Most of them are couched in unhelpfully impenetrable jargon that renders their theories inaccessible to clients and often to students. Arguably, we continue to exaggerate the special qualities, techniques and skills associated with each approach, instead of endeavouring to simplify, to identify what is truly helpful and what is gratuitous theorising. What does all this splintering or fragmentation tell us about the nature of counselling and counsellors?

6

Counselling, Religious
Concepts and Critiques

> We psychotherapists must occupy ourselves with problems which, strictly speaking, belong to the theologian.
>
> Jung ([1933] 1984: 278)

> There is always an unconfessed hope, a secret conviction even, that all this cultivating of little personal salvations, this gentle tending to circumscribed and limited anomalies, will somehow in the end add up to a comprehensive moral purpose, a kind of humanistic Kingdom of God.
>
> Halmos (1965: 29)

While counselling has been with us for only a few decades, religion is as old as humanity itself, and older indeed than even philosophy. It is essential to place counselling in a religious perspective because the concepts of conscience, covenant, community, altruism, love, confession, enlightenment, and many others are so central to religions and have obviously informed counselling theory and practice. It is in fact remarkable that secular counsellors are able to train as counsellors, learning about acceptance, empathy, genuineness and the importance of attention to others generally, without necessarily understanding even some of the vast history of religious concepts which have preceded counselling concepts. Such neglect may be due in part to a certain hostility towards religion engendered by Freud's view of it as a universal obsessional neurosis.

Another reason for looking at religion, or spirituality (some writers regard these as quite separate matters) is that the humanistic and transpersonal therapies contain a great deal of religious material. Gestalt therapy has its 'Gestalt prayer' and a 'person-centred creed' has been put forward (Mearns and Thorne, 1988). Holiness may not be completely different from the kind of holistic concerns of the transpersonal counsellors in particular. Saintliness and radical sanity may be more than vaguely related. Jung drew from many traditions, including the major religions, mysticism, mythology, anthropology, mythology and astrology. Assagioli, Wilber, Grof, Rowan and others have borrowed from religious disciplines and given therapy generally an important spiritual dimension. It is claimed by some that no self-respecting counsellor or therapist can afford to be ignorant of this dimension and that it cannot be written off as some sort of universal neurosis, but may indeed hold the key to radical personal transformation effected by psychological means. In this chapter I confine my attention mainly to aspects of Judaism, Christianity and Buddhism, and commonalities and conflicts in counselling and religion.

Judaism

Smart (1971) describes the ancient Hebrews as primitive nomads who believed like other primitive people in the presence of *mana*, or hidden, spiritual forces in nature generally, but especially as *elohim* (divinities) in the sky and in certain sacred objects. From the earliest of times in Judaism we see the concepts of a singular God (Yahweh), of the importance of history and ancestral images, of the Law (or Torah) as portrayed in the Pentateuch (the first five books of the Bible), of a covenant between God and mankind (the Ten Commandments), of ritual, ethics, justice, divine intervention, of a promised land, and a powerful sense of community. The belief in a special relationship with the one true God, who had issued laws to be followed and provided a constant sense of guidance, meaning and historical consequence, permeates Judaism to this day. There was in fact an ancient Jewish tribe called the *Therapeutae*, monks who lived near Alexandria and practised the philosophical art of *therapeutein*, or healing, for example, and it may be no accident that the Jewish influence on the development of psychotherapy has been so immense.

We cannot fully appreciate how much has been lost in our age without some understanding of the powerful transmission and impact of religious messages. While many of us may believe that injunctions handed down to us by parents contaminate and inhibit rather than enlighten or guide us, we perhaps forget the positive contribution they have made in history and may yet have to make. The Jewish scriptures are full of such injunctions, laws, or distilled wisdom. The Jews learned that God was 'the Lord' – 'I am that I am' – and was a jealous God who issued very clear instructions: not to lie, steal or cheat, not to hate or to practise illicit sex or idolatry. Browne's (1962) anthology captures the essence of Jewish wisdom. From *The Book of Proverbs* come these early psychological insights:

> Every man knows his own bitterness,
> And in his joy no stranger can share.
>
> Even in laughter the heart may be aching,
> And the end of joy may be sorrow.

More questionably, from a present-day, humanistic perspective (also from *Proverbs*):

> Train up a child in the way he should go,
> And even when he is old, he will not depart from it.

The *Psalms of Wisdom* declare:

> How happy is the man who has not walked in the counsel
> of the wicked.

Taking this translation at face value, the counsel of the wicked reads like an atmosphere or 'company' and suggests a useful metaphor for our contemporary counselling. 'Counsel' is perhaps more than mere advice, but a kind of ethical climate. To walk in the counsel of the loving or truth-seeking would then read as indicating an ethical climate of integrity, likely to lead to happiness.

The *Apocrypha* contains much wisdom and counsel in the form of aphorisms. From *Wisdom Concerning Wise Men And Fools*:

> The man who keeps the Law controls his thoughts,
> And wisdom is the consummation of the fear of the Lord.
> The man who is not shrewd will not be instructed,
> But there is a shrewdness that spreads bitterness.
> A wise man's knowledge abounds like a flood,
> And his counsel is like a living spring.

Keeping the law and controlling one's thoughts will not have universal appeal today, yet we could interpret this in terms of the 'laws' of integrity or congruence (in counselling parlance) and the benefits of vigilantly monitoring one's thoughts (as recommended in cognitive therapy). The fear of the Lord is not a popular concept today, unless it be interpreted as a respect for cosmic, ecological and psychological principles. We may sometimes reject the notion of the 'wise man', but we have our own, comparable concepts, such as the self-actualising or fully functioning person. Even counsellors and therapists openly or tacitly accept that better counselling is likely to be found in (or from) people who have lived fully, examined their own minds and hearts and perhaps the theories (wisdom) of others. Sternberg (1990) and others have developed a study of wisdom from psychological and philosophical perspectives which promises to add much to our understanding of how maturity and expertise may enhance counselling.

From the Talmudic period, Jehuda ben Tama proclaimed:

> At the age of five one is ready to study the Bible, at ten to study the *Mishna*, at thirteen to observe the Commandments, at fifteen to study the Talmud, at eighteen to get married, at twenty to start earning a livelihood, at thirty to enter into one's full strength, at forty to show discernment, at fifty to give counsel, at sixty to start feeling old . . .

Of course, the statement that one is in a mature position to 'give counsel' only when one is 50 is now highly contentious, but it is still generally accepted today that counsellors probably have more to offer when they are somewhat mature in age and attitude, and it is evident that many counsellors are in fact older, many entering the profession later in life. I have also heard it said that a counsellor in an employee assistance programme cannot be credible unless he or she is at least 45 years old.

Solomon ben Judah Gabirol (also known as Avicebron) wrote a collection of maxims called *The Choice of Pearls*. In this, a man tells a sage, 'I perceive that human beings do harm, so my soul counsels me not to mingle with them' (Browne, 1962: 268). The translated phrase 'my soul counsels me' is interesting from our point of view because it could mean 'It is my opinion', 'I deduce that' or 'I feel inclined'. But it could also be taken to mean that the man has a conscience, or a clear relationship with his soul, or deeper self, by which he is (or feels) counselled. The sage in fact replies that he should not shun company, but be careful how he is affected by it.

The philosopher Bahya ben Josephibn comments that crying is beneficial in infants 'for in the brains of infants there is a humour which, if it remain there undischarged, would produce evil results. Weeping dissolves this humour and drains it away from the brain, and thus the infants are saved from its injurious effects' (Browne, 1962: 296). There are indications here of an early theory of cathartic release which has been returned to in the work of twentieth-century therapists like Reich, Janov and Stettbacher.

From an example of medieval Jewish literature, *The Counsel of a Nameless Poet*:

> Take thy friend into thy most secret counsel, but of a thousand choose one. Then turn from thine own unto his advice, provided thy intellect be as clear and serene as his; for thou possibly wilt see only that which meets the eye, whilst he will see the matter from all sides. (Browne, 1962: 314)

Here, counsel (most secret counsel) means confidence, and the person is urged to be discerning as to the choice of a 'counsellor'. Provided we do not wrongly dismiss the concept of advice here, I think we can see an early example of identifying the benefits of finding an objective other, with whom to share a problem. Seeing the matter from all sides, and seeing more than meets the eye, is precisely what most counsellors and psychotherapists train and aim to do.

It is impossible to do justice to the centuries of Jewish literature, philosophy, theology and psychology, but these examples convey, I believe, some of the early insights and wisdom of Jewish culture. Since many have claimed that psychoanalysis, and possibly most psychotherapy, stems essentially from the Jewish experience, it is vital to pause to consider its immense influence. Its ethical strength and painstakingly studied wisdom have been carried through into the thought of many.

The work of Martin Buber, the Jewish theologian and philosopher, has been briefly mentioned in Chapter 3. Buber's simple concentration on the 'I and Thou' relationship, on the significance of the human encounter, has had a profound effect on counselling and psychotherapy. Buber's writings stand today as a stern reminder that people are not objects and that our interactions – everyday or therapeutic – are always in danger of being converted into subtle abuses of each other. Friedman (1993) has extended Buber's principles explicitly to the domain of psychotherapy and to the creation of an approach known as dialogical psychotherapy. Friedman is critical of approaches which over-psychologise human affairs and fail to acknowledge and incorporate direct interhuman encounter. Friedman, like Buber, derives meaning from the works of the *Hasidim*, a movement of mystically inspired Jews originating in the early eighteenth century. Although Hasidism honours individual uniqueness, it stresses loving community and commitment. Friedman is therefore critical of psychoanalysis and other approaches: 'The search for linked causes, the distrust of motives, one's own and others', the distrust of the conscious, the conceptual and the 'merely verbal', the loss of trust in the immediacy of our feelings, intuitions and insights, the loss of trust in our own good faith and that of others, enclose us round in a well-nigh hermetically sealed psychic ecology' (1993: 129). Hasidism, and dialogical psychotherapy, emphasises personal and communal responsibility.

It is Freud, of course, who is held up as the Jewish father of psychoanalysis. Although he claimed not to be a practising or believing Jew, many are convinced that psychoanalysis could only have emerged from a Jewish context. 'I believe it is beyond coincidence that the most disturbing and ambivalent theory of the human psyche in the nineteenth and twentieth century (psychoanalysis) was invented by a Jew,' says Dale (1988: 71). According to Dale, religious and cultural Judaism, and the many persecutory experiences of Jews, have sensitised them to introspection, led them to the helping professions, and made them uniquely susceptible to depression and manic-depressive illness. Dale is not alone in declaring that survivors of the Nazi holocaust and their descendants carry untold psychological scars. In Pirani's (1988) view, the Jewish founders of psychotherapy systems (especially Freud and Klein) have bequeathed a depressed vision of the world, concerned almost exclusively with suffering and depth, while more hopeful, transpersonal systems stem from Jung and his followers.

Freud may have been consciously indifferent to Judaism, or hostile to its religious aspects (as an atheist), but many, including Bakan (1990), claim to detect strong Jewish influences in his work. Bakan focuses particularly on the influence of the Kabbala, or Jewish mystical tradition, but also traces some of Freud's thinking to Maimonides, the medieval sage. Maimonides wrote *The Guide of the Perplexed*, which contains a great deal of instruction in dream interpretation as well as allusions to the metaphysics of sex. Not all Freud scholars are impressed by Bakan's thesis, and indeed Vitz (1993) even argues that Freud was far more influenced by Christian literature and theology than by Judaism. However, Freud's *Totem and Taboo* and *Moses and Monotheism* reveal clear preoccupations with Jewish themes, among them a concern about incest and ritual.

How much of Freud's (and others') ritualistic inclinations may have been passed down into, for example, clinical taboos, strict time-keeping practices, and so on? It has been suggested that analysts and therapists take their holidays 'religiously' in August simply because that it what Freud did. The Jewish psychologist Brandt, regarding psychoanalysis as a 'Jewish science', argues that it relies on the verbal and interpretational skills so central to Judaism. Jews freely demonstrate their emotional life, according to Brandt, their history is reflected in the way in which psychoanalysis dwells at length on personal biographies, and analysis is built on a theory of mental conflict which reflects the anti-Semitism that Freud would have been so familiar with. Of great importance, too, is the observation that clinical psychoanalysis is essentially a minority interest in the same way that Judaism is only for the chosen few (Brandt, 1982).

Counsellors may ask themselves to what extent the model they follow contains or is influenced by Jewish thought. Certainly a glance at some of the leading figures in the original and contemporary worlds of therapy shows this impact: Freud, Adler, Abraham, Federn, Rank, Klein, Binswanger, Moreno, Reich, Perls, Fromm, Berne, Beck, Ellis, Erikson, Bettelheim, Maslow, Frankl, Kernberg, Heimler, Mahrer, and many other contemporary therapists are of Jewish descent.

Christianity

The life and mission of Jesus Christ was characterised by preaching, miracles, healing and an unreserved commitment to God. Jesus claimed to fulfil and transcend Jewish law. He regarded himself not merely as preaching a new gospel but as an embodiment of a thoroughly new and definitive interpretation of God and the kingdom of God on earth. Jesus himself is often referred to as 'the wonderful counsellor' and it is necessary to give attention to his message, to Christianity broadly and the relationship between it and psychotherapy.

Jesus offered inspired moral guidance, for example in The Sermon on the Mount, which was of a new order, emphasising love, forgiveness and understanding. His message was partly concerned with how to live a righteous life, but was also a new teaching about the significance of others (love your neighbour as yourself), about the need to forget oneself so as to find God, and an expectation of seeing a new, transcendent reign of God on earth. He told people not to be anxious about tomorrow but rather to trust in providence. A new, worshipful community was declared. The concept of repentance, of turning from egoistic pride to love of others and of God, is a cornerstone of the Christian life. Sin, pride, evil and possession by devils are to be overthrown by the grace of God, by the Holy Spirit ushering in the conversion experience of rebirth. By leading a good life, we open the door for supernatural power to thoroughly cleanse us and release us into a qualitatively new experience of everyday living. Religious, and especially mystical, experience has had a profound impact on psychotherapy, and in many ways the therapist's agenda to induce radical transformation of the personality can be equated with just such religious states.

Jesus considered himself to be, and millions of Christians over the last 2,000 years have worshipped him as, the son of God, the very embodiment of God. As such, his earthly existence was filled with extraordinary events marking him out from other preachers. His supernatural power was apparently such that he could heal leprosy by touch, restore sight to the blind and even survive his own death. We must each make up our own minds about the reality of these claims, but if Jesus indeed performed healing miracles, then Weatherhead (1952: 47) is right to 'compare the long, laborious methods of psychoanalysis with the speedy way in which His patients were restored to health'. The reports of miracles do at least oblige us to consider whether instantaneous and lasting cures for physical and mental illness are possible and, if they are, how we may discover the power to practise them. Weatherhead notes that even the early apostles rapidly lost the power to effect miraculous healing. With this loss, 'less is demanded from the healer. More is demanded from the patient. The onus is put on the patient to have "faith", but the power to call forth faith is sadly lowered' (Weatherhead, 1952: 87). This phenomenon of waning power has also been noted in therapeutic movements: the original founders have apparently dramatic successes, the early followers have a little less, and the members of the official institution gradually become faithful, but perhaps uninspired, followers.

St Paul noted that 'The good that I want to do, I fail to do' (Romans 7: 19). This observation, that we are frequently unable to execute actions which we consciously will, has remained problematic to our own day, although Freud shed some light on it by demonstrating that we often unconsciously oppose our own conscious wishes and intentions. The kind of logic that this insight leads to has prompted some commentators to suggest that 'God' should be equated with our own unconscious, or with the deeper, unknown, powerful parts of our own mind. Christian theology has often been riven by debates as to whether God is a 'wholly other', independent supernatural agency, or simply part of human nature, and nature generally. The ultimate conflict between humanistic values in counselling and a theology of the supernatural reveals itself in trans-personal therapy's reclaiming spiritual experience, on the one hand, and movements like Alcoholics Anonymous commending faith in a Higher Power, on the other. In order to understand both the rich and problematic legacy of Christianity for counselling, a brief review of certain aspects of Christian life and healing movements is required.

It is easy for many of us in the late twentieth century, in a secular society, to forget the contribution of Christianity to moral guidance and cohesion of community. The Church has for centuries provided a physical, moral and intellectual structure for ordinary people to understand and shape their lives. The Bible has been a source of comfort and instruction to millions for centuries. Only in relatively recent times, with the advent of historical research and scholarship, and from scientific progress, has faith in its literal meaning and supernatural authorship been seriously undermined. But there have been scores of other Christian guidebooks and sources of inspiration. *The Imitation of Christ*, written by Thomas à

Kempis in the fifteenth century (trans. Sherley-Price, 1952) provided counsels on the spiritual and inner life, for example. Sherley-Price refers to à Kempis as 'a wise and trustworthy counsellor to all who seek to know and fulfil the true purpose of human life' (1952: 11).

The counsels of à Kempis are short instructive pieces of spiritual guidance on matters of purity of mind, humility, patience, bearing the trials of life, avoiding pride, distractions and despair. A reading of the *Imitation* reminds us that there was (and still is for active Christian believers) not only a source of moral guidance in such writings but also a real sense of the presence of Christ. à Kempis talks of the friendship of Christ and urges readers to 'hold converse with Jesus'. By contrast, he advises us to avoid talkativeness generally (or what we might call small-talk).

> The reason why we are so fond of talking with each other is that we think to find consolation in this manner, and to refresh a heart wearied with many cares. Alas, however, all this is often to no purpose, for this outward consolation is no small obstacle to inner and divine consolation. (à Kempis 1952: 37)

Although he lived a monastic life and would therefore be likely not to commend talkativeness, we might ask to what extent we rely on conversation with others (whether counsellors or friends) instead of cultivating a deep inner life of our own. And for many of us, of course, there is no belief in a Jesus with whom we can converse. It may be, however, that figures like Jesus represent archetypes of truthfulness, goodness, freedom, meaning and service that most of us consciously or unconsciously seek to emulate to one degree or another.

Theologians have long debated the merit of natural religion, or one version or another of the idea that everyone has direct access to God, to a true self, inner divinity or states of transcendence and ecstasy. The Gnostics, for example, considered heretical by orthodox Christians, placed ultimate value on personal experience. It is self-knowledge which shows the way to God, and the Gnostic was said to be a 'disciple of his own mind, discovering that his own mind is the father of the truth. Whoever follows the direction of his own mind need not accept anyone else's advice. . . . Have a great number of friends, but not counselors . . . But if you do acquire a friend, do not entrust yourself to him. Entrust yourself to God alone as father and friend' (Pagels, 1982: 139). Gnosticism is much more concerned with the subjective self than with the meaning of Judaeo-Christian history. Gnostics looked for the good within themselves and were concerned with inner depth, tendencies which respectively correspond somewhat with tenets of the person-centred and psychodynamic traditions of counselling. There is little evidence that twentieth-century therapists have culled their ideas directly from movements such as Gnosticism – Jung, sometimes called a modern Gnostic, is the exception – but it seems likely that certain concepts and methods are recirculated throughout history under different names and within various disciplinary constellations.

Mysticism generally, in Christianity and other religions, has sometimes offered a great deal to those outside orthodox structures who seek richness of meaning in their lives. Mystical experience has been said to dissolve the everyday sense of individual separateness, time constraints and suffering. True mystical experience does not mean, of course, imaginary or inauthentic states of mind, but a genuine breakthrough into a sense of timeless, unproblematic, selfless being. St Paul, St Bernard of Clairvaux, Meister Eckhart, John Ruysbroeck, Walter Hilton, Julian of Norwich, St Teresa of Avila and St John of the Cross are some of the best known Christian mystics. The unknown author of *The Cloud of Unknowing*, a religious tract written in the fourteenth century, instructed readers to put a 'cloud of forgetting' between themselves and everyday distractions, as part of the process of reaching God. The intellect was regarded as a barrier and sin was to be overthrown completely, with a disciplined contemplative life paving the way. Quakerism, founded by George Fox (1624–1691), in its focus on the Inner Light, on silence and spontaneity, on waiting and presence, can also be compared in many ways with the practice of counselling and therapy, and perhaps in particular with the person-centred approach. It is not so far-fetched to compare such spiritual projects with the psychotherapeutic task of unearthing and outgrowing psychological obstacles to self-actualisation and to a life of authenticity, the humanistic and existential schools of therapy being particularly committed to this quest.

The likeness between the counselling relationship and the traditional Christian pastoral relationship is, I think, fairly clear. The parish clergyman acted, and often still acts, as a guide and mentor to his parishioners. A major part of the value of the clergy until about the seventeenth century was their provision of the hearing of confession. According to Thomas (1971: 157) the Church of England 'discarded regular auricular confession but the clergy still wished to keep their role as counsellors and advisers to their flock'. In effect ministers of religion were the psychotherapists of their day, offering help and comfort to the melancholic and suicidal. Indeed, as Hurding (1985) reminds us, Jesus was referred to in the New Testament as *parakletos*, or a person called in to help, an advocate, comforter, supporter or counsellor. This has always, then, been part of the priestly vocation. In the light of twentieth-century psychoanalytic and other therapeutic knowledge, the clergy have adapted their attitudes and methods to take advantage of specific psychological healing methods. Anton Boisen, an American founder of pastoral theology and clinical pastoral training, employed Freudian, Jungian and other secular insights in his work, as did Leslie Weatherhead in Britain. Hurding (1985) spells out the ways in which Christians can use secular psychotherapeutic knowledge, but like many other Christians sees it as falling short of the power inherent in Christ.

Christians have developed their own unique counselling approaches which are not based on secular theory. I will briefly refer to Jay Adams' nouthetic counselling, for example, which is firmly grounded in belief in the Bible as the sourcebook for counsellors. This scriptural counselling holds that sin is the cause of all psychological distress and that secular psychology has nothing to contribute to any genuine healing process. Gary Collins' approach, often referred to as 'discipleship counselling', follows Adams in being based on a teaching and admonishing model. For Collins, the term 'counselling' can be used of teaching, preaching and explaining the Christian message in many situations, including 'public counselling', 'community counselling', 'mutual aid and self-counselling' and 'lay counselling'. As Collins puts it, 'Counseling is a type of caring or people-helping that must involve all compassionate Christians. Many problems do not need a specialist's involvement. Most can be handled by lay counselors' (Collins, 1986: 74). Such counselling is effected by encouragement, exhortation and enlightenment. Care of the environment, planning for the communal future, and other areas of life, are all referred to by Collins as forms of counselling, which is an interesting but perhaps over-extended use of the word.

Frank Lake's clinical theology, an amalgam of theological insights and a range of psychotherapeutic theories and methods, warrants special attention for several reasons. Lake considered that counselling went hand in hand with the work of the Holy Spirit, and that there was a correlation between the suffering of the individual and that of Christ. He experimented with LSD and deep breathing techniques, becoming increasingly influenced by primal therapy. Towards the end of his life, Lake believed that considerable damage was done at the intrauterine stage of human development and that this could be undone therapeutically. He drew inspiration equally from Christian writers like St John of the Cross and Kierkegaard, and a variety of therapeutic writers. In his book *Tight Corners in Pastoral Counselling* (Lake, 1981), he presented material on intrauterine and birth trauma, again showing correlations between Christian suffering and the pain of all individuals. The title of the book, and the depth of the therapeutic work discussed there, make it clear that Lake did not hold the opinion that counselling was somehow shallow in comparison with psychotherapy. This view, that any counsellor may find him or herself confronted by a client's early childhood, birth or intrauterine suffering, is confirmed by Thorne (1991).

Justice cannot be done in this context to the many contributions of Christian thinkers to the field of counselling. I should like to refer to the work of Paul Tournier, however, and his practice of 'dialogue counselling'. Qualitative human relationships are a central concern in Christianity, and Tournier sees dialogue taking place between counsellor and client, but also between each and his or her awareness of God. Tournier uses eclectically the insights of secular therapies but adds an emphasis on confession. Tournier noted the common need to unburden, but also observed that a remote listener might be off-putting; he was therefore quite open to making self-disclosures in his own counselling of others. There are similarities between Tournier's approach and that of Carl Rogers, except of course that Rogers had no Christian affiliation. Rogers talked often about individuals' longing to be heard, and this longing is related, I believe, to the tradition of confession. Confession means to acknowledge and be acknowledged.

People have confessed to priests, to their own diaries and even in public meetings, through the ages. St Augustine's *Confessions* are the prime example of soul-searching and personal insight made into literature. We may need to be reminded that confession has also featured centrally in other cultures, for example among American Indian tribes (La Barre, 1964). Weatherhead (1952) cites many poets as examples of authors of written confession, suggesting that the creative act is frequently cathartic. Freud goes as far as to say, 'Confession is liberation and that is cure. The Catholics knew it for centuries, but Victor Hugo had taught me that the poet too is a priest; and thus I boldly substituted myself for the confessor' (in Vitz, 1993: 104). Foucault (1975) commented on the resemblances between Catholic confession and psychoanalytic free association, arguing that both practices persuade people that they have hidden inner secrets to express and that the sanctioned listener has the perceived power to absolve. Lest we imagine that private confession has no relationship to larger power structures, consider Dreyfus and Rabinow's (1982: 174) summary of Foucault's views on this:

> At least in the West, even the most private self-examination is tied to powerful systems of external control: sciences and pseudo-sciences, religious and moral doctrines. The cultural desire to know the truth about oneself prompts the telling of truth; in confession after confession to oneself and to others, this *mise en discours* has placed the individual in a network of relations of power with those who claim to be able to extract the truth of these confessions through their possession of the keys to interpretation.

Hymer (1988) has made a study of the place of confession in psycho-therapy, arguing for a psychoanalytic rationale of the function of confession. Confession may not serve only cathartic functions but also developmental needs, testing the therapist, exhibiting grandiosity, working through vulnerability, and so on. In passing, it is interesting that Hymer ranks confession to cab drivers as being perceived as a slightly lower risk than to clergy or therapists, with friends, parents and lovers being the highest risk groups. This confirms the value of the neutral stranger, the person we do not have to live with but to whom we can take our 'nasty bits'. Much of the power of Alcoholics Anonymous and other similar fellowship groups can be attributed to the requirement that members, known only by their first names, confess in front of each other. Much more strangely, the *Guardian* (30.7.94) reported an American telephone help-line created by a 'Mr Apology', who invites and listens to every kind of eccentric and criminal caller who wishes to telephone and confess anonymously. Its creator, who is untrained, regards it as a secular confessional.

William James ([1902] 1982) was the pioneer of the psychology of religious experience. His monumental work addresses the phenomena of healthy-mindedness, the sick soul, the divided self, conversion, saintliness, mysticism and philosophy of religion. He cites a testimonial about the reality of God: 'God is quite real to me. I talk to him and often get answers. Thoughts sudden and distinct from any I have been entertaining come to my mind after asking God for his direction' (James, [1902] 1982: 71). Direct guidance from God may be still experienced by many Christians, but equally, many people who are in the perplexed state of the person cited by James would seek a counsellor, and would feel a need to talk with a counsellor in the absence of any conviction about the presence and power of God to fulfil this role.

From a religious, cultural and historical perspective, it is worth attending to James' writing on the 'religion of healthy-mindedness'. James was writing at the turn of this century and had completed most of his work before Freud had issued his. Christian Science had been created by Mary Baker Eddy in about 1870. In brief, Christian Science is founded on the premise that God is all, that the Spirit of God is all and can vanquish all illnesses. Although Weatherhead (1952) was sceptical, if not disdainful, about the claims of Christian Science and some of its business methods, James ([1902] 1982) regarded it as essentially one among several other potent, American Christian projects. Referring to the 'mind cure' movement, James asserted that 'the extremely practical turn of the American people has never been better shown than by the fact that this, their only decidedly original contribution to the systematic philosophy of life, should be so intimately knit up with concrete therapeutics' (James, [1902] 1982: 96). Emerson's transcendentalism, Berkeleyan idealism, spiritism and Christian Science are some of the strands of this religion of healthy-mindedness, which is based on American enthusiasm and optimism. This has continued well beyond James' time, into the positive thinking of Norman Vincent Peale, Ron Hubbard's Scientology, est, neuro-linguistic programming and many other variants of optimistic, psycho-religious therapies and cults. It is also a major part of the more orthodox humanistic therapies and may account partly for the discrepancy that exists between these and the European, deterministic models of therapy.

I have referred in Chapter 4 to some of the counselling and care-giving organisations which emerged from a Christian, pastoral context. The Samaritans was initiated by a Christian minister and its very name bears witness to the Christian concern to reach the desolate. Alcoholics Anonymous grew, in the United States, from Christian inspiration. British Marriage Guidance Councils arose in the 1930s, inspired by the work of the Reverend Herbert Gray, a Presbyterian minister. The Catholic Marriage Advisory Council, Compassionate Friends and many other agencies were launched by direct Christian efforts. The Westminster Pastoral Foundation, the Dympna Centre and other counselling and training organisations are of Christian origin. Many individual counsellors (as well as social workers and probation officers) are either ex-priests or committed Christians. Many leading psychotherapists, such as Fairbairn, have had Christian affiliations. Herman (1987: 91) even manages to correlate Kleinian concepts with Christian experiences: 'Like Mrs Klein, the Gospels say there is no knowing until the very end whether we can keep hold of our good object in the inmost heart when the winds of fate ride high and hatred converges from all sides.' Halmos (1965) has pointed out that the growth of counselling and other personal services was increasing at the same time (from around the 1950s in the UK) that the population of clergy was declining, but has this been a real change or mainly the substitution of one psycho-religion for another theistic religion?

Overlaps and conflicts between Christian faith and secular counselling

Part of the thesis presented by Halmos (1965) in his seminal book on counselling is that it is an activity based on faith and love. Counselling, understood as a practice common to psychotherapists, psychiatrists, social workers and other helping professionals, has taken over from both political activism and formal religion. Counsellors believe in the power of love over hatred, they promote a philosophy of autonomy, and their work is a form of communion. 'Professionalisation,' says Halmos, 'has proved an excellent camouflage for the counsellor's *agape*', or Christian love (Halmos, 1965: 31). Even Freud at times spoke of the psychoanalyst as a 'secular pastoral worker'.

Robinson (1986) gathered together evidence for the overlaps between psychotherapy and the Judaeo-Christian religious tradition. Both are concerned with restorative functions and the good life. Both use ritual and promote the seeking of meaning and healing. Both use the 'therapy of the word'. A priesthood of kinds is seen in both, involving a training and initiation process and a hierarchical organisation. In both religion and psychotherapy there are charismatic founders and sacred texts. Both contain elements of esoteric knowledge and both promise some form of deliverance. Religion has been called a haven (Spilka, 1986) and psycho-therapy has been labelled a religion (Vitz, 1977). Maslow (1968: 5) specifically equates 'failing to do with one's life all that one knows one could do' with sin. There can be no doubt that, whatever the differences between therapy and religion, there are enormous overlaps and that each has borrowed and benefited from the other.

The psychoanalyst Peter Lomas declared 'I feel a little as if I am a kind of priest in disguise – a priest in the very broadest of terms, not a Christian priest. It could be said that I am in the business of "character building"' (Dryden, 1992: 13). The much-cited statement that 'No one ought to practise psychotherapy unless he has the wisdom of Socrates and the morality of Jesus Christ' (reported by James Glover in his 1925 address to the British Psycholgical Society) is another indication that the therapeutic and religious spheres are seen by some to overlap enormously. One writer has also astutely pointed out that personal investment in terms of belief, training, time and livelihood is at stake for any clergyperson or psychotherapist who might lose their faith or in any way publicly express serious doubts about their profession. 'The consequences of the therapist's losing his faith are no less severe than those of a priest's losing his faith. It is not surprising that both are rare occurrences' (Fish, 1973: 8).

What are the main conflicts between religion, and especially the Judeo-Christian tradition, and counselling and therapy? Let us look first at psychological critiques of religion. Freud maintained a sceptical attitude for most of his life, regarding religion as an obsessional neurosis and being suspicious of alleged religious experience as an illusory 'oceanic feeling', probably a memory and/or wished-for repetition of infant or intrauterine bliss. It is understandable, if life is inherently limited, if we are mortal and prone to disappointment, that we seek comfort in images and practices relating to non-empirical beings like God. But this is an illusion and, if one is interested in pursuing truth to its conclusions, the illusion of religion is an impediment.

The catalogue of objections to Christian belief includes its patriarchal assumptions and organisation, and hence its oppression of women and damage to their well-being; its negative view of sexuality generally and especially of pre-marital and homosexual sex; its propagation of the sense of guilt, worthlessness and fear of God; and its encouragement of people to look outside themselves for salvation, even in serious delusional convictions of being, or being in contact with, supernatural persons. Ellis (1986) has been one of the main critics of psychologically dysfunctional religiosity, and many counsellors have encountered clients (including the sons and daughters of the clergy) whose problems derive directly from an oppressive religious upbringing. In some cases, powerful injunctions are so obstinate that excessively religious clients may not be able to benefit from therapy, especially if they sense that it may challenge their faith. Rollo May (1992), along with many other writers on therapy, has also cautioned against the abuse of talking therapies by practitioners who have an unrecognised Messiah complex.

Such criticisms may be and have been turned back on counselling and therapy, however. Among those who are most vocal in this respect are Vitz (1977) and Hurding (1985). Vitz's attack centres on the view that psychology and psychotherapy have helped to cultivate a kind of 'selfism'. 'Psychology as religion has for years been destroying individuals, families, and communities' (1977: 10). Selfism, or self-worship, is promoted by most therapeutic approaches, including the psychoanalytic, humanistic and existential. These encourage parent-blaming, narcissism, neglect of community and God. Vitz predicted that within 10 years (from 1977) people would be bored with the cult of the self, but there is little sign that this is true. Hurding (1985), who demonstrates a comprehensive understanding of the many secular approaches to therapy, warns that they are ultimately relatively empty and misdirected precisely because they operate without reference to God. Hurding is critical of transpersonal therapies in spite of their concern for transcendence because they rest largely on mystical principles and ignore the unique demands of Jesus Christ. Frankl (1977) argued that there is a void at the heart of twentieth-century life, that this existential vacuum can only be filled by God, and that we have a religious unconscious; we repress our own spiritual longings. Frankl's logotherapy is one way of attempting to liberate these longings.

Buddhism

Siddhartha Gautama, the Buddha, was born in the sixth century BC and, as legend has it, forsook his privileged lifestyle in order to discover the everyday conditions of most people's lives and the way out of suffering. His search included a period as a mendicant and study with various sages, culminating in intense ascetic meditation, the realisation that such austerity might be too severe or even unnecessary, and finally, in enlightenment. It is not, perhaps, too far-fetched to compare the Buddha's search with the journey made by many in our time through therapies, systems of meditation, gurus, cults and wisdom literature.

Like Christ, the Buddha preached and established a community. It is often said that Buddhism is not a religion, since it posits no God, but that it is, rather, a way of life. Although Buddhism as a historical movement has been subjected to the same process of dividing into schools and traditions as other major religions, there are certain core tenets to be examined for our purposes. According to Buddha, 'all is suffering'. In other words, the human experiences of birth, separation, illness, want and death entail suffering, dissatisfaction, or *dukkha*. In our ignorance of the true nature of reality, we constantly crave for what we do not have, and lead lives of relative misery. Thus Buddhist teaching has much in common with Vedanta, with Krishnamurti's enduring themes and with mysticism generally. Our typical daily existence is made up of misperceptions about life, self and how to be happy. We regard the self as something real and permanent, when it is not, we are possessively attached to others even when we know that separation and death is inevitable. We do not learn from our mistakes and thus repeat our errors in cyclical fashion. The Buddha's noble eightfold path to self-development points to a way out of this. It has been suggested that Buddha's method emulated the classical ancient Indian form of diagnosis of illness: identifying what is wrong, what the cause is, searching for a cure, and prescribing a remedy (Smart, 1971).

We must understand and overcome desire, hatred, delusion and fear. To do this, right understanding, right thoughts or motives, right speech, right action, right means of livelihood, right effort, right concentration and right meditation are required. 'Right' is not the opposite here of wrong but indicates a quality of what is most appropriate and skilful. Although a path is spelled out, desire to achieve self-centred results from following it will, paradoxically, cancel out progress. A link may be seen here with psychoanalysis and the idea that both the analyst's aim-attachment and the patient's phantasy of a happy outcome constitute impediments to profound change. But just as the Buddha broke through illusion (*maya*) and experienced *nirvana*, so enlightenment is available to all others. Nirvana is said to be a state of mind or final realisation of the true nature of reality in which one experiences 'the end of woe' (Humphreys, 1951) as the illusion of a separate self gives way to the knowledge that one is the universe. Buddhism worships no God but counsels us to work out our own salvation, or freedom from suffering.

The clearest effect of Buddhism on western counselling and therapy has probably been via Zen, a particular expression of Buddhism which emphasises direct experience of reality in the here and now. Perls, and many others in the early development of humanistic psychology and therapy, were impressed by Zen teaching and have acknowledged its contribution to their methods. Fromm (1986) claimed to see parallels between psychoanalysis and Zen, particularly between the mechanisms and aims of de-repression and enlightenment. Brandon (1976) commended the spirit of Zen in helping ventures generally, showing how its sense of compassion and urgency can heighten commitment and effectiveness. Brandon's bestselling *Zen in the Art of Helping* has had an iconoclastic and inspirational impact on social workers, counsellors and therapists, who concede that all the theorising and training in the world cannot directly meet the actual needs and nuances of any encounter with a client. The influence of Zen is not confined to humanistic therapies. Even a form of behaviour therapy – dialectical behaviour therapy – includes 'encouragement to accept feelings and situations in the tradition of Zen Buddhism' (Koerner and Linehan, 1992: 434). Watts (1975) argued that Buddhism more closely resembles psychotherapy generally than it does either religion or philosophy. Reynolds (1980) shows that Zen is integral to more than one model of Japanese therapy.

If only skilful living – a mental state of vigilance and situational artistry – can adequately overcome our everyday problems in living, then as counsellors and clients we should be learning how to live skilfully, how to avoid destructive habits and fears. To what extent does counselling resemble a Buddhistic analysis and treatment of human problems and a potent strategy for ending suffering? Bohm (1994) postulates that learning the skill of observing one's own thought processes from moment to moment can be likened to learning physical skills. Hence, personal meditation, a kind of continuous, holistic and subtle tracking of the tendencies of our thoughts and feelings, might be regarded as a skill to be learned as a kind of fundamental mental hygiene which transcends the somewhat fragmentary efforts of therapists and counsellors.

Cognitive therapy aims to familiarise us with our everyday subtle problematic thoughts, person-centred therapy with our organismic valuing process, focusing with our bodily sensations and psychoanalysis with our repressed motivations. Buddhist and other forms of meditational experience attempt to familiarise us with all our conscious and unconscious, cognitive and affective facets. Although meditation may need to be taught by a teacher (Deikman, 1982), it is really only effective as an ongoing practice when discovered by each person him or herself, according to Krishnamurti. Krishnamurti has always denied the need for and usefulness of such teachers, a point echoed by the title of Kopp's (1972) *If You Meet The Buddha On The Road, Kill Him!* Similarly, Mahrer's experiential psychotherapy is based on the premise that the therapist's task is to enter the client's stream of experience and to coax the client further into it, rather than introducing the distraction of someone in the role of therapist.

Many besides Watts (1975) consider Buddhism an essentially psychotherapeutic enterprise, if not the most radical kind of problem-solving, or problem-eradication (Hall, 1979). Wilber et al. (1986: 271) point out that Buddhist meditational texts claim to lead the way to 'nothing short of a life without the experience of emotional pain'. But Buddhism has its critics. It is often said that Buddhism and certain other oriental religions are fatalistic in that they teach acceptance of outer conditions and focus on the self and its dissolution and devalue the significance of individual human beings. It has also been noted that many western seekers have embraced forms of Zen and other mystical systems in the hope of a quick and effortless breakthrough into higher states of consciousness. Wilber et al. (1986) warn against such pathological attractions to Zen Buddhism in particular, and note that it is unwise and potentially dangerous to attempt to bypass necessary developmental stages on the road to non-egoic consciousness. This being said, it should also be noted that various extraordinary, meditational states of mind may be encountered spontaneously or accidentally in the course of counselling and psychotherapy. Such is the strangeness of the psychoanalytic climate and the freedom to 'free associate', for example, that some clients may find themselves propelled into unfamiliar, perhaps fleetingly liberated, mystical states of mind.

A note on other religions

It is not possible to dwell further on the many religions and their divisions, but no marginalisation is intended by this. Hinduism and Islam are of course tremendously significant forces, both historically and currently, and Jainism, Confucianism, Taoism, Shinto and others ideally would also merit close attention. Most religions have their own God or gods, their own worldview and mission to convert others to their faith. Obviously those religious systems incorporating belief in reincarnation espouse quite a distinctive, different outlook for individuals. Unhappiness in your present life may be interpreted as stemming from a previous incarnation and/or as likely to be remedied in a future incarnation. Indeed, certain forms of transpersonal therapy and hypnotherapy include the claim that it is possible to explore previous incarnations.

The *Bhagavadgita* is one of the most formative texts of Hinduism, dating probably from the second century BC and offering teaching on the transcendental nature of the Self. Bhaktivedanta Swami Prabhupada's commentary on the *Gita* underlines the devotional nature of the work and the need for a relationship of discipleship:

> In every step there is perplexity, and it behoves one therefore to approach the bona fide spiritual master who can give one the proper guidance for executing the purpose of life. All vedic literatures advise us to approach a bona fide spiritual master to get free from the perplexities of life, which happen without our desire. They appear like a forest fire, which takes place without being set by anyone. Similarly, the world situation is such that perplexities of life automatically appear. (Bhaktivedanta, 1975: 24)

The person who succumbs to these perplexities is 'he who does not understand the problems of life'. Anyone who is serious about understanding life's problems (one's own and those of the world) avoids over-attachment to family and friends, and their views, and seeks 'the science of the solution' with a spiritual master. It may be facile to compare this relationship directly with the contemporary therapeutic one, but there are likenesses. The client in counselling or therapy faces perplexity, seeks out an objective professional, and engages in the pursuit of understanding and problem-solving. Counsellors and therapists studiously avoid labels such as 'master' or 'guru', yet the profession is steeped in dyadic terminology (counsellor and client, countertransference and transference, and so on) and in discriminations between the properly trained and accredited, and those who are not so. A bona fide 'psychological master' would be hard to identify: is it someone who is actually in touch with profound or transcendental truths, or who has simply submitted to one accredited training or another? Henry David Thoreau is said to have referred to most other world literature as 'puny and trivial' compared with the *Bhagavadgita*, and we are bound to ask ourselves what kind of relationship exists between it and the literature of twentieth century psychological analysis and problem-solving methods.

Consider, briefly, yoga in its ancient and modern forms. Organised into a systematic body of knowledge by Patanjali, yoga refers to union, yoking, communion and attention. The *Gita* suggests that the real meaning of yoga centres on deliverance from pain and sorrow. Yoga in its many forms seeks to control and fulfil body, mind and soul. Part of yogic character building involves *Svadhyaya*, which is the education of – or drawing out the best from – a person. 'When people meet for *svadhyaya*, the speaker and listener are of one mind and have mutual love and respect. There is no sermonising and one heart speaks to another. . . . The person practising svadhyaya reads the story of his own life, at the same time that he writes and revises it. There is a change in his outlook on life' (Iyengar, 1966: 40).

Yoga philosophy includes analysis of the subtle movements of thought, from disarray, agitation and dullness to attentiveness and concentration, and finally to a self-transcending unlocking of the divinity within oneself. Sustained yogic attention to breathing, care of the body and meditation, paves the way to freedom from personal pains and problems. Pieces of yogic knowledge may be seen in cognitive therapy, in the Alexander Technique, postural integration and other contemporary therapies.

Most religions also have their fundamentalist and liberal traditions. Islam is known as probably the most monotheistic of religions; in other words, belief in and worship of the one true God, or Allah, is a central and immovable principle. The *Koran*, Islam's supreme authority, tells us that 'The guidance of Allah is the only guidance'. The strength of Islam lies in this pure conviction and in its anti-idolatrous stance. Kakar (1984: 34) argues that:

> In contrast to much of Western psychotherapy which is organised around increasing a man's sense of *freedom of choice*, the Muslim and many other non-Western therapies are organised around another central human need: the restoration of a sense of *centrality* in time and space which in the Western world view has been almost destroyed by the Copernican and Darwinian revolutions.

The assumption made by most western counsellors, that autonomy is an inviolable principle, is seriously challenged when working with Muslim clients who place their religious responsibilities above their individual autonomy. Nevertheless, May (1988) regards Muhammed as one among many 'physicians of the soul', and Vilayat (1993) employs Sufi principles in his approach to counselling. Sufism is the mystical discipline within Islam, concerned with the true Self or inner centre, and utilises dreams, chanting and dance in order to introduce people to spiritual rebirth.

Is counselling a secular religion?

This question might be better phrased as 'Do psychology and psychotherapy constitute a secular religion?'. The very words, with their 'psych' prefix, suggest immersion in the world of the psyche, or soul, which is of course also the domain of religion. Originally, the psyche connoted soul, life or breath, and was drafted into its current English usage in the seventeenth century. Although it now has many applications, it is understood to refer to mind. Counselling, I have argued, may be regarded as the selfsame activity as psychotherapy, concerned with mental processes. Some argue that counselling and therapy should be primarily concerned with the human soul or spirit, while others, particularly those wedded to the more behavioural approaches, prefer to regard observable behaviour and changeable thoughts as legitimate terrain. Putting aside these disputes for the moment, it seems clear that counsellors occupy a place in society previously seen as the rightful domain of priests. Counselling, like religion, is psycho-centric, taking our inner lives as paramount. Rollo May is only one of those who regard psychotherapy as 'psycho-religious therapy' (Clare and Thompson, 1981: 17). Szasz (1988: 67) is in no doubt that 'the birth of psychiatry occurs when the study of the human soul is transferred from religion to medicine, when the "cure of souls" becomes the "treatment of mental diseases", and, most importantly, when the repression of the heretic-madman ceases to be within the jurisdiction of the priest and becomes the province of the psychiatrist'.

Counselling and psychotherapy represent ideologies. They present an explanation of suffering and suggest methods for overcoming it. London (1986) regards psychotherapy as a 'moral force' filling the gap previously occupied by strong religious belief; indeed, he sees religion, philosophy and therapeutic ideologies as taking turns historically in meeting needs for meaning. But there is no God as such in counselling, and there is no Church. Counselling is about problem-solving, personal growth and betterment, and is highly individualistic. It is also broadly hedonistic, in that the pleasure or reduction of suffering of its clients is a primary goal. Duty and self-sacrifice are not generally commended by counsellors. Counselling may be seen to imply perfectibility, or a kind of personal heaven on earth. The exception to the individual focus of counselling is when counselling or therapy is conducted in groups or when therapeutic communities work together. Where two or three (or more) are gathered together in the name of truth, compassion and community, spirituality and psychological exploration may become the same, and love may be experienced.

Counselling and therapy are about 'me, here and now' and are thus relatively ahistorical and individualistic, divorced from a sense of collective destiny. Counselling uses the language of growth, awareness, de-repression, and so on, and may have overshadowed terms such as kindness, honour, love, truth, goodness, conscience, right and wrong. It is part of the overall amoral, hedonistic values of our time. Vitz and other critics may be right that it therefore promotes selfism. Perhaps we can only say at this point that the values of counselling and therapy have the as yet largely unrealised potential to inform a new, spiritual transformation within society.

Therapy as psychospiritual quest

I am grateful to Bettina Peterseil for the following personal account, which gives a first hand picture of one person's powerful experience of therapy and her perception of it as the beginning of a larger quest.

> Since I can remember I had been looking for love, peace and happiness outside of myself. My search had been a restless one. It had carried me from one country and one relationship to another. There had been a deep void in me and for many years I had desperately hoped to fill it. Then came the day when my pattern of life broke into pieces. The last of many relationships had failed, and I just knew that the same would happen to me over and over again if I did not

change. I was longing deeply for a stable relationship. New countries failed to fill me with excitement. I felt strongly that I needed help to bring a change about. At this stage I was a very lonely, forlorn and closed up, restless young woman.

A book was given to me. It was Arthur Janov's *The Primal Scream*. I felt that with this I was given the answer. This was what I needed to change my life. I identified with almost every described unhappiness in the book. Two years later I was able to start a variety of primal therapy in Germany, my country of origin. Never before had I thrown myself with such an amount of hope, eagerness and with such totality into anything. Here for the first time in my life was I surrounded by people who shared openly with others, in the safety of dimly lit rooms and padded walls, all their unhappiness without reserve. Here I did not feel alone any more. For the first time in my life I felt safe to show my pain, here I learned to let go of streams of frozen tears and hidden anger. Here we all bonded with each other over the agony of our past. For the first time I was relating to others, without the fear of losing them if I showed my needs and my anger.

After two years I realised that I had looked at many of my pains and had now enough understanding of my past and my resulting life pattern to be able to let go and go out into the world. I joined a final week of therapy that focused on death and letting go, which seemed appropriate to me when I was preparing to let go of my therapy. This proved the climax of my therapy experience. I once more looked in my mind at every member of my family and let go of them one by one, especially my mother, who was then still alive. We were still very closely attached to one another emotionally. In fact she died hundreds of miles away at the very moment I was letting go of her within the safe space provided by therapists and padded walls. This experience, more than anything before, deeply changed my whole life. Two years of constant letting go had prepared me for this moment. Learning about my mother's death, I felt a deep joy. We had simultaneously released each other. I felt that this release had been an act of love and forgiveness, enabling me to move on to a new level of consciousness.

A few months later I met a man who became my husband, and from there on both our lives changed so dramatically. A state of peace and happiness, briefly experienced at our first encounter, the remembrance of a long forgotten truth in myself, which I had always searched for, made us join our lives. Up to this point, despite my longing for a stable relationship, I had held a horror of staying in a fixed place with the same person, and I had been repelled by the idea of family life and a home of my own.

As we realised later, we had started together on a spiritual quest. During the course of this quest my entire former life style changed dramatically. We moved from the city to the country. We left jobs and friends behind, old values were exchanged for new ones. I changed my way of eating. We had started on a journey where we were asked to let go more and more of our past, of all values we held dear. Today I am in a continuous process of letting go of my entire former thought system. This process will go on for the rest of my life. During the first years of our quest my therapy experience helped me immensely. My first stable relationship with a man brought up many still deeply buried feelings about my childhood past and later relationships. Then becoming a mother confronted me once more, and in a much deeper sense than in my therapy, with myself as a baby and my own unmet needs. The constant process of letting go of the past in me, now helped us along on our new path. The easy access to my emotions had now become a tool I brought along with me, which made it possible to move along smoothly on our path into the unknown. Later new tools also helped.

In therapy, I had begun to look at myself instead of looking outside of myself.

Thus discovering my own past, I still projected the bad and the good outside of myself on to family members, teachers and others. In the next stage I learned that all I had until now safely projected outside of myself was actually in me. During the course of our quest I myself became the bad parent I had before seen outside myself. Since then, like a spiral my life has turned further and further inward. I see myself today in an ongoing process of letting go of all projections good or bad, learning to accept, even forgive my unhappiness. I move further and further towards my true self, which is peace and happiness. An important first step on this life path was my therapy experience many years ago.

7

Counselling, Philosophical Concepts and Critiques

Psychotherapy is . . . at bottom a truth-seeking venture.

Irvin Yalom (1991)

The psychotherapist carries on his work with an almost wholly unexamined 'philosophical unconscious'. He tends to be ignorant, by reason of his highly specialized training, not only of the contemporary philosophy of science, but also of the hidden metaphysical premises which underlie all the main forms of psychological theory.

Alan Watts (1975)

Philosophy, sometimes defined as the love of wisdom or love of truth, may be considered to date formally from the fifth or sixth centuries BC in Greece and India. However, as Frankfort et al. (1964) show, if we allow that primitive myth is a form of symbolic or allegorical philosophy, then philosophy – as an attempt to understand the nature of reality, the function of the state, the values of life and the 'good life' – may be considered to be much older. Indeed, some writers argue that philosophy represents a certain intellectual development from religion generally. I am not about to attempt to present even a truncated history of philosophy, but rather to present a case for the importance of certain aspects of philosophy for counselling. The first of these aspects is that philosophy is a longstanding venture, whereas counselling and psychotherapy, in their contemporary and professional forms, are merely a century old. The second aspect is that the questions asked, the methods used and the subject matter covered by philosophy overlap considerably with those of counselling.

It is essential to place counselling in some sort of philosophical context for many reasons. Needleman (1982) argues that 'the weakening of philosophy in our century has resulted in a form of collective and indi- vidual pathology that has far deadlier consequences than is generally imagined'. He asserts that we are living in a time of 'metaphysical repression' and that the task of philosophy is to help us lift this repression. As he puts it, if man does not 'remember' his truth-seeking nature, 'he will be "lived" by the emotions, opinions, obligations, terrors, promises, programs, and conflicts that compromise the day-to-day life of every human being'. Philosophy deals with the big questions of life, yet, says Needleman, 'we have all but given up hope of ever seeing them asked or answered, [these] questions that somewhere deep within us, in the child within us, we long to think about, dream about'. Unfortunately, 'official philosophy' has done us few favours, since it has so often concerned itself with mere philosophical arguments rather than with passionate, shared truth-seeking. Urmson and Ree (1992: 131), in describing the history of philosophy, cite Quine's view that 'there are two kinds of people interested in philosophy, those interested in philosophy and those interested in the history of philosophy'. It has also been wittily put that a philosopher is 'a blind man in a dark room looking for a black hat that is not there'.

It is not, unfortunately, surprising that many counsellors see little connection between philosophy and counselling when even many philosophers feel forced to apologise for the aridity of much of their discipline. Needleman is a rare exception as a philosopher. Ayn Rand (1982), like Needleman, was a passionate advocate for meaningful philosophy, arguing that philosophical principles are implicit in the kinds of everyday phrases we commonly use (for example, 'It may be true for you, but it's not true for me'; 'I can't prove it, but I *feel* it's true'; and 'this may be good in theory, but it doesn't work in practice'). The word 'philosophy' is also used in everyday phrases such as 'My philosophy of counselling is . . .' and 'She takes these things philosophically'. Rand cautions, however, that:

> As a human being, you have no choice about the fact that you need a philosophy. Your only choice is whether you define your philosophy by a conscious, rational, disciplined process of thought and scrupulously logical deliberation – or let your subconscious accumulate a junk heap of unwarranted conclusions, false generalisations, undefined contradictions, undigested slogans, unidentified wishes, doubts and fears, thrown together by chance, but integrated by your subconscious into a kind of mongrel philosophy and fused into a single, solid weight: self-doubt, like a ball and chain in the place where your mind's wings should have grown. (Rand, 1982: 5)

Rand further cautions against the 'open mind', which too easily becomes the 'wide open mind' of no substance. Instead, she advocates an active, critical mind which resists 'fashionable catch phrases' and 'every new variant of the same old falsehoods'. She concurs with Needleman that explicit philosophy currently holds no sway, but asks, 'When philosophy collapses, why are there no thinkers to step into the vacuum and rebuild a system of thought on a new foundation?' The tentative answer seems to be that human beings, subtly encouraged by governmental policies, accept mediocrity and become 'indifferent to the issues of truth and falsehood'. Although I do not want prematurely to anticipate my conclusions, I must state here my suspicion that counselling both attracts human beings (both clients and counsellors) who hunger for truth, yet simultaneously sells them somewhat short by encouraging acceptance of an implicit philosophy of pragmatism and hedonism, rather superficial psycho-epistemologies, and an indifference to the big ethical or metaphysical questions 'somewhere deep within us'. Counsellor trainers do not generally encourage counsellors-in-training to ask unsettling questions about the intellectual rigour of counselling theory, for example; neither do counsellors encourage their clients to ask questions which are outside the range of convenience of counselling psychology. Rand's reference to pragmatism as a 'concrete-bound, range-of-the-moment, anti-conceptual mentality' might uncomfortably describe much counselling and counselling training.

Many writers on the history of psychology and psychotherapy cite classical philosophers as originators of psychology. Capretta (1967), for example, mentions the particular contributions of Descartes, Hume, Locke, Kant, Wundt, Brentano, William James and others. Many of the concerns of philosophy overlap with those of counselling. Counsellors can potentially learn a great deal from philosophy, or at least from those aspects of philosophy which are more than sterile logical arguments. However, as I hope to make apparent, philosophy also implicitly challenges many of the assumptions, claims and linguistic liberties of counselling. Before dwelling on these further, I wish briefly to refer to the work of Krishnamurti which, although hard to categorise, may be considered philosophy.

In Krishnamurti's many speeches and writings, he repeatedly criticised organised religion, philosophy, politics and psychotherapy systems on the grounds that they fail to grasp the holistic and fluid nature of life, they parcel up and propagate fragmentary understandings of human problems and ultimately distract people from serious, committed, self-initiated truth-seeking. Krishnamurti was no casual, flippant iconoclast, but a dedicated enquirer into the nature of human suffering and the possibility of emancipation. I mention his work here because I believe him to have been a true philosopher, in the Socratic sense, and in some ways (although obviously not in the accredited sense!) a true counsellor. Indeed, the publisher's blurb on one of his books (Krishnamurti, 1975), claims that he has 'devoted his life to speaking and counseling, . . . always pointing the way for each person to find himself'. Krishnamurti was sought out all his life by numerous individuals wishing to discuss problems in living. He was not a pragmatic counsellor but, like the Buddha, was concerned with holistic and enduring transformation of the human being. Instead of asking questions about 'presenting problems', 'problem-management' or 'problem-resolution', he asked 'Why do we have problems at all?' Instead of analysing the unconscious he asked questions such as, 'What is the so-called unconscious, does it really exist, and if it does, is it perhaps as trivial as the conscious mind?' These are radical, philosophical enquiries which are implicitly challenging, if not threatening, to the fabric of the professional counselling world.

The philosophy–psychotherapy interface

The centuries-long habit of asking questions about why we are here, how we are best to understand life and how it may best be lived is one that clients in counselling ask both explicitly and implicitly. People who are depressed may ask, out of their depression, why they were ever born and what the point of continuing to live may be. Such questions are often written off as merely symptoms of depression, and indeed for people who are gravely depressed these may be mainly personal laments rather than philosophical questions (although this distinction may be questioned in the light of Tillich's (1962) existentialist treatment of 'the courage to be', as expounded in his therapeutically potent book).

Human beings have always had an irrepressible need to probe the possible reasons for their existence and the best way to live. Many specific philosophical questions, for example in the field of ethics, are now asked frequently in counselling. The rights and wrongs of abortion, suicide, divorce, and so on, are today much more likely to be taken to counsellors than to philosophers. An exception to this was reported in the *Observer* (23.1.94): a French philosopher, Marc Sautet, apparently conducts individual philosophical consultations in Paris at £35 an hour, as well as leading philosophical holidays to Greece; people experiencing anxiety about death, for example, seek answers or dialogues with Sautet's help. Perhaps Persaud (1993), a psychiatrist complaining about the ubiquitousness of counselling, would approve of Sautet's lead: 'counsellors often treat a group of people who might better be served by priests and philosophers, not by therapists' (Persaud 1993: 283).

Boethius's influential classic *The Consolation of Philosophy*, written c.500 AD and widely translated in the Middle Ages, expressed the writer's need during imprisonment and facing death to make sense of suffering. It has been called a 'moral medication'. Boethius referred to philosophy as his nurse and derived comfort from considering his fate as part of God's providence. In this and Stoicism generally lies the power of the individual to transcend adverse circumstances, an ability which many contemporary therapists of the cognitive variety prize highly. If we are able to understand and accept the necessity or inescapability of an event, then equanimity, at least, may be restored. Part of the function of counselling may be said to be to console or offer solace to suffering individuals. Such consolation may be derived from the counselling relationship or from the sufferer's own efforts to understand adversity. Boethius's work is in fact part monologue and part dialogue with a divine spirit. We may consider that consolation means 'the alleviation of sorrow', which is of course a major task of the counsellor.

There are, of course, uses of philosophy that are not merely of a consolatory nature. Most clients experiencing acute ethical dilemmas are quite unlikely to consult official philosophers for guidance, but it is arguable that counsellor training should include modules on certain elements of philosophy. Apart from philosophy generally, attention to moral philosophy or ethics has clear applications to the work counsellors do. Kelleher (1993) produced a booklet following a television series on just such moral dilemmas, which shows vividly the great need that may exist for instruction in practical ethics. Kelleher, incidentally, cautions that there may be real limits to what we can learn from the classical philosophers, since many of them were bachelors and rather removed from ordinary life. Storr (1988), to the contrary, regards the life of relative solitude chosen by philosophers like Kant and Wittgenstein as a possible prerequisite for creativity.

Although philosophy is probably an activity or discipline currently in broad decline (some have spoken of 'the death of philosophy'; others have suggested that its apparent death corresponds with the current material-istic hegemony), a number of counsellors and therapists have testified to the benefits they have found in it. Rollo May (1992) sees fit to mention explicitly the influences of Socrates on Adlerian psychology, of Plato on Jungian and Freudian thought, and of Marcus Aurelius and Augustine generally. He regards Descartes as pivotal for the debate on the mind–body problem in psychotherapy, and Spinoza as significant for his analysis of passion and reason. Many of these figures are contrasted with Rousseau and the romantic movement, emphasising the value of the emotions. Schopenhauer and Nietzsche raised crucial issues of the will, the self and power, and have even been referred to as 'philosophers of the uncon-scious'. Many credit Nietzsche as the originator of the idea that individual authenticity must override social conformity.

Freud is known to have attended many lectures given by the philos-opher Brentano. Albert Ellis has frequently cited Epictetus, the ancient Greek philosopher, as one of the well-springs of his own approach. R.D. Laing and other existentialist therapists based much of their approach on the writings of Kierkegaard, Heidegger, Husserl, Merleau-Ponty and Sartre. Judith Baron, General Manager of BAC, has alluded to the influence of John Stuart Mill's philosophy of individual liberty on her commitment to social work and counselling (Baron, 1994). Richardson (1989) has presented his concerns about the often unexamined philo-sophical assumptions of psychotherapeutic schools, even questioning whether psychotherapy itself is not a grand unconscious search for meaning. Heaton (1993) complains that we have accepted the scientific paradigm uncritically, and that Pyrrhonian scepticism is still relevant for its power to question dogmatic therapeutic (and other) positions.

Jung suggested that 'there are many well-educated patients who flatly refuse to consult the clergyman. With the philosopher they will have even less to do, for the history of philosophy leaves them cold, and intellectual problems seem to them more barren than the desert' (Jung, 1984: 260). This statement reflects a widespread twentieth-century disaffection with religion and philosophy. Purton (1993) describes his own search for meaning in philosophy, followed by a more satisfactory search in psychotherapy. Nevertheless Purton regards Wittgenstein as one of the most helpful of modern philosophers, since he pointed out many of the problems of language and perception which are common to philosophy and counselling. Indeed, Eagleton, writing on Wittgenstein, suggests that 'the philosopher's job isn't to deliver us the secret of the universe – that's for the poets – but to act as a kind of therapist, disenchanting our minds of the pseudo-problems which beset them, and so packing us off poorer but more honest' (*Guardian*, 18.3.93). Finally, the influence of Lacan, Foucault and Derrida and of postmodern thinkers generally has begun to have its mark on the world of counselling and therapy (McNamee and Gergen, 1992).

Some common themes in philosophy and counselling

The injunction of the Delphic oracle, 'Know Thyself', is surely one that is central to the entire psychotherapeutic enterprise. While respecting the gods of his time, Socrates became the fiercest proponent of intellectual freedom and committed enquiry into the nature of virtue. He departed from the 'pre-Socratic sophists' in his disciplined commitment to logical truth-seeking and its embodiment in his own life and actions. His main method of philosophising was by dialogue with others, seeking to identify their strongly held opinions and then to expose the fallacies contained within them. He commended the importance of the soul above attachment to material wealth or position. His mother was, according to tradition, a midwife, and he often spoke of himself and his philosophical art as a kind of midwifery – helping others to give birth to the truth within themselves. Such was Socrates's commitment to philosophy, that he was put to death by the authorities in a manner anticipating the self-sacrifice of Jesus Christ. Such was his understanding of the injunction to 'Know Thyself' that he was equally committed to exposing the false and avoidant within himself, in human nature in general, and in his society: introspection, dialogue and public preaching were inseparable activities.

In our own time self-knowledge has arguably become a largely intro-spective activity characterised by the accumulation of private insights about our childhood development, our typical thoughts and feelings, and our interpersonal behaviour. Rarely do we ask who this 'self' is about whom we are busily accumulating knowledge and, as Schechtman (1994) has shown, it is probably only since Locke's theory of personal identity (that our continuity as a distinct self or person rests on being able to remember our personal past) that we have taken psychological continuity for granted. Contemporary self-knowledge is frequently mediated by the professionals, paraprofessionals, mystics and pseudo-mystics of our time, and is certainly divorced in most cases from courageous social action and vigorous dialogue. The 'Socratic dialogue' that has become part of the technical equipment of cognitive therapists, consists mainly of disputing with clients their irrational thoughts and predictions in a strictly limited, personalistic sense. Such is the pervasive influence of the (sacred?) concepts of autonomy and hedonism in counselling and society generally, that cognitive and other therapies invariably stop short of questioning them.

With Plato emerged the importance of the idea of the truth behind appearances and it is clear that a great deal of modern therapeutic theory, stemming from Freud, dwells on the premise that appearances often, if not always, conceal subtler truths. Plato is credited with originating the very concept of mental health, and of postulating a tripartite understanding of the mind (reason, spirit and desire) which corresponds roughly with Freud's ego, superego and id (Norman, 1983). Perhaps one of the main attractions of counselling and therapy is a fascination with getting behind appearances. Unfortunately it may be the case that behind many appearances lie yet further mere appearances and that 'the truth' is and will remain elusive. For example, training psychoanalysts may relish the prospect of mastering the art of getting behind other people's appearances but there is little evidence that they are encouraged seriously to probe for the truths behind the psychoanalytic establishment (Masson, 1991). What I intend to do in this chapter is to raise some of the questions which permeate counselling ideology and practice, but which seem rarely to be aired and debated critically. The approach taken is based on the concept of philosophy as critical intelligence and affectionate scepticism, and not on the precepts of official philosophy.

Cause and effect

Freudian and post-Freudian therapies rest on the notion that something innate or something that has happened in infancy leads to psychological problems. In other words, something from your past or embedded in your mental apparatus influences your present behaviour and inhibits your freedom. One commonly hears statements such as 'He is depressed because he has not satisfactorily resolved his anger at the death of his mother', or 'She cuts herself because she was sexually abused as a child', or 'I have difficulty relating freely because I am still stuck in the script given to me by my parents'. Most therapeutic models rely heavily on the past–present connection. Either we have failed to negotiate the 'depressive position' (Klein), or we have succumbed to the 'conditions of worth' imposed on us by our parents (Rogers) or we are locked into a 'repetition compulsion' (Freud). Even the more here-and-now-oriented therapies, such as Gestalt therapy and rational emotive behaviour therapy, tend to offer explanations of cause and effect which may be ahistorical but far from acausal: 'Your life is miserable because you act inauthentically, or because you upset yourself.' Therapies certainly differ in the weight they place on *what* they consider to have rendered you dysfunctional or neurotic, but all of them rely on one theory or another of cause and effect, or aetiological model.

There are, of course, many alternative views, one of which is that life is simply chaotic and that human beings are prone to good and bad behaviour, happiness and unhappiness, in an unpredictably shifting series of fortunes (Vicinczey, 1969; Rhinehart, 1994). We may feel compelled to produce approximate explanatory theories to account for our individual human histories, and we may invent interesting therapeutic theories with apparently predictive powers. Yet it remains the case that there are more things in heaven and earth than are dreamt of in the philosophies of counsellors and therapists. Transpersonal counsellors may scoff at the small-minded deterministic philosophies of behaviour therapists, but they themselves espouse a particular set of philosophical constructs which are in turn thought absurd by others (Ellis and Yeager, 1989). An alternative view advanced by the existentialist therapists is that the world, and hence any theory of cause and effect, is to be understood – or understanding is to be created – by each individual (Deurzen-Smith, 1988). If your construction is that the world is an unpredictable place and the future is waiting to be shaped by you, then that is the way it is (or appears to be) for you. If your construction is that the world is in God's hands, then that is the way the world is for you. Sex therapists are divided on the issue of the causes of vaginismus, for example, and have to admit that their clients report a wide range of putative causes (Ward and Ogden, 1994). Counsellors owe it to their clients to examine just what their own philosophical assumptions are so that they do not unconsciously misunderstand or conflict with those of their clients. It is surely arrogant to suppose that because you have found the psychodynamic grail, for example, all your clients should share your views about psychological determinism. As Deurzen-Smith (1988: 1) puts it: 'To the extent that the client does not fall in with the idea that her thoughts and actions are unconsciously determined, she cannot be helped by psychoanalytic counselling.'

Humanistic counsellors attach far greater importance to the concept of self-determination and free will than either behaviourists or psychoanalysts. In the tradition of Rogers, Moreno, Perls, Berne, Frankl, Mahrer and others, people are considered to retain vast reserves of energy, positive motivation, goodness and an ability to rise above the shackles of their upbringing, culture and 'the slings and arrows of outrageous fortune'. The emphasis is not on compromise with the past but on unknown and unlimited potential. 'Life is what you make it' is the clarion call, rather than 'You are largely what your mother or culture has made you'. The emerging school of solution-focused brief therapy also breaks from determinism, shows relatively little interest in the past of the client, seeking instead evidence of the client's ability to function non-pathologically. This approach is future-oriented and is satisfied with using 'skeleton keys' to understand the client and the way he or she functions, in contrast to those approaches that are preoccupied with the minutiae of pathological cause and effect (Cade and O'Hanlon, 1993).

The *BAC Code of Ethics and Practice for Counsellors* (BAC, 1992) stresses the counsellor's ethical responsibility to 'respect the client's ability to make decisions and change in the light of his/her own beliefs and values'. The client's 'capacity for self-determination' is held in the highest regard by that document. Yet the nature and individual extent of this capacity is nowhere examined. Of course, in a professional code, a philosophical discourse would be impossible, but is nevertheless implicit. Regard for self-determination, however, should not be promoted without some analysis of what it is and what some of its diminishing characteristics may be. To promote the idea of the client as agent is one thing, but to appear to dictate to counsellors that they should respect self-determination without questioning it, is another. Is self-determination invariably a good quality? Do some people have a greater capacity for self-determination than others? Are there any legitimate grounds for respecting the ways in which we are *not* self-determining (Gazzaniga, 1992)? Are there any occasions on which it would be appropriate to override a client's self-determination (for example, when he or she is about to commit some perilous act)?

The question of free will and determinism must be faced and discussed by counsellors and clients alike. If my problems have been in some sense caused by my parents, by my teachers, by accidents in my childhood or later, by social circumstances, and so on, then precisely what does it take for me to overthrow my problems? What exactly is the free part of me that is able, first, to recognise such causes and then to put their effect aside? One of the strengths of counselling, perhaps, is its provision of a hopefully objective outsider who can help the client to identify unnecessary restraints (past causes) and to leave them behind in order to exercise freedom in the present and future. Clearly, however, the effects of certain past events (for example, living within the holocaust experience, being raped or assaulted) are far less easy to shake off than others. The reverse side of this argument, one that is well portrayed by Thomas Szasz, is that we cannot necessarily attribute our own distress or distressing actions to mysterious or even known causes, since we always, at least to some extent, retain the faculty of freedom and responsibility.

I hope these examples indicate that the question of cause and effect is not merely 'academic'. Might we question too whether professional organizations are inevitably philosophically biased and even philosophically oppressive? Certainly in the UK the humanistic ethos of counselling is so powerful that it would be well-nigh impossible for any serious questioning of self-determinism to make much impact on its codes of ethics. Many of the issues relating to determinism and free will were discussed by Rogers and Skinner (in Kirschenbaum and Henderson, 1990) and it may be arguable that we are all both determined and, paradoxically, free. Indeed, philosophers refer to this position as compatibilism, arguing that we have free choices no matter what has gone into our make-up (Honderich, 1993). But such debates need to be aired in some way within counsellor training.

The problem of knowledge

Epistemology – 'the theory or methods of the grounds of knowledge' – is a central philosophical preoccupation. How do we know what we know, or believe we know? What is valid and what invalid evidence? How do we make decisions? How do we know that we are not deceived? Such questions can easily deteriorate into arid, official philosophy. When we ask, however, 'What shall I do about my marriage?' or 'Shall I kill myself?' or 'Why am I so depressed?' or 'Do you think counselling will help me?' or 'How can I know whether counselling, psychotherapy, drugs or a holiday is best for me?' or 'What would be the best counsellor training course for me?' or 'How can I know which is the most effective form of therapy?', epistemology becomes a concrete and acute concern. We seem to live in an impatient and unthinking age where either impulse or apathy often rules. We do things because they feel right or comfortable, or because we have always done things in a certain way. Most of us are probably unused to thinking logically, calmly and systematically about personal or social problems.

Counsellors are often struck by the claim of some clients that they do not know why they are having panic attacks, why they are depressed, anxious and so on. People are often apparently divorced from the obvious about themselves. Someone may tell you that he is experiencing mysterious panic attacks; a little probing soon reveals that the person's wife died last year, he has just lost his job and has no close friends. Something has happened to this man, and probably to many people, whereby the obvious becomes mysterious. We may describe this process as dissociation, as being out of touch with one's feelings, or by using any other psychotherapeutic terminology. In simple terms, however, this man has had an overload of stressful life events and temporarily cannot, or thinks he cannot, cope. The counsellor will help him to become aware of the obvious and to accept that his reaction is within the normal range, and that it will probably get better. This might be called commonsense, yet many clients attribute great powers of perception and cure to counsellors, and many counsellors are perhaps only too happy to accept such flattering feedback. Noll (1994) uses the term 'aristocratic epistemology' of this kind of phenomenon. Critics of psychoanalysis and psychotherapy have suggested that common-sense, or even temporarily unknown causes, are sometimes disguised by therapeutic writers in varieties of esoteric language as subtle knowledge available only to the highly trained (Farrell, 1981; Gellner, 1985; Grunbaum, 1984).

People come to counsellors wanting to know why they feel as they do, and how they can feel better. In such a predicament, they clearly think of themselves as ignorant and counsellors as knowing or powerful or skilful. Many counsellors, particularly the person-centred kind, maintain the belief that only the client knows what is wrong and how to change it. Others, such as behaviour therapists and cognitive-behaviour therapists, see them-selves as somewhat expert consultants. Reality therapists may regard their task as essentially straightforward, while psychoanalysts consider that lengthy exploratory psycho-surgery is always required. The client knows he or she is in pain, distress, confusion or doubt, and *believes* that the counsellor or therapist has expert knowledge and skill. The counsellor may believe this too. The interested outsider, however, might well ask, 'How is it that counsellors and therapists are trained in such a wide variety of approaches, each holding its own explanation of the causes of and cures for psychological distress?' Can every one of these explanations be equally valid? How can we know, how can we find out, the truth of the matter? How can we distinguish between charlatanism and a profession resting on a sound knowledge base?

Let us take a concrete example of the problem of knowledge in the sphere of personal, psychological problems. Suppose I have marital difficulties. My wife and I cannot agree on whether our problems stem mainly from her or from me. A friend sugests that our problems are 'in the marriage itself', or in the interaction between us. We discuss this but cannot agree on where I, she and 'the marriage itself' begin and end. We decide to consult a couple counsellor. The counsellor, who has been trained psychodynamically, believes (or knows?) that our problems have some historical force; perhaps I 'married my mother', my wife was attracted to behavioural resemblances between me and her father, and so on. Perhaps by disentangling all these unconscious and half-conscious motives and attractions, we can remedy the problems we are having. Yet I am aware that another counsellor believes something quite contrary to all this, and works quite differently. She considers that we must look at our different assumptions, our cognitive styles and typical behaviours. Yet another friend suggests from a feminist perspective that as a man I am obviously mainly at fault, my wife is oppressed, and so on. How are we to know to whom to turn for help? Perhaps we would be better off talking to a priest, or to other couples? Perhaps we must entertain the idea that marriages are not guaranteed to last forever. Whoever we turn to, including so-called non-directive counsellors, will have an assumption about marriage. Whoever talks with us will soon begin to formulate opinions (although these will probably be called hunches, assessments, or clinical conjectures).

Take another perspective on the problem of knowledge. I am aware when teaching students of counselling that they frequently assume that I know more than they do. This may sometimes be the case. I may have more experience, I may have done more training, read more books and written books. But does this mean that I know more about human nature, interpersonal relationships, how to help people, and so on? Logically, perhaps it should. Yet all that I have learned I have learned from others, whether in person or from books or other materials. I may have learned faultily, I will have listened in a biased way, I will have learned only what suited me, and so on. I may have immersed myself in an approach to counselling that, 50 years from now, turns out to be proven nonsense. Yet my students are still inclined to listen respectfully, indeed credulously, to what I say. How can they judge the truth or usefulness of what I say and do? How can they judge the merits of any of the central texts in counselling and psychotherapy? What is it that tells us whether something is true, genuine and of likely therapeutic benefit? Many issues concerning tradition and training in the therapies are addressed by Spurling (1993). Newman (1991) casts an interesting light on clinical epistemology when he asks clients how they know, for example, that they are depressed; where did they get this knowledge, how did they learn to identify and name their feelings as depression?

Appearance and reality

One way of understanding the present field of the talking therapies is to divide them roughly into approaches which are concerned with the obvious, observable and rational, and approaches which focus on what is subtle, hidden and deep. This kind of division can be seen in Plato, in mythology, in the existentialist distinction between existence and essence, and in many other guises. At one level we live simple, linear lives from cradle to grave. At another level, we constantly encounter problems and signs of hidden forces or hard-to-understand dynamics. At one level, we may say that the solution to agoraphobia is to go out, to leave the house and confront discomfort, to overcome the illusion of a current threat. At another level, we are accustomed to the idea of investigating the hidden, subtle, putative causes of agoraphobia and regarding the phobia as symptomatic of deeper problems. On the face of it, problems can be easily solved by accepting inescapable realities or changing what is in your power to change. In everyday experience, life is filled with obstacles that we believe we cannot overcome, or which cannot be overcome without encouragement or expert assistance.

Winnicott (1988) suggested that there is a psychoanalytic explanation for the preoccupation many philosophers have with the question of reality. Babies who experience early good enough mothering come to know instinctively that this experience gives them the illusion of contact they need for healthy development; they grow up knowing and accepting that essentially they will always be alone. They are not preoccupied with philosophical questions about direct contact with reality. By contrast, babies who experience less than this good enough quality of mothering do not develop such a healthy attitude. 'A sense of threat of loss of capacity for relationships hangs over them all the time. For them the philosophical problem becomes and remains a vital one, a matter of life and death, of feeding or starvation, of love or isolation' (Winnicott, 1988: 115). Although Winnicott does not make the claim explicitly in this particular text, we may infer that he – and many other analysts – regard much philosophy as a neurotic result of damaging early personal experiences. In this sense, psychoanalysts claim to have a grasp of what is real and what is not real that is superior to that of philosophers.

Classical psychoanalysis is the exemplar of an approach which seeks depth and subtlety. Rational emotive behaviour therapy, particularly as practised by its founder Albert Ellis, is an exemplar of an approach which takes the bull by the horns. Two such approaches are in complete conflict. In psychoanalytic terms, Ellis' approach is simplistic, aggressive, addresses only the level of 'secondary process' of logical mental control and is likely to have only short-term success. Ellis claims that psychoanalytic theory is largely nonsense and that clinical psychoanalysis is certainly inefficient. The unconscious is all-important in psychoanalysis, yet non-existent in rational emotive behaviour therapy. There is a realm of 'primary process', or timeless, irrational, dream-filled experience which features little in the theory and work of the cognitive-behaviour therapists generally. Some commentators may say that this level of experience may exist, but is not necessarily implicated in people's everyday problems and does not help them to overcome real dilemmas. For the past several decades, anyway, we have had disagreements in the therapy field, many of which are characterised by a pull towards either depth or surface.

Goldberg (1977: 8) complained that 'practitioners often act like romantic poets who believe that the power and efficacy of their practice resides in its mystique'. Those trained in the depth psychological approaches are often disdainful of the more practical, reality-based, short-term approaches such as reality therapy, rational emotive behaviour therapy, solution-focused therapy, and so on. Real change takes time, according to those who espouse a belief in the invariable need to dig deep beneath appearances. Enduring change requires extensive and subtle probing and interpetation. What clients bring to therapy are merely presenting symptoms or calling cards and it is the therapist's expertise which identifies deeper psychic realities. Depth psychologists are not concerned with finding remedies for their clients' (or patients') immediate crises, since they know that these crises mask subtler unconcious conflicts. Many humanistic therapists too have a depth agenda for their clients, some speaking of an initiation into one level of deeper reality after another (Hart et al., 1975).

As Goldberg and others have argued, it may be abusive to insist to clients that their own interpretation of their troubles must be incorrect or incomplete, because the therapist has the power to see through appearances. On the other hand, would it not be remiss of a therapist to deal with a client's panic attacks peremptorily with behavioural techniques, when those attacks might conceal all manner of traumas such as rape, childhood sexual abuse or birth trauma? Extremists on each side of this debate might be prepared to dismiss the reality of early traumas or the helpfulness of direct methods of ending panic attacks. The problem remains, however, of how to decide which approach is intellectually and practically more adequate, certain attempts at striking a balance notwithstanding (Greenwald, 1974). As clients and as counsellors we are often asked to put our money on one horse or the other. If I approach a psychodynamic counsellor with my career dilemma or insomnia, he or she is sure to see behind these concerns. Conversely, if I approach a cognitive-behavioural counsellor with a sense of generalised anxiety and doubts about whether my mother really loved me, he or she is sure to want to elicit specific, workable, current goals.

Consider the concept of will and weakness of will within this context of appearance and reality. On the surface, I wish to change certain aspects of my life, let us say my job and my relationships with colleagues. I more or less know what I need to do – be more assertive, take more risks, believe in myself – but I baulk when action is required of me. All I should have to do is will myself to confront my boss about her unfair treatment of me, yet I avoid this. My counsellor agrees a plan of action with me, a homework assignment, yet I 'cop out'. Alternatively, I have a counsellor who persistently analyses my lack of progress at work in terms of how I felt about my mother and how I feel about the counsellor. Neither approach, let us suppose, moves me on any further.

Another way of looking at this problem is in philosophical terms (Charlton, 1988). If I ask 'What is will, and what is weakness of will?' I may be able to reframe the problem entirely. Instead of regarding this as some awful personal cowardice or mystery, I might conceive it as a universal philosophical problem: everyone appears to be free, yet everyone seemingly experiences degrees of inhibition of freedom. Apparently we wish to better ourselves, to make ourselves happier and more fulfilled, yet in reality something holds us back. Counsellors may refer to this as a 'yes but' phenomenon. Freud argued that certain things are necessarily repressed in the unconscious, yet Sartre disputed this interpretation of events and preferred instead the explanation of 'bad faith': we know, in fact, that we are choosing to avoid something, that we lack courage. Explanations of what lies behind appearances (in this case, the appearance of free will) absolve people of responsibility. It can be, and is indeed by many, argued that the more we accept responsibility for ourselves in all areas of our lives, the less need is there for depth explanations or depth therapy.

The difficulty inherent in this argument is the common experience that certain unpleasant moods and bodily sensations are often difficult to understand and to shift. I do not know why I have a headache or why I suddenly feel depressed. I try to think more positively and to behave differently, but all to no avail. There may be some hidden psychogenic causes for these feelings, or there may not be. I may be highly susceptible to certain noxious pollutants in the environment, yet if I am looking for psychological explanations, I will miss this possibility. So a further problem when considering appearances and reality is that depth and surface refer not only to psychological events but to organic, environmental and other phenomena. What may appear initially to be a weakness of will or the presenting symptom of a long-repressed bad memory, may turn out to be the first signs of an unavoidable physical illness. Similarly, it can be argued that what may appear as a psychological crisis is in fact a spiritual or transpersonal crisis. And, conversely, what sometimes seems like a mystical experience is in reality a symptom of psychosis. What we take today to be satisfactory psychological explanations may well turn out in the light of much future genetic research to be very wide of the mark (Gazzaniga, 1992).

Reason and emotion

Another unmistakable conflict throughout the talking therapies is that between reason, or thought, and emotion, or feelings. Are we primarily thinking beings whose personal problems stem from and must be corrected through our thinking processes, or are we primarily feeling beings who must trust and regain contact with the full range of our feelings if we are to function better? Of course, many will argue that we are both these, and more. Lazarus (1989), for example, suggests that our functioning is best described in terms of behaviour, affect, sensations, imagery, cognitions, interpersonal factors and biology. Others insist that we are spiritual and social beings above all. Bohm (1994) argues that our thinking and feeling processes are simultaneous. The thinking-feeling dichotomy, however, is fairly persistent.

According to cognitive-behavioural therapists, what we think dictates how we will feel. If I interpret an adverse event in my life as catastrophic, I will inevitably feel very depressed or anxious. If, in therapy, I can learn to moderate my thoughts and to interpret adverse events as uncomfortable but not terrible, then I will be far less disturbed. This approach assumes that everyone is able to gain sufficient control over their thoughts to begin to make such changes; many people in fact protest that they have little such control and that feelings may be much more dominant in their lives than thinking. Lazarus in fact considers that we all have our particular primary modalities, or ways in which we mainly react to events, sometimes cognitively, but often affectively, behaviourally, somatically, or whatever. For the most part, therapies can again be roughly divided into those placing emphasis on thinking and those placing emphasis on feeling.

In general, the humanistic therapies (person-centred, Gestalt, psychodrama, primal, experiential, and so on) value the experience and expression of strong feelings more highly than the use of the intellect. Naturally, philosophy, particularly official, academic philosophy, favours the intellect. You cannot systematically *feel* your way through an explanation of human behaviour and human problems. Indeed it is debatable whether you can be at all systematic when dealing with emotions. Janov and Holden (1975) claim that feelings are the very cornerstone of sane human functioning and that in primal therapy they can be systematically explored; they have a logic of their own. In this view philosophy, and intellectualising generally, is regarded more often than not as a kind of defence mechanism, or warding off of psychological pain. In psychoanalysis, too, intellectualising on the part of a patient is regarded as a defence mechanism. Oddly enough, proponents of primal and Gestalt therapies have usually regarded psychoanalysis as excessively intellectual and emotionally superficial.

Humanistic therapists and sympathisers, sometimes referred to as a third force in psychology or psychotherapy, seem impatient with the logical-positivism of science and scientistic methods and discourse. Keen to overthrow the dualistic thinking of Descartes and the myth of any real distinction between body and mind, humanistic practitioners have perhaps explored varieties of feeling states that had lain dormant or had been disrespected for a long time. Tedious logical analysis appeared not to make much headway after many centuries, until Kierkegaard, Nietzsche, Rousseau, Schleiermacher and others wrote about states of agitation, anguish and exaltation. Perhaps *incoherence* as a common human state should be on the agenda, and perhaps excessive reason should be put into perspective. Existentialism 'gave philosophy a subjective, quasi-psychological twist, making it the study of human consciousness' (Stevenson, 1987: 91). How can consciousness be studied and explained without in some way abandoning the sovereignty of the intellect? There is much more to human consciousness than logic and conscious reason. Feelings may be described and dissected, but in the process they are distorted and lost.

What place do feelings have in counselling? Obviously many people come in crisis, for example when freshly bereaved or divorced. Often the very thing they need to do is cry, and perhaps scream and shout. There may be no logical or philosophical value in crying and screaming, but there is demonstrated cathartic value. Small wonder, however, that Ellis and others within the cognitive-behavioural camp express concern that strong feelings run the risk of engendering infantile, regressed, irrational and demanding behaviour. As often as not, the labels by which therapies are known betray their real values. Rational emotive behaviour therapy gives prominence to the 'rational'. Psychoanalysis is 'analysis'. But psychodrama is 'drama' and experiential psychotherapy is 'experiential' (feeling-biased). Almost certainly in clinical practice feelings are expressed in cognitive therapies as much as thinking and analysis takes place in feeling-based therapies. By its very nature, philosophising is rather logical and therefore may tend to under-rate the role of feelings. 'The heart,' said Pascal, 'has its reasons which reason knows nothing of.'

Autonomy

Autonomy is the sovereignty of the self, the right to self-determination. Although we have implicitly covered much of this ground in the discussion on cause and effect, it is important to pause to consider the concept of autonomy, which often has the flavour of a sacred right and is intimately associated with the concept of authenticity and our right, if not duty, to be authentic (Maslow, 1968; Taylor, 1991). Counsellors are expected to respect and safeguard the autonomy of the client and no other concept is quite so central to counselling and psychotherapy (Holmes and Lindley,

1989). One of the greatest and most succinct expressions of the belief in the centrality of autonomy was provided by Isaiah Berlin:

> I wish my life and opinions to depend on myself, not on external forces of whatever kind, I wish to be the instrument of my own, not other men's, acts of will. I wish to be a subject, not an object; to be moved by reasons, by conscious purposes, which are my own, not by causes which affect me, as it were, from outside. I wish to be somebody, not nobody; a doer – deciding, not being decided for, self-directed and not acted upon by external nature or by other men as though I were a thing, or an animal, or a slave incapable of playing a human role, that is, of conceiving goals and policies of my own and realising them. (1969: 131)

Autonomy is one of Lukes' (1973) constituent parts of the ideal of individualism, along with dignity, privacy and self-development. Autonomy stands against conformity, slavery and anonymity, as seen in Berlin's statement. It is perhaps so much a part of our own culture that we can hardly conceive of any serious doubt about its inviolability. But its importance may be primarily in the stand it takes against slavery, objectification and alienation. Carried to unthinking extremes, like any concept, it may have its dangers. It has been pointed out frequently that our age, and the practice of the therapies within it, is perhaps excessively self-centred or narcissistic. Psychology's, and counselling's, promotion of the individual may have led ironically to the enthronement of the individual and his or her rights, to the detriment of human connectedness and sense of social cohesion. Counsellors may inadvertently have exaggerated the merits and extent of autonomy, of individual freedom and choice, overlooking the question of moral responsibility and obligations to others. London (1986: 65) cites C.P. Snow's admonition concerning our tendency to 'sit back, complacent in one's unique tragedy, and let others go without a meal'. Consideration for the other is the theme of Sampson's (1993) dialogical view of psychology. Sampson is critical of the private inner world promoted by traditional psychology and psychotherapy, and advocates instead a shift towards greater respect for others, other cultures and dialogue generally. Friedman's (1993) views on dialogical therapy suggest that autonomy without full-bodied dialogue is empty.

Worldviews

I have sometimes put the question to students, 'How do you see the world? What is your predominant conception of human existence? Is it meaningful or meaningless, tragic or comic? Is there a God or not?' Often trainee counsellors have not seen the immediate relevance of such questions to the practice of counselling, and often they cannot begin to conceptualise their views at all without some difficulty. This is not surprising, perhaps, since such thinking is not encouraged in our schools and is barely a feature of our age at all. If we have a contemporary worldview at all, for many of us it is implicitly a pragmatic 'look after number one, strive to excel, and hope to survive' ideology. Or for some it is a somewhat rigid, prescriptive set of moral and political views known pejoratively as political correctness. Although some maintain religious and political allegiances, I suspect that many individuals now live relatively unexamined lives, or lives dedicated to rather circumscribed hedonistic goals. Perhaps for many of us there exists a kind of muted hedonism and resignation; we quietly hope to prosper as individuals and we despair of finding genuine leadership or community. In many ways, counselling may be a search for purpose, meaning and meeting in sanctioned interpersonal settings.

Van Deurzen-Smith (1988) argues that clients in existentialist counselling must be helped to understand their own worldview, their own values, before progress can be made. What is life? What is death? To what extent do I see myself as responsible for my own life and its meaning? If counsellors cannot answer such questions for themselves, how will they assist clients struggling with them? Spires and Dryden (1988) examine different visions of reality in various approaches to therapy. Using the visions of reality classified as romantic, ironic, tragic and comic, they suggest that humanistic therapies, for example, have a large emphasis on romantic visions, while psychoanalysis emphasises a tragic, and behaviourism a comic vision. This schema is explored more fully by Messer (1992). For Szasz (1991), however, most if not all psychotherapy is a denial of the tragic nature of life, refusing to accept the possibility that life is full of adverse circumstances which can only be met with courage and realism. A part-echo of this view is found in Craib (1994).

One of the problematic features of counselling and psychological enterprises generally is that they have a subtle, or not so subtle, tendency to become quasi-worldviews. Just as Freud applied psychoanalytic ideas to society and culture generally, so many people today think psychologically, or practise a form of psychological reductionism. Everything can be interpreted in individual, 'depth' terms, everything can be traced back to the motivations of individuals, or to collective motivations. Every utterance, every piece of literature or work of art can be understood in these terms. Unfortunately, the depth psychologies have this seductive nature, that they appear to offer possible answers to everything, much as religion has a tendency towards totalitarian explanations. Life cannot be seen as simply what it is, but must be interpreted as the manifestation of psychological forces. People cannot be regarded as free and fallible agents but must be seen as psychologically driven, the dupes of their own unconscious or their own irrational thinking. As Stevenson (1987) argues from a philosopher's perspective, there are many possible worldviews, or theories of human nature, none of them entirely satisfactory.

It is not feasible to examine the whole range of possible philosophical problems. However, we must note that counselling has in some way to deal with the problems of mind and body, with the idea of the self, with the meaningfulness or otherwise of the specialised concepts and language with which the entire counselling and psychotherapy enterprise is saturated. The self is particularly problematic, since it is central to considerations of individual suffering, the individual psyche, and questions concerning the reality of a self or selves. We talk about a 'real self' as if it is something lying waiting to be discovered as the fruit of a sufficiently heroic therapeutic journey, for example. Related to this are concepts like the 'inner child' which can become so commonplace in counselling as to take on an apparently unquestionable reality of their own. I sometimes wonder if clients are not convinced by their counsellors of the existence of some sort of homunculus (the ghostly inner child) sitting physically inside their bodies somewhere, gratefully receiving the belated affirmations and 'strokes' of their owner. In other words, interesting, transient and potentially therapeutic images may easily be mistaken for realities.

Mair (1992) and Gergen (1990) have criticised therapists for generating and reifying such metaphors. Few answers are available as yet (philosophical texts taking questionable therapeutic constructs to task are still rare) but such questions must be asked if we wish to avoid propagating magical, dishonest and ultimately ineffective ideas. In many ways the field of theoretical and philosophical psychology is now leading the way in this area (Sampson, 1993; Schechtman, 1994; Slife, 1993), as well as Foucauldian commentators such as Newton (1995), who challenge the sometimes facile and deceptive tendencies of current psychotherapeutic discourse. Spinelli (1994) argues for the usefulness of Wittgensteinian analysis of language in understanding therapy contextually so that, for example, we might benefit more from asking 'When is therapy?' than 'What is therapy?'

8

Counselling, Sociopolitical Concepts and Critiques

> People do not come to counselling centres with neatly packaged difficulties responsive only to internal reflection and the gaining of insight. They come with personal tragedies overlaid with financial problems, with relationship difficulties exacerbated by disadvantages of housing and environment, and with private miseries compounded by mental and physical illness.
>
> Carole Sutton (1989a)

Counselling is characterised by one-to-one, private conversation. The body of knowledge upon which counselling is founded derives from, or is usually closely associated with, psychology, a discipline that is itself largely focused on the individual. Freudianism and the talking therapies generally have often been contrasted with Marxism, the former intent on studying the individual psyche, intrapsychic conflict and biographical detail, the latter on large scale, societal struggles, on history and a programme for social change (Fromm, 1980). Of course, both enterprises acknowledge and to some extent embrace the concerns of the other, but arguably Freudianism or psychological discourse generally is currently in the ascendant. Robinson (1990) suggests that Marx is now largely ignored and that the radical left among Freudians (for example, Reich, Roheim and Marcuse) are of historical curiosity value more than having any real impact on the current conservative world. As Robinson also points out, for many critics Freud is the epitome of the anti-utopian thinker.

In this chapter I propose to raise some of the main salient issues in the interface between the individualistic orientation of counselling and its sociopolitical context. As Bimrose (1993) comments, this subject has been paid lip-service by many counsellors but counsellor training courses still betray the fact that it is viewed as marginal in practice. Perhaps this should come as no surprise, since many counselling and psychotherapy trainees have begun their interest in this field as clients and as the research of Pistrang and Barker (1992) suggests, it is probable that a majority of clients attribute greater value to psychological explanations of their distress than to socio-economic explanations. Indeed, Halmos (1965) partly equates the growth of counselling with the discrediting of political solutions.

What do we mean when we mention 'social context'? As the quotation from Sutton (1989a) suggests, individuals seeking counselling contain and bring with them problems of relationship, personal economics, housing, oppression, illness and so on. An immediately illuminating point here is that Sutton speaks from the context of a counsellor associated with clients from the 'lower' social classes who receive counselling in voluntary and statutory agencies. Affluent clients often do *not* have any pressing economic, housing and similar problems, often buy their own counselling or therapy and present personal problems which their lower class counterparts would not necessarily define as problems at all. The term 'social context' might better be rendered into the plural, since we clearly inhabit very different social contexts. The discrepancies in wealth within the so-called developed world are themselves magnified in contrast with the levels of poverty within the so-called third world. Smail (1987: 86) has pithily commented on 'the worlds of difference between Mother Theresa of Calcutta and the average Hampstead psychoanalyst'. In spite of recent critiques of Mother Theresa's politics, the contrast remains an important one.

The social context in which we live may be understood to refer to the impacts of gender, race, education, sexual orientation, disability, age, environment, class and economics. Added to this list might be the historical context in which we live; the impact of ongoing or transient wars, natural catastrophes and economic slumps. None of us is born into a social vacuum and no one develops as a child unconditioned by particular social factors. In psychology generally, and counselling psychology especially, however, these factors have not been traditionally regarded as of paramount importance. Most theories of psychological dysfunction have centred on, for example, birth trauma, intrapsychic conflict, developmental problems, parental deficits, sibling rivalry, childhood trauma, faulty adjustment, irrational personal beliefs, and so on. Accordingly, theories of personal liberation have centred on the re-tracing of past emotional hurts, identification of personal *scripts* and *schemata*, resolution of transference and programmes of personal re-adjustment. In a field which manages to hold such a wide diversity of theories, including the behavioural and transpersonal, for example, it is evident that very few have centred on, if they have even considered, the significance of social context, social conditioning and social change. (Often such terms are used, but synonymously with 'familial' or 'interpersonal'.) Critics of counselling understandably complain that clients are helped simply to adjust to a sick society.

Perhaps the main impetus for counselling to address the social and political has come from proponents of feminism and anti-racism. Feminist therapy and transcultural therapy have gained some sort of identity, at least (Chaplin, 1988; Sue and Sue, 1990; Walker, 1990). We have feminism to thank for the argument that the personal is political. In other words, we have begun to understand that what happens in our everyday lives and relationships is deeply affected by, and in turn can and should affect and transform, politics. From feminism we learn that individual travail is not merely a result of unresolved childhood hurts but a consequence of the longstanding, institutionalized oppression of women which is so pervasive as to have been accepted until recently as natural and inevitable. The growing vociferousness of women, black people and other oppressed groups, has in recent decades challenged the complacently intrapsychic theories and practices of counsellors, psychologists and other human service professionals. Such trends will continue to influence and transform counselling but in turn the insights of psychotherapy and counselling will also shed light on some of the causes and possible cures of social oppression. In the present chapter, then, I aim to examine some of the many sides of the argument, rather than adopting either an anti-counselling or anti-political stance. This dialogical position seems in fact to be a promising development generally (Samuels, 1993).

Social explanations for psychological problems

It is asserted by various writers that society or civilization is itself sick and pathogenic. One argument runs thus: that human beings have adapted successfully to the rigours of the earth's climate, to competition with animals and to the earth's resources generally. Human language and culture has led to advanced technology and to a pace of life, however, with which many individuals cannot keep up. Within humanity itself there are wide discrepancies of wealth, intelligence and ability, and it is as if the competition that humans have won against nature has converted into a competition of human being with human being, of nation with nation. Men have oppressed women, whites have oppressed blacks, adults have oppressed children. The need for people to live in dense communities for protection and convenience has in turn led to overcrowding and aggression. The need for social regulatory functions has led to dehumanizing educational systems and dehumanizing political systems generally.

The nuclear family, itself apparently crumbling in our own age, has introjected many of these struggles and stresses, so that children have become powerless victims who themselves frequently perpetuate aggressive or other anti-social behaviour when they become adults. Social mobility has perhaps undermined some of the supportive structures previously supplied by lifelong work colleagues, neighbours and extended families. Society needs its members to curb and contain their spontaneous behaviour (including sex), and so people frequently become psychologically and psychosomatically ill (Robinson, 1990). Individual human beings, however basically decent, are under pressure to survive economically as part of an economic system from which they feel alienated. Language and community have become vehicles of deception and suspicion rather than of empowerment and cooperation. Human beings find themselves obliged to be at least partially dishonest with each other and even with themselves. All these factors add up to a stressful existence and to an unsurprisingly chronic degree of mental distress. Some of these arguments are sum-marized by Fromm (1963; 1980). More recent analyses of the stressful demands of modern life (Kegan, 1994: Newton, 1995) argue that even counselling and psychotherapy have themselves become pressures upon us, asking us to live up to ideals of psychological independence and authorship that we often simply cannot reach.

Crime, alcoholism, drug addiction, suicide and relationship breakdowns are arguably some of the universal and visible signs of our sick civilization. Coinciding with the rise of psychology, psychotherapy and social science generally, religion has been in decline in the west. Moral explanations for human distress and destructive behaviour have weakened in the face of many relatively convincing psychological explanations. Perhaps what were once regarded as signs of sin or personal degeneracy are now more commonly accepted as signs of a decaying social fabric. Increasing crime rates are often debated in terms of a link with unemployment and poor welfare provision and even the more right-wing of commentators do not find such explanations completely absurd. Many voluntary and statutory organizations are funded in recognition of the common links between alcohol abuse, drug addiction, unemployment and crime. There may be relatively little political commitment to improving conditions for the poor and oppressed but the principle of a connection between poor social conditions and personal distress and crime commands some intellectual respect.

In their study of the connections between social and personal problems, Mirowsky and Ross (1989) ask why some people are more distressed than others and identify lack of control over one's life as a major factor. They argue, as many others have, that there are clear, direct links between socio-economic status and lifestyle, and mental and physical health and illness. There is a higher incidence of depression among women than among men and a higher incidence of depression among women who work and look after their own children than among women who have no children or those who are helped with childcare. Mirowsky and Ross suggest that role strain and overload lead to depression. The isolation experienced by women who take care of children at home is often a contributing factor in depression. I infer from my own experience of once working in a mental health agency that a disproportionate number of women suffering from depression, anxiety and agoraphobia had endured years of home-bound isolation, loss of contact with other adults, loss of esteem, and lack of support. Not only did they feel depressed or anxious, but they commonly reported that they had no conscious idea why they felt this way.

Mirowsky and Ross (1989) assert that low socioeconomic status is the primary factor contributing to mental distress. Describing the broad socio-economic differences in terms of 'poor and uneducated' and 'well-to-do and educated', they claim that these differences 'dwarf the difference between men and women', and that 'high socioeconomic status improves psychological wellbeing and low status increases psychological distress'. The equation here is that the less you have to begin with, in terms of social advantages and coping resources, the more likely you are to fail economically, to experience distress and to dwell within a cycle of deprivation. The authors point out that black people typically have lower levels of education and income than whites and are thus extremely vulnerable to poverty and psychological distress. People with children to take care of – men as well as women – are likely to experience greater economic hardship and distress than those without children. As Samuels (1993) cautions, it is dangerous to view and thus stereotype all such classes as if they individually experience the same kinds and levels of distress, but broadly speaking, the picture is clear: certain social conditions are much more likely to foster psychological distress.

I once met a man who had literally been born in prison. His mother had been a convicted offender. He had subsequently grown up in the care system and had graduated from one institution to another, had associated with offenders all his life and had been involved in many crimes. He had also experienced a series of damaging relationships with women. I have witnessed, with a sense of dismay and powerlessness, the cycle of deprivation in process, in a young woman who had grown up 'in care', became pregnant twice in her teens, and her babies had themselves to be taken into care. Social workers and probation officers often become relatively immune to such stories because they are staple fare in their profession. Consider an ironic counterpart to such instances. Many middle class and upper middle class children in the UK are sent to 'public' boarding schools where they learn to cope without their parents; such experiences are considered character-forming. When adults, these children frequently become social leaders (politicians, administrators and businessmen), since it is still the case in the UK that the 'top people' are drawn from a few elite schools and universities. Political leadership may therefore often be characterized by people who have learned to dissociate from their feelings of vulnerability early on in life. They may then exert inordinate influence over the life of a nation, based on their own (some might say) schizoid personalities. As individuals, they may not consciously experience distress themselves but they are certainly capable of blocking the progress of any compassionate welfare programmes for their lower status fellow citizens. These are perhaps contentious claims but they are important and not untypical analyses from a psychological perspective.

This forces us to ask whether anything can be done to prevent widespread psychological distress and what is an appropriate treatment or strategy for those already distressed in circumstances relating to poverty, unemployment and isolation. It is difficult to imagine, although logically possible, that counsellors and other helping professionals would altogether dismiss such considerations. 'It's not my job to change society, but to help individuals' is an understandable statement but a limited aspiration. It is evident, however, that in certain quarters it is the assumption that the individual client or patient (and his or her internal world) is the therapist's sole concern (Pilgrim, 1992). This is short-sighted and, we might argue, deeply unethical. If counsellors are genuinely committed to understanding and alleviating psychological distress, are they not abusing their position when they turn a blind eye to social explanations of distress? Strupp (1982a: 111) clearly thinks not: 'Do not look to us for revolutionary social change; do not expect us to change an imperfect world where poverty, technology, racial discrimination, pollution, and man's inhumanity to man have created a plethora of problems that we deplore but do not have the power to change.'

Many of the causes of distress are obvious to counsellors from their own clinical experience. Albee (1990: 377) refers to psychotherapy as 'a window on the damage done to children [and] . . . the damage done to everyone by a social system that encourages mindless competition and implicitly embraces the philosophy of social Darwinism.' Can psychotherapsists, then, in good conscience, ignore such findings and concern themselves exclusively with each client? Counsellors in private practice face a particular ethical dilemma, since it is only their paying customers on whom they can rely for a livelihood. They are not paid to do social research or to lobby parliament. Yet many counsellors probably ask themselves if there are not more effective ways of combating psychological distress than attempting never-ending, piecemeal individual solutions.

If psychological distress is largely caused or exacerbated by unemployment, economic stress, overwork, poor housing, isolation, oppression and lack of opportunity, then it is probably not helped significantly by minor, individualistic counselling interventions for a relatively small number of people. Mays and Albee (1992) point out that ethnic minorities experience greater poverty and social stress than their white counterparts, yet they neither use nor staff psychotherapeutic services commensurate with their needs, in relation to the extent that white people utilize and staff such services. It has also been objected that ethnic minorities and the poor generally contribute in their tax payments towards psychotherapy services that in fact benefit only a small proportion of white middle class people.

Albee (1990) argues that it is in the very nature of psychotherapy to defend the social status quo and that there are not – nor can there ever be – enough psychotherapists to make a socially significant impact on the epidemiology of psychological distress. As he puts it, 'psychotherapy may partially reduce the handicaps of a few of the emotionally damaged but this kind of war on emotional poverty cannot succeed because it does nothing to alter the social forces that keep producing more victims than are helped' (Albee, 1990: 134). Albee and his colleagues advocate programmes of primary prevention as an effective alternative to counselling and psychotherapy. Counsellors who promote individual counselling and greater funding for it, thereby divert money and commitment from preventive projects and from due consideration of the principles involved. If you argue for public money to be spent on counselling, are you discouraging debate on the social causes of psychological distress? If so, you may become aligned with the oppression of the poor and disadvantaged. If, as Hillman and Ventura (1992) and Sennett (1986) suggest, we have helped to shape culture towards respect for private, interpersonal and intrapsychic reflection to the detriment of public concern and political action, then we run the risk of becoming a cause of social problems ourselves.

Psychological attitudes to social problems

Many attempts have been made to explain society's ills in psychological terms. We have already considered the idea that the price of civilization is social neurosis. Required to be good, productive citizens, we learn from childhood onwards to suppress our more instinctual drives or inclinations, to relate politely, to work uncomplainingly and to schedules set by others. Whether in capitalist, communist or other regimes, we live in societies which wield power over our wealth, health and very lives. Parents often receive the blame for doing psychological damage to their children, but the truth may be that most parents, often living lives of quiet desperation (socio-economically speaking), experience very little choice in how they relate to their children and what values they pass on to them. Transgenerational habits and traditions mix with current economic family pressures and parental exhaustion to exert powerful influences on children. Many of these influences are resisted, especially in adolescence perhaps, but the conflicts created between parents and children frequently go underground to become the stuff of the so-called unconscious. Mainstream Freudian and neo-Freudian ideology and practice seems largely to ignore, however, any serious analysis of the interface between the family and the society in which it exists.

I do not want to lump together all psychologies and schools of psychotherapy, since I am aware that their proponents view themselves as often more socially aware than each other. Group, family and systemic therapists, for example, often see their own endeavours as having an impact on the wider community that is far greater than that achieved by individual therapists. Many humanistic therapists believe themselves to be committed to struggles for social justice and transformation, even if their psychoanalytic or behavioural counterparts are rather tame politically. Very broadly speaking, however, the psychological approach to personal and social problems is characterized by a focus on the individual, his or her inner life and immediate relationships. As we have seen, the concept of individual autonomy is at the heart of counselling ideology. Individuals should be regarded as free, self-determining, active agents; their personal concerns should be taken deadly seriously; their uniqueness should be honoured. Furthermore, so this ideology implies, it is only when we respect individual autonomy that people begin to act in a spontaneously pro-social manner. Psychoanalysts, psychotherapists and counsellors have the tools to help their clients radically transform their own lives and, in turn, transform the world. This represents a certain form of psychosocial logic which is quite prevalent in counselling circles. Lift the chains from individuals' minds and the good life, the utopian society, will follow.

In this latter vision, things just fall into place. Thus, Janov believes that people who have undergone primal therapy will seldom have any interest in formal politics: 'They do not want to control anyone else's life, and therefore have no political ambitions, indeed, very few ambitions except to live a life in peace. . . . Primal man is governed by his feelings' (Janov and Holden, 1975: 455). Broadly speaking, all will be well in the society created by humanistic therapy, because therapy restores true human feelings and these feelings restore true community, sane society, and so on. Unfortunately, this argument is reminiscent of the kind of religious sentiment – quietism – that promotes the view that attention to the inner life, the soul, and communion with God, is all that counts and will certainly bring about the good society if one has sufficient faith. Let us look after ourselves, our own psyches, feelings, hurts and healing, and social solutions will materialise effortlessly, runs this argument. Furthermore, all such arguments are usually bolstered by psychological analyses of what has gone wrong with society, why people are evil or crazy, why institutions function as they do, and what the psychologists can do about it.

Psychological analyses of social problems often do produce explanations that have some credibility. For example, it probably is the case that many dictators and many democratic leaders have been driven by their own inner demons, their own painful childhood experiences and lack of self-esteem, to gain power over others (Miller, 1987). It probably is the case that many genocidal leaders are full of hate learned from wretched early childhood experiences. It is quite possible that politicians – who are mostly men – are so removed from their own feelings of need and vulnerability that they cannot understand the real needs of others. The problem with such analyses is that they lead nowhere: dictators do not seek therapy. Conversely, those who seek therapy, and live within its ideology, rarely seem to seek real political power or influence.

Apart from the naive view that social transformation automatically follows from individual therapy or counselling, there is a greater danger. To illustrate this I give a personal example. Some years ago I underwent therapy in Los Angeles. Just before my first session I heard that the woman who ran the psychotherapy institute owned a Rolls Royce. This seemed of some significance to me and I mentioned it during my session. I was asked what this meant to me. In fact, the therapist kept pressing me about what it meant until, as I recall, she made the point that I was obviously envious, that everyone probably would have a Rolls Royce if they could afford one, and that it was my task, if I wanted to cease being neurotic, to stop being envious and start getting in touch with my own feelings. Even as I write this, I can see some sort of logic in these remarks.

If I had that kind of money, I probably would have a big or fancy car, and perhaps what prevents me from having that kind of money is a passive–aggressive attachment to envy, a need to denigrate the achievements of others, and so on. This may be true and I may be quite wrong in questioning whether people deserve to buy Rolls Royces from the proceeds of selling therapy to others. The danger in this argument, however, is that anything can apparently be justified in this way. The reason I am not richer or more successful is that I refuse to get in touch with my angry feelings about my powerful father, let's say. The reason that some people stay at the bottom of the social ladder is that they misdirect their energies and fantasies. This logic culminates in Schutz's (1979) claim that whenever we are robbed, raped or in any way hurt, it is because we unconsciously want or attract these events. Only by gaining full consciousness and honesty do we transcend all these games of self-defeating behaviour and go on to embrace a fulfilling life for ourselves.

Many forms of therapy have their own explanations of this kind. In rational emotive behaviour therapy, for example, we are taught to accept that life is often a hassle, that it is not, nor ever will be, exactly the way we want it to be. We had better adjust our expectations of life, and not demand from it things which are not forthcoming. We may be *concerned* about social injustice and we may choose to try to do something about it, but we will not inordinately upset ourselves over it. As reported in Samuels' (1993) accounts gathered from many depth psychologists, a typical analytic response to political material brought into the therapy session is, perhaps, to acknowledge the 'reality issues' therein, but then to focus on the individual, intrapsychic meaning of these political concerns. Our perceptions, or 'phantasies', are usually held to be more crucial than external realities. Terrified of significant people in our early lives, we may repress such original terrors and unconsciously attach the terror to the enemies of another nation state; feeling unsafe because of repressed memories of personal traumas, we may unconsciously convert this into feeling unsafe in the world and dedicating our lives to political activism in relation to pollution, nuclear proliferation, mistreatment of animals and other evils. Locked in an unconscious Oedipal conflict, you may act this out politically by opposing all authoritarian regimes, for example. The classical Freudian view has it that unconscious individual dynamics repeat themselves on the wider stage of human history (Freud, 1930).

Chasseguet-Smirgel and Grunberger (1986), in contrasting the views of Freud with those Reich, argue for the 'primacy of internal factors' and against the 'illusion' of liberation through sexual fulfilment and a Marxist society. Chasseguet-Smirgel and Grunberger call 'romantic and fashionable' the idea of 'changing the world'. According to them:

> Because political ideologies analyze sociopolitical facts in terms of a projective, and sometimes persecutory, system of interpretation, they tend to disconnect these facts from their unconscious roots . . . Human beings can only act, and create, on the basis of their internal, psychosexual model. We project this model

on to the world when creating political systems, institutions and economic structures, thus making them in our own image. In other words, this kind of projection is a translation of psychic space into social space. (Chasseguet-Smirgel and Grunberger 1986: 212)

The daunting logic of the position of these authors is that no one who has not been fully analysed by an orthodox psychoanalyst can be sure that any of their sociopolitical concepts or actions is anything but an unconscious projection. In a rather softer but essentially identical vein, Lindner (1986) recounts the story of a communist union leader he analysed, and ends with the analytically triumphant testimony that 'In the course of his analysis Mac learned that the Party *was* his neurosis. When he concluded his analysis, it went with his symptoms. About six months after we had terminated, Mac quit the Party. He no longer needed it' (Lindner, 1986: 111). Newton (1995) suggests explicitly that modern employee counselling services have flourished alongside the weakening of unions and that the channelling and interpreting of grievances as individualistic and therapeutically adjustable is one of the main functions of such services.

While psychotherapeutic accounts do not invariably denigrate all aspects of political analysis and social change, Chasseguet-Smirgel and Grunberger see no possibility for any amalgam of Freud and Marx and promote the view that human beings create illusions inevitably, unless psychoanalysed. Weatherill (1991) seems to echo some of the fears of Chasseguet-Smirgel and Grunberger, arguing that the human potential movement's advocacy of self-empowerment 'encourages a grandiose defence'. As I have stated, I believe that there is often much sense in simple psychological analyses of politics and political leaders, but I consider totalitarian psychotherapeutic thinking to be both absurd and dangerous, undermining as it does any faith in commonsense and direct political action.

Psychosocial change projects

I am using the term 'psychosocial' not in its clinical sense, relating to individuals' adjustment to their interpersonal worlds. By psychosocial change projects I am referring to historical and current attempts to apply the insights gained from psychotherapy and counselling, broadly speaking, to understanding and improving social conditions. Interestingly, it is Alfred Adler, whose theories have been among the least exploited in recent decades, who may be considered the psychotherapist who originally had the greatest interest in sociopolitical factors. Adler's concept of 'social interest' emerged at the time of the First World War and denoted a 'social feeling', a 'love of one's neighbour' and an overcoming of egocentricity. This was and is in contrast to the classical psychoanalytic suspicion that altruism is often simply a defence mechanism. Adler sought to concretize his social interest in the establishment of child guidance clinics and in general maintained contact with various educational and social institutions throughout his life. It is probably no accident that Adler's theories received far less attention than those of Freud, Jung and other depth psychologists and that Adler was sometimes criticised for speaking mere commonsense.

It is also significant that most contemporary cognitive-behavioural therapists acknowledge some debt to Adler. Indeed, a line of theoretical descent can be traced from Adler to Harry Stack Sullivan, Karen Horney, Erich Fromm, Victor Frankl, Rollo May and other existentialist and humanistic therapists. Many of these practitioners placed emphasis on the everyday and the interpersonal as significant factors in emotional disturbance and its amelioration. Ellenberger (1970) sees fit to include Binswanger, Glasser, Albert Ellis and Eric Berne in a list of practitioners who owe something to Adler. Each of these, albeit in very different ways, has attended to social factors, perhaps especially to the need to make therapy more comprehensible and accessible to larger numbers of people and to make it relate clearly to the interpersonal and social sphere. This represents a swing away from depth psychology and its theoretical speculativeness, towards concern for pragmatism and demonstrable effectiveness. It also embodies a respect for the here-and-now of clients' lives and an acknowledgement, for example in the existential concept of the *Mitwelt* (public sphere), that wrestling with the sociopolitical is an important part of clients' realities.

Wilhelm Reich stands out among early therapists who derived their inspiration from Freud, yet moved on to create entirely distinct theories. Reich advocated not a mere understanding of sex and the danger in its suppression, but a sexual revolution. As Chassegruet-Smirgel and Grunberger (1986) point out, Reich attempted to formulate a species of Freudo-Marxism based on theories of sexual and somatic freedom, which estranged him from both Freudians and Marxists. Although Reich has no great following today, he influenced considerably the humanistic therapists who practise bodywork and all practitioners who incorporate an under-standing of the function of the psychosomatic in emotional disturbance and health. Figures such as Reich have also contributed in some measure to a sense of social unrest. Chassegruet-Smirgel and Grunberger, for example, associate Reichian theory with the French student revolution of 1968. The radical educator A.S. Neill also credited Reich with influencing him and his own ideas for free schools.

Erich Fromm, in collaboration with Sullivan and Horney, and inde-pendently, developed his own version of psychoanalysis which he referred to as humanistic psychoanalysis. This was informed by a study of Hegel, Marxism and religion and emphasised a human need for relatedness and rootedness. Like Reich, Fromm drew heavily from both Freud and Marx and saw a need to move beyond them (Fromm, 1980). Fromm asked in *The Sane Society* (Fromm, 1963) whether we are sane as a society, and why rates of suicide, homicide and alcoholism, for example, are so high.

He posited the view that what we have come to regard as normality may in fact be a kind of pathology, and argued that greed and ambition, which we easily exalt as capitalistic virtues, are forms of insanity. Just as couples may become enmeshed in a *folie à deux*, so society may be seen as a *folie à millions*.

Fromm suggested that we suffer from schizoid self-alienation and employed the jarring phrase that 'man is dead'. To overcome this, a new consciousness is required which transcends narrowly religious, psycho-analytic or socialist solutions. Fromm commended education as one path towards this new consciousness and urged the creation of possibilities for meaningful adult education. In somewhat utopian vein, Fromm argued that people at around the ages of 30 or 40 should be freed to change employment completely and to study again. In some ways, this is exactly what some people do when they enter counselling or psychotherapy and go into training, and it may be that the counselling movement represents an instinctive bid for new learning and community on the part of mature people.

The 1960s were perhaps the heyday of the idea of a psychosocial revolution. The restlessness of youth and rejection of war, along with a period of relative prosperity, spawned a short era of colourful social experimentation. Writers such as R.D. Laing (*The Politics of Experience*), Timothy Leary (*The Politics of Ecstasy*), Aldous Huxley (*Island*) and Hermann Hesse (*Steppenwolf, Siddhartha*) generated and encapsulated a spirit of urgent re-examination of social values. This movement, if it was a movement, was driven by a mixture of eastern religious concepts (especially Zen Buddhism, yoga and meditation), by psychedelic drugs, sexual permissiveness, pacifism, rejection of authorities and a swelling of utopian hopes. The human potential movement in the USA was fuelled, in centres like Esalen in California, by the relatively new therapies of psychodrama, Gestalt, encounter, re-evaluation counselling and many others. Today this movement has been toned down considerably, or is perhaps being reborn in mellower form in the so-called New Age move-ment. Then and now, experiments with communal living, non-possessive relationships, ecologically responsible attitudes and exploration of spiritual potential, represent hope for a radically different society. According to humanistic writers such as Rowan (1983), no worthwhile psychotherapy or counselling can ignore the social dimension and all psychotherapy has a responsibility to challenge social norms rather than to encourage clients to adapt to a sickening society.

The re-evaluation counselling of Harvey Jackins (1978) deserves special mention because it is one of the few attempts to weld psychotherapeutic and political principles into a cohesive action programme. The cathartic methods of re-evaluation co-counselling are not essentially different from many other humanistic approaches. What does distinguish Jackins' approach, however, is his insistence on co-counselling being taught in classes, being practised between equals and being promoted as a social movement. Not only is intrapsychic pain to be discharged, but distress patterns that have been culturally learned and which inhibit personal and social liberation. Thus, 'freedom from unaware racism', 'Jewish liberation' and all other forms of anti-oppressive commitment are vigorously promoted. In Jackins' view, we are hurt and diminished throughout life by internalizing oppressive attitudes in the same way in which we develop idiosyncratic personal hurts. Although various forms of co-counselling have developed which do not follow Jackins' political agenda, they do all share a belief in the power of citizens to co-operate in ridding themselves of limiting attitudes and behaviour. This challenge to the professionalization of the healing of individuals and society represents an important critique of counselling which has not been satisfactorily addressed by research or by rigorous intellectual analysis. If anything, the forces of professionalization are clearly winning the battle against do-it-yourself movements such as co-counselling, and the 'barefoot psychoanalyst' is probably more of a romantic symbol than a thriving reality.

In less revolutionary vein, but certainly germane to our discussion, the emergence of group and family therapy must be considered for its contribution to psychosocial change. First, it is significant that practitioners have been willing to look beyond the individual counselling or psychotherapy client to the micro-social system of which she is a part. Family therapy in particular recognizes that families themselves may be sick or dysfunctional and that the apparently sick individual may be the 'symptom' of this familial or systemic sickness. Secondly, it is evident in group therapies of various persuasions that individuals who have not previously known each other will usually quickly learn to project their own fears and fantasies on to each other, on to the group as a whole and on to the leader, if it has one. Group therapy has acted as a tremendous opportunity to focus on interpersonal (and by implication, social) dynamics. Indeed, the whole area of social psychology – a discipline which is, oddly, largely omitted from the training of counsellors and therapists – has thrown up promising but under-used material for observing, understanding and predicting social interactions and sociopolitical phenomena. The 'large group' based on humanistic and analytic principles has been used to focus on cross-cultural and other forms of social conflict. Again, however, there has not been the level of professional interest shown in group therapy that has been demonstrated in individual therapy, in spite of a certain amount of research suggesting that group therapy may be equally efficacious.

De Maré et al. (1991) write about their experiences of conducting large groups of up to about 70 participants. They demonstrate that dyadic therapy replicates early childhood experience, where the person is involved in conflict and care struggles with one other caregiver; small group therapy replicates the dynamics of families. The larger the group becomes, the more attention is turned away from internal, private conflict and its resolution, towards the airing of cultural conflicts, public debates and their attempted resolution. In the large group dialogue becomes necessary as people share their idiosyncratic feelings, explore their somewhat tribalistic views, and negotiate their way through layers of resistance to hearing others' realities; hatred of those who are different is commonly transformed, eventually, into new understanding. A state of 'koinonia' or 'impersonal fellowship' may be reached in which is glimpsed, perhaps, the possibility of some hopeful new cultural order. Although these views are rooted in psychoanalytic theory, they suggest interesting links with the dialogic and group processes advocated by Newman (1991), Bohm and Edwards (1991) and Sampson (1993).

Feminist therapy and counselling is not a monolithic structure and many writers trace its origins to ancient feminine wisdom (Chaplin, 1988). In its contemporary sense it emerged in the 1960s in a wave of conscious-ness-raising groups, political activism and challenges to patriarchal forms of therapy. The feminist therapist Judy Freespirit (1976) crystallizes much of the Zeitgeist in her attack on some of the male therapists she had been client to. She regrets that she had chosen men as therapists in the mistaken belief that they must be more professional, with their MD and PhD degrees, than many of their lesser-accredited female colleagues. Addressing one of these men, she says, 'Do you know what I had to do each week to earn that $15 and thereby begin to learn to trust? I cared for a two-year-old girl for twelve hours a day, five days a week. For this I was paid $20, approximately $5 of which went to pay for feeding her two meals a day, so my net earnings were just enough to cover our one precious hour at $15' (Freespirit, 1976: xiv). She complains that her therapist always refused to call her by her first name, thus discounting her feelings and her very identity. She concludes her address by declaring that 'I feel cheated and misused and I'd like to blow up the whole plush ninth floor of that ugly black box of an office building where you have encased yourself in such luxurious air-conditioned splendor, bought with the blood, sweat and psyches of so many contact-starved patients. . . . How many women are you mind-fucking, Dr B?' (Freespirit, 1976: xv).

It would, however, be a caricature to portray feminist therapy as purely anti-patriarchal therapy. It has been and is about exploring long-ignored or belittled aspects of women's lives, it is about supporting women and promoting their own feelings and values. It is also about pointing out needs for assertiveness training, and for careful attention to be paid to the interface between individual suffering and real sociopolitical oppression. Important questions for counsellors focus on the extent to which they may harbour conscious or unconscious sexist attitudes. Certain observers are so pessimistic about the possibilities of men being able to understand such issues and being able to avoid either subtle or gross forms of interpersonal oppression, that they suggest men should never counsel women. Yet others assert that a great deal of healing can take place when women can learn to trust men in a therapeutic setting. There is no doubt that the insights of feminist therapists have had a major impact on public awareness of a wide range of subjects, including women's body-image, sexual abuse, men who batter women, child-rearing and the long-range effects of mothering. Men's groups, looking intensively at the difficulties men experience in relating non-competitively, non-aggressively and in a non-sexist manner, have also been driven by the insights of feminism and feminist therapy.

A current model of 'social therapy' which, like Jackins' re-evaluation counselling, rejects conventional psychology and psychotherapy, deserves special mention. Newman (1991), along with colleagues, or comrades, has developed a flexible model of individual, brief and group therapy which derives its understanding from the needs of oppressed groups who are not well served by traditional white Eurocentric psychology. Newman takes seriously the failure of the counselling and therapy industries to understand and address the desperation of people living on low incomes, in poor housing, suffering from institutionalized racism, drug addiction and the cycle of deprivation generally. Employing the political analysis of Marx and the linguistic analysis of Vygotsky, Newman suggests that the received language of psychology is alien and unhelpful to oppressed people, who are better empowered by using language which is their own and methods which emanate from their own experience. Thus, transference is a nonsense in this context and better understood as alienation in the Marxist sense. Alienation permeates society, through the family and into the very souls of human beings. In social therapy, people are helped to 'gain a quite specific, active, practical contact with the social origins of the products of bourgeois society, including their lives as a component of that social reality'. Professionals have a greater investment in providing drugs, rehabilitation programmes, therapies and theories, than in radically challenging acceptance of social conditions. People may best overcome their depression, for example, by actively understanding its roots in society and engaging in making changes to their environment, rather than by consuming the pearls of wisdom of therapists. Beyond 'society', people are urged to understand history, to understand that they can change it and that their involvement in so doing is likely to be health-promoting. The belief that oppressive conditions really can be changed, and always change historically anyway, can lend a sense of power and purpose to those most devalued by contemporary power structures.

The values of counselling

I think it is true to say that efforts to combine politics with therapy have been quite marginal within the broad therapy world. I also question just how meaningful it really is to introduce the concepts and practices of 'red therapy', 'social phenomenology', 'social dreaming', 'deep ecology' and so on. Are such terms real agents for change or transient inspirations and entertainments? Even the term 'empowerment', originated by the radical educationalist Paulo Freire, and held in such esteem by feminist and humanistic counsellors, may be considered more a satisfying concept than a powerful and observable reality. Such concepts have a natural attraction but are problematic. Power is, of course, a vital sociopolitical principle. Counsellors like to regard themselves as helping their clients to regain their own, innate power. Counsellors do not consciously seek to have power over clients. Yet the concept of empowerment in a counselling context necessitates the 'empowering' and the 'empowered' – 'come to us and we will empower you (we have the psycho-technology)'.

Within counselling, there is another important endeavour to understand clients' socio-economic struggles and to activate the means to improvement. Rather than introducing special schools of political therapy, counsellors may attempt to extend their empathy into clients' political concerns. Rowan (1983) discusses the importance of 'listening with the fourth ear', or heeding the client's everyday, external, 'real world' concerns. Indeed, it is the official position of organizations like BAC that counsellor trainees should be exposed to the subject of social contexts and that counsellors should be sensitive to clients' socio-economic realities. It is an appealing proposition that by employing a profound form of empathy, or depth-listening, one can tune into the ways in which others' social contexts impinge upon them (Levin, 1989). Workshops offer counsellors the opportunity to learn what it might feel like to be gay, if one is heterosexual, to be black, if one is white, to be a woman, if one is a man, and so on. Counsellors are urged to try to understand others in such ways and to take this understanding into their one-to-one work with clients. However, this approach has been challenged, since there are real limits to empathy. Even in a quite mundane way, I am acutely aware of not being authentically understood as a parent by people (including counsellors) who do not themselves experience the ongoing stress and drama of being a parent. I do not feel authentically understood as an originally working class person by those who were born middle class. By inference, I am sure that I do not have an authentic grasp of what it is really like to be a woman, to be black, homosexual, disabled or chronically unemployed.

This brings the discussion towards the question: who are the counsellors? Some stereotypes suggest that counsellors are middle-aged, middle class women, do-gooders and generally liberal or 'left-wing types'. Counsellors are certainly not predominantly working class, nor predominantly right-wing! In order to train to become a counsellor or psychotherapist one needs to be reasonably well-off, or at least to enjoy disposable income. It is not unreasonable to suppose that the counselling world reflects certain political sympathies or ideologies. It is probably largely the case, as I have shown in Chapter 3, that working class people in distress receive help from statutory and voluntary organizations, while the middle classes make much more use of private resources.

When people choose to train as counsellors and psychotherapists, they are choosing a certain form of help, a certain identity, which includes the choice not to become a social worker, advice worker or nurse, for example. It also represents the choice not to be primarily involved in direct politics. Why people become counsellors is not a subject I can go into in depth in this book, but the choice has a political dimension. Albee (1990) has much to say about the uncritical espousal of therapeutic ideology and the talking therapies as professions. The point to be made here is that when counsellors tell themselves they are listening with the fourth ear, they may be deceiving themselves about being politically sensitive, when in fact they may be simply perpetuating the values of bourgeois quietism. Although many counsellors are probably very modestly remunerated for their work, it is also important to bear in mind that in Italy, for example, £1 billion are spent each year on psychotherapy (Bourne, 1993) and that a top psychoanalyst in the United States can earn $286,000 per annum, compared with the President's $200,000 (*Observer Magazine*, 2.1.94).

Holmes and Lindley (1989) ask whether psychotherapy is a luxury but conclude that it should be available as a form of primary health care, and should be viewed as on a par with state education. Acknowledging that those from poorer socio-economic backgrounds and cultures may often be wrongly diagnosed or be offered supposedly appropriate therapies (psychopharmacotherapy, behaviour therapy, family therapy and brief therapy), they agree that work must be done to correct such biases. However, these authors are in favour of a community psychotherapy which would serve the needs of all sections of the population. This ambition challenges the elitism of classical psychoanalysis in its principles and methods. It is difficult to see how psychoanalysis, or indeed any of the untestable and interminable therapies could be justified as forms of state-funded health care. This is one of the reasons why there seems to be some hope in the development of the brief therapies in community mental health settings (Barkham, 1989; Budman and Gurman, 1988; Cummings, 1988; A. Ryle, 1990). While many therapists object to allegedly truncated therapy, there are signs that a focus on how therapy may be effective in a short time will benefit both the profession of psychotherapy and future state-funded citizens in need of therapy. Ideally, perhaps, everyone should have access to exactly the kind of counselling or therapy they need (however long it may take), but realistically this is unlikely ever to receive state funding. Commentators such as Albee (1990) would also argue that such funds would be more efficiently, and perhaps more ethically, devoted to the prevention of mental distress than to the profession specializing in shutting the stable door after the horse has bolted.

Many therapists have a preference, declared or undeclared, for working with supposedly well-motivated, psychologically minded clients. The acronym YAVIS – young, attractive, verbal, intelligent, successful – sums up this favoured group. These are people whose lives are probably socio-economically stable and even thriving. Others, described by the acronym HOUND – humble, ordinary, unattractive, non-verbal, dumb – are not sought after as clients. Those who are struggling simply to survive in a society in which they are on the bottom rung will not prove much fun for those counsellors itching to get on with the business of promoting personal growth. In this sense, counselling may be criticized for giving unto those who have. The have-nots will have to make do with soup-kitchens, social security offices, and occasional befriending and advice! This may seem a sweeping and unfair comment, but as I have mentioned earlier, a newspaper article on the response to the spread of AIDS noted that the rush to counsel people with AIDS was not matched by a rush to provide the more menial services often needed in the later stages of the disease, such as home-help, cleaning, cooking and lifting. Psychotherapy and counselling appear to have a certain glamour. Landsman (1982: 269) indeed claims very starkly that in the USA 'the rich get psychoanalysis, the poor get shock therapy, and the prisoners and institutionalised retardates get behavior modification'.

Does counselling reflect the values of privacy and intimacy to the detriment of the public and political spheres? This is certainly the position espoused by Hillman and Ventura (1992) and to some extent by Samuels (1993). When clients bring up political and social material in their therapy sessions, is this to be regarded as symbolic of personal problems or in an entirely different light? We have become so accustomed to the notion that our personal problems and preoccupations are associated with what is 'deep' or what lies in the personal past, that we perhaps largely ignore the impact current events, directly and through the media, have on us. We are bombarded by television images of violence and news of public scandals and economic doom. We may be daily beset by worries about whether we can pay the mortgage, whether we will be made redundant, be bombed by a terrorist group or suffer from any one of a variety of contemporary ills outside our control. We may complain about these to our partners and friends, but at the same time experience a gnawing sense of political impotence. Is this experience invalid in therapy? Is counselling in some ways used as an oasis of reflection in an insane world?

As Chesler points out, 'an incest survivor with insomnia or panic attacks often cannot sit in a room long enough to have her consciousness raised; an anorexic or 'overweight' woman who is primarily concerned with losing weight or looking 'pretty' may not be able to notice others long enough to engage in political struggle with them' (Chesler, 1990: 318). This latter point endorses the argument that for many people a certain amount of therapy is necessary before they are ready to take on any political insight or responsibility. The more damaged you are, runs the argument, the longer it may take to put you back together, so that eventually you may gain political and transpersonal, as well as individual, understanding and fulfilment. At odds with this view is the proposition that a world crisis cannot be averted by waiting for millions of citizens to have therapy, but must be met by immediate, holistic consciousness that transcends all self-absorption (Bohm and Edwards, 1991).

Are counselling and psychotherapy value-free enterprises? One view has it that the talking therapies are pragmatic and/or clinical, individualistic ventures which have no relationship with the political sphere. Kovel (1988) disputes this assertion, and uses the illustration of transactional analysis which is frequently employed in individual therapy, in training, in management development programmes in business, military and other settings. According to Kovel, TA is 'unabashed about its congruity with consumerist culture . . . [and] . . . helps people get along with each other and the order of things' (Kovel, 1988: 142). In other words, TA may be used as a slick, apparently apolitical means of achieving superficially harmonious human relations. This perspective on TA is certainly not shared by writers such as Clarkson (1987), who offers some explanation for the processes of guilt, responsibility and social awareness in TA terms. Steiner and others have previously presented TA, incidentally, as a politically radical therapy in Wyckoff (1976). However, it remains the case that few if any therapeutic systems take any explicit and sustained political position. Rose (1989) offers an account of the arguably sinister uses of psychology and psychotherapy in Britain. Rose is critical of TA and other 'technologies of autonomy' on the grounds that they provide an illusion of privacy, freedom and mastery. We buy such illusions and thus keep ourselves and the psychological experts happy, but we may be no nearer to any political or social truths or solutions. Sampson (1993), critical of 'the autonomy obsession' within our society and certainly within our helping professions, urges us to engage in dialogical enterprises rather than turning our attention in upon the so-called self.

As Mair (1989: 282) says of therapists: 'Perhaps we do not want to be too closely associated with the murky depths or the underbelly of society. We want to be legitimate professionals, respected in the world of bright and light. We want to be chartered and registered, sanctioned and approved, fully paid up members of the legitimate realm.' In other words, although counsellors are privy to the confessions and complaints of numerous individuals about the society in which they live, and even though counselling may in fact be one of the primary avenues for psychosocial strain to express itself, counsellors and therapists attempt to maintain a professional, socially acceptable face. Counsellors cannot be ignorant of the many ills generated by society, but neither are they disposed to risk any serious challenge to the powers that be, because their own professional identity and livelihood is on the line. I have wavered over whether to use 'counsellors' and 'therapists' separately here. A group of student psychotherapists I once worked with voiced their suspicion that counsellors perhaps collude with their clients in encouraging quick, superficial adaptation, whereas psychotherapists inevitably plumb the depths and implicitly encourage their clients to express their unease with social norms. The obverse of this is the argument that counselling is more accessible and democratic, and psychotherapy more elitist.

The relatively new European Association for Counselling included in its preliminary definition of counselling the assertion that 'counselling is an interactive process between a counsellor and client(s) which approaches, in a holistic way, social, cultural, economic and/or emotional issues' (EAC, 1994). Could this imply that counselling could have real sociopolitical muscle, perhaps? It appears that counselling centres have sprung up rapidly in Sarajevo to meet the needs of large numbers of bereaved and traumatised young people. At the same time, reports from war scenes around the world spell out the warning that millions of traumatically orphaned and bereaved children and young people represent predictable social problems for years, or possibly generations to come. In Iraq following the Gulf War, it is said that 'all Iraq's children – a third of the population is under 15 – need counselling so that normality and childhood can be restored' (*Guardian*, 30.12.94). The children are traumatised by widespread loss of parents and siblings, by having witnessed horrific bombings and the sight of dead and mutilated adults and children, and by being chronically anxious about their own mortality. Counselling can help a great deal in such situations, and must obviously be provided, but it is difficult not to agree with Albee (1990) that radical education and prevention projects must not be eclipsed, since counselling alone cannot, as a one-to-one activity, have sufficient social impact to significantly affect society-wide trauma.

We may wish to ask ourselves: is counselling apolitical or metapolitical? Does counselling generate a false consciousness? Is counselling, perhaps, some sort of social movement? Do counsellors and their trainers give sufficient critical thought and personal commitment to the matter of social contexts? I end this chapter with a pertinent quote from Friedman's biography of Martin Buber, in which it is implicitly questioned whether we are really serious at all about social justice and change.

> Partial explanations, such as Marx's concept of the radical alienation of man through economic and technical revolutions, and Freud's concept of individual neuroses, do not yield an adequate understanding, any more than existential analyses. 'We must take the injured wholeness of man upon us as a life burden in order to press beyond all that is merely symptomatic, and grasp the true sickness.' The true sickness Buber described as 'massive decisionlessness', dualism, the radical separation between ideas, ideals, and values and personal existence on which the spirit no longer has any binding claim. (Friedman, 1982: 180)

9

The Identity of Counselling:
Science, Faith or Art?

> We belong to a profession whose members cannot decide whether they
> are scientists or philosophers, technicians or artists. We cannot agree on
> whether therapists should be trained in schools of medicine, education,
> liberal arts, or social work. . . . We cannot decide whether therapy is
> essentially a profession or a business.
>
> (Kottler, 1993: 111)

Having asked whether counselling can really be defined, can be distinguished from other similar historical, interpersonal endeavours and can
survive its critics' analyses, we must now further ask whether it is more
legitimate to refer to counselling as a science, a faith or an art. We might
also ask if it is a profession, a business, a sport, or something *sui generis*,
but the first three categories are sufficiently taxing in themselves. There are
many who would defend the claims that counselling (or psychotherapy) is
a science (Davar and Bhat, 1995; Malan, 1979), a faith (Halmos, 1965)
and an art (Bugental, 1992). There are also those who view it as a
disciplined amalgam of all three or as an amateur human activity drawing
on all three. In addition, some consider it a field of legitimate interdisciplinary standing (Thorne and Dryden, 1993). I have examined many
of the aspects of counselling which relate to faith and religion in Chapter
6. Here I examine mainly the significance of the distinctions between its
scientific and artistic or creative aspects.

Counselling as science

Wilhelm Wundt called what was one of the very first psychology courses
Psychology as a Natural Science in 1862. Slife (1993) comments that this
signifies the aim of psychology from its inception to become a natural
science, following the model of Newtonian physics. Certainly Freud
regarded psychoanalysis as a scientific enterprise, modelling it partly on
Helmholtzian physics, and many practitioners since Freud have emphasised the importance of the scientist-practitioner, or clinician who applies
knowledge from the fields of neurology, psychology, psychiatry, psychoanalysis, and so on, to actual human distress, and whose work is
constantly subject to research influences. In fact, Bettelheim (1989)
suggests that Freud's scientific emphasis has been misunderstood due to

mistranslations of his works, and that Freud's was primarily a humanistic, not scientific undertaking. According to Bettelheim, Freud wished to protect analysis from both physicians and priests.

But what is science? It is sometimes regarded as synonymous with knowledge and mastery, but in a more specialised sense is 'a branch of study which is concerned either with a connected body of demonstrated truths or with observed facts systematically classified and more or less colligated by being brought under general laws, and which includes trustworthy methods for the discovery of new truth within its own domain' (Onions, 1983). I will not enter into the debate about the differences between hard or natural science and social or human science, but certainly in the natural sciences, including medicine, we expect to find objectivity, consistency, demonstrability, testability and predictability. It is on these last two counts in particular that psychotherapy and counselling are seriously questioned, since much therapeutic theory concerns constructs about intrapsychic processes that cannot be seen or tested directly and most clinical work does not proceed according to predictable steps. Some critics have condemned both psychoanalysis and behaviour therapy alike as pseudo-scientific, sometimes arguing that psychotherapy is primarily about consciousness, which is not readily categorised or quantified (McCall, 1983). From feminist and philosophical perspectives, too, classical science has been criticised as being remote from the kind of humanistic meaning pursued within counselling (Strawbridge, 1992).

Eysenck remains unrepentantly critical of talking therapies. I am grateful to him for providing the following concise summary of his views on this matter.

People who seek counselling usually need help along two lines. One is practical, i.e. advice on how to deal with bureaucracy, banks and other practical issues. No doubt counsellors should be invaluable for giving such advice. The other kind of need is for some form of emotional therapy, usually for some type of neurotic illness or symptomatology, suffered either by the client himself or some friend or member of his family. Treatment of this type depends for its success very much on the personality, experience and good sense of the counsellor; it is in essence what has been done over thousands of years by priests, doctors, friends, family members, etc., and such advice and help should by no means be denigrated.

It is when counsellors believe that what they are doing is scientific, and based on solid principles, that the evidence is clearly in the negative. Consider a recent paper by Svartberg and Stiles, entitled 'Comparative effects of short-term psychodynamic psychotherapy: a meta-analysis', published in the *Journal of Consulting and Clinical Psychology*, 1991, 59, 704–714. This analysed the outcome results of psychoanalytic therapy, compared with no therapy at all, in 19 separate studies, carried out by properly qualified people. The brief outcome was that overall there was no difference between psychoanalytic therapy and no treatment. Now consider that therapists were much better trained than most counsellors, had much longer experience, and yet failed completely to produce any kind of improvement in their patients. Their help was not superior to the kind of advice given by priests, parents, friends, etc.! I fear that anyone who still believes in the effectiveness of psychotherapy would have some difficulty in arguing against these (and many other similar) results.

There is good evidence that behaviour therapy is greatly superior to such psychotherapy, or no treatment at all, but few counsellors are properly trained in behaviour therapy. If they were, then the situation would be very different; behaviour therapy has a proper scientific basis, and strong evidence to support its claims. I would like to see counsellors adopting a more scientific approach, but this is only likely to happen when they realise that the usual type of psychotherapy often practised in fact has no scientific basis, and no empirical claims to being better than placebo treatment, or no treatment at all (see Eysenck and Martin, 1987).

Eysenck's claims are of course disputed by most counsellors and therapists (see Dryden and Feltham, 1992b), many of whom assert that on the basis of their own and their clients' subjective experiences there is no doubt that counselling is usually very effective. At the same time, many have little or no interest in arguing that counselling is a science and many indeed prefer to be altogether distanced from scientific models of counselling. Yet even humanistic therapists like Rogers have insisted on the importance of research as well as or apart from clinical practice which may validate what is being done and explain some of its operations. Unfortunately, at least in my view, the current net result of a vast amount of research is disappointingly inconclusive and in some cases self-contradictory. The gains from research to clinical practice seem minimal, even though it is interesting to know that clients on average attend, say, only eight sessions of therapy, or that there is currently little demonstrable difference in effectiveness between therapies. Research in this field yields interesting minor finds but seems quite unlikely to turn up anything dramatically new or unexpected. To be fair to researchers, they have had to grapple too with the question of what precisely counselling and psychotherapy are: forms of treatment, education, social control or ritual and redemption (Orlinsky, 1989)?

Among practitioner–researchers, Hans Strupp has vigorously set forth his view that psychotherapy most certainly is scientific:

> At its best, psychotherapy is not faith healing, religious conversion, or brainwashing, nor does it traffic in the sale of friendship, as has been alleged. Admittedly, it may share some elements with all of these activities, but that is not its defining characteristic. What sets psychotherapy apart from other forms of 'psychological healing' – and of course medicine – is the planful and systematic application of psychological principles, concerning whose character and effects we are committed to become explicit. As psychotherapists and researchers, we want to learn more about what we are doing; we want to be able to do it better; we strive to be objective; and we are willing to work hard toward this end. To me, these are the beginnings of science, if not its essence. (Strupp, 1982b: 333)

Pooled clinical experience (for example, the most common explanations for and the most fruitful approach to use in relation to anorexia nervosa) does, perhaps, form a knowledge base which could be described as science-like. Professionalism in counselling which is based on deep clinical experience, attention to certain research indications and thoughtful innovation may be the closest to science counselling will ever come. Even the observational care of the counsellor and the explicit therapeutic attempts to encourage clients to become 'personal scientists' observing their own behaviour can be referred to generously as scientific. Personal construct therapy and transactional analysis are pertinent examples here. (Incidentally, TA has the curious distinction of being simultaneously one of the most popularised and most scientific-*looking* of counselling models, with its many diagrammatic explanations, matrices, and so on.)

Certainly the attempt to produce manualised therapy, with instructions for therapists to follow in particular kinds of cases, resembles some scientific procedures. The stubborn fact remains, however, that where human beings in their diversity are concerned, the variables facing counsellors are simply too myriad to succumb to precise scientific understanding and clinical prediction. The complexity of human development – involving little understood genetic factors, circumstances of birth, sibling rivalry, interwoven with school bullying, emotional effects of house moves, shades of emotional, physical and sexual abuse, accidents and ill health, grinding economic worries, divorce and separation, social and cultural position and life chances – surely precludes any precise science of analysing and rectifying individuals' problems.

To some extent Malan (1979) and Janov and Holden (1975) represent exceptional aspirations. For Malan, the phenomena of defences, anxiety and hidden feelings are 'scientific facts' and 'any theory of the human psyche, and any form of psychotherapy, *must* be incomplete unless it incorporates the psychodynamic point of view' (Malan, 1979: 254). Janov has argued that primal therapy has neuroscientific correlates and that independent physical measurements will validate his work. Unfortunately, earlier practitioners such as Hubbard and Reich have made pseudoscientific claims which have probably deterred most therapists from ever considering a close marriage of concepts from the talking therapies and neuroscience (Gardner, 1957; Gazzaniga, 1992). Others, however, remain convinced that close relationships between specific brain functions and mental dysfunction and psychotherapy can be or will be demonstrated (Levin, 1991). To some extent too, Lazarus' (1989) multimodal therapy represents an attempt at systematic assessment of each client's unique constellation of problematic modalities and an effort to apply suitably eclectic techniques. Lazarus is ready to admit that we have a long way to go before psychotherapy comes of age scientifically, however.

It has often been said that in psychotherapy there are no silver bullets; there are certainly no laser-accurate interventions. There is, however, the aspired-to skill of finding and delivering the *mot juste*, the phrase, silence or gesture that may potently strike the right chords and deeply affect and benefit the client. Words, tones of voice, facial gestures can and do, as we all know from our intimate contacts, have tremendous visceral impact, for better or worse. The counsellor aspires, perhaps, to learn and refine the art or science of therapeutic response.

Counselling as art

While the term 'psychotherapy' has a medical or scientific flavour, play therapy, art therapy, dance and movement therapy hardly have a scientific ring to them. Therapists, particularly those who invent new approaches, seem to relish polysyllabically garnished neologisms! Psychoanalysis, communicative psychotherapy, psychosynthesis, transactional analysis, cognitive-analytic therapy, rational emotive behaviour therapy, multi-modal therapy – the list is long indeed. Add 'integrative' and it sounds even better: hence, integrative psychosynthesis! I am unsure whether this suggests that therapists and counsellors wish to be perceived as scientific, or simply that they enjoy wordplay. (Another explantion, of course, is that commercial and proprietorial motives lie behind the nomenclature.) Carl Rogers seems to have done his share of wrestling with the name problem, beginning with non-directive, then client-centred, now person-centred counselling. This latter term sounds friendly, almost managing to suggest that perhaps rival therapies are impersonal or machine-centred! We might ask seriously, however, what thought processes transpire when creators of therapeutic systems set out to describe and define their approaches as something quite different from predecessors: above all, a distinctive name has to be found and a good deal of artfulness goes into this creative process.

My remarks here are meant to hint that counsellors and therapists probably have an ambivalent relationship with science: the therapeutic relationship and process are about humanness, subjectivity, feelings, trust, warmth, intuition, listening, being in touch, genuineness, spontaneity, risk, challenge, improvisation, interpretation, visceral awareness and generally being able to tolerate ambiguity, and so on. Only when it is written about, studied, researched or documented for an insurance company or award-granting body does all of this need its pseudoscientific clothing, perhaps.

Freud was something of a polymath, managing to relate to the science and art of his day and of antiquity. Today, it is much more common for counsellors and therapists to be allied in some way with the arts or the field of the interpersonal generally. Psychoanalysis is often allied with literary and artistic criticism and analysis. Jungian therapy is intimately associated with imagery and symbolism. The evocative or expressive therapies make ample use of all media, including dance, singing, chanting, drama, photography and massage. The techniques of sculpting, psycho-drama and Gestalt chairwork are well known for working therapeutically with projective material. Visualisation adapted to various approaches is a common technique. Storytelling is a central part of the counselling process and narrative approaches to therapy are currently gaining greater status. A facility with words is one of the most significant (if least studied) parts of the counsellor's craft. Bugental (1992), in describing the art of the psychotherapist, makes use of a musical analogy. In order to explain his concept of 'interpersonal press' (sensitivity to others and the ability to verbalise this flexibly), he refers to a musical keyboard and suggests that the octaves parallel certain definable interpersonal skills (silence, bridging, restating, summarising, and so on). As with piano practice, conscious and constant use of and experimentation with all such skills is said to develop the counsellor's art.

Intuition, attunement with feelings and intimate talk is traditionally the domain of women and, of course, counselling itself is characterised by a majority of its practitioners and clients being women. Typically, a majority of the founders, theorists, researchers, administrators and key teachers in the field are men, however. But the educational backgrounds of most counsellors and psychotherapists are more likely to lie in the arts than sciences, whereas psychologists, psychiatrists and (traditionally) psychoanalysts are by definition likely to have medical and scientific backgrounds. It is surely no coincidence that the talking therapy professions most arts-inclined are counselling, psychotherapy, family therapy and social work, whose staff are predominantly women. Reactions against the hard end of the medical model – ECT, psychosurgery, psychopharmacology, classical behaviour therapy etc. – have come from what might be termed the 'feminine values' of respect for nurturance, empathy, feelings and so on. The tools of the counsellor's trade are more often the senses – listening, observing, contact – than the intellect and its scientific creations.

The historical swing in the UK, from medically trained psychoanalysts to lay analysts, represented an acknowledgement that non-scientists could often offer as good a service as others. (Indeed, it is often claimed that scientifically trained practitioners, psychologists for example, are handicapped as counsellors or therapists because they think in narrow categories and are over-reliant on somewhat mechanical interventions.) Many of the early British analysts came from the artistic and philosophical Bloomsbury group and its associates – Adrian Stephen (brother of Virginia Woolf), Joan Riviere, James Strachey and others. Indeed, Leonard Woolf published Freud's early work at the Hogarth Press. The evolution of psychoanalytic talking therapy as something of an art form is therefore also connected with its partly British formulation, the American scene being much more rigidly shackled to science.

Allowing that the roots of the talking therapies extend back into religion and philosophy, and also into ancient literature generally, we must not forget that most classical writers, from Dante, Shakespeare, Goethe, Blake, Dostoevsky and Lawrence, have wrestled with the perennial themes of human suffering and folly, love, death, and our attempts to slay our dragons. The poet Matthew Arnold in (sections from) *The Buried Life*, for example:

I knew the mass of men conceal'd
Their thoughts, for fear that if reveal'd
They would by other men be met
With blank indifference, or with blame reprov'd . . .

But often, in the world's most crowded streets,
But often, in the din of strife,
There rises an unspeakable desire
After the knowledge of our buried life . . .

A longing to inquire
Into the mystery of this heart that beats
So wild, so deep in us, to know
Whence our thoughts come and where they go.

This poem, written in 1852, depicts poignantly the need to be heard and understood that is now so clear in counselling and that has been expressed both directly and symbolically throughout human history. More recently, the poet Philip Larkin – in *This Be The Verse* – demonstrated starkly that one need not be a psychoanalyst, nor write in technical terms to understand and convey what we now almost take as a truism:

They fuck you up, your Mum and Dad,
    They may not mean to, but they do.
They fill you with the faults they had
    And add some extra, just for you.

Rieff (1973) considers D.H. Lawrence one of the 'psychologising prophets' who, in *Psychoanalysis and the Unconscious* and *Fantasia of the Unconscious* put forward his own views on the need for a pro-sexual, anti-repressive, creative new humanistic religion. Lawrence condemned the coldness of science and its refusal to embrace and understand the irrational. But setting himself against Freud, too, Lawrence stressed the significance of will and desire over intellect, anticipating perhaps in some sense the tenets of humanistic psychology.

This very brief diversion into literary history is intended only to remind us that artistic threads are to be found in and outside of our present day psychologies. It may well be the case that many who become counsellors today would have been priests or artists in previous times, but that counselling – as the heightened use of the senses in imaginatively entering others' worlds and interpreting their biographies with them – has become almost a more valued or needed art. Perhaps, just as religion, philosophy and politics, and also science in many ways, are often perceived as discredited, irrelevant or even harmful, so contemporary art has come to be perceived by many as having little to say. The interpersonal arts seem to have emerged at just the time when an ideological and aesthetic vacuum has reached its most dangerous point.

Many would concur with the view that counselling is primarily an interpersonal art or craft which draws from science and from many other disciplines too. Indeed, Kottler (1993: 237) argues somewhat poetically that 'science is its brain, creativity is the heart of therapy'. The National

Training Laboratories which began in the USA in the 1940s and thrived for a while as sensitivity training groups incorporated the notions of human science and interpersonal experimentation. This is but one example of 'human science'. Whatever the counsellor knows is subject to modification in the therapeutic situation; scientific knowledge may or may not prove useful in each counselling session. Furthermore, science itself is as open to criticism as an ideology as any other, and many have argued that science and technology are the religions of the age, with their own destructive 'shadows'. Halmos (1965) has put a clear case for faith as a counsellor's guiding principle and the 'renunciation of science' complements this. Halmos warns that a balance of subjectivity and objectivity must be sought but it is in the nature of counselling that a 'social science lag between what we feel we must assume and what we can verify' is inevitable (Halmos, 1965: 125).

One of the central problems for counselling is that it cuts across academic disciplines, historical ideologies and contemporary professions. The problem is not unique to the UK. Mahrer (1989) has discussed the very same problems in Canada, for example, in the context of arguing for a more accountable and generic psychotherapy training programme. Decisions and plans relating to clarifying the identity of counselling and rationalising it will inevitably be fraught with difficulty and take many years to address and resolve. What is interesting is the persistence of the phenomenon of talking therapy across so many diverse settings. It is as if history itself is recording that the suffering individual wishes to speak and be heard, no matter what havoc is created!

10

The Future of Counselling: a Personal View

Having looked at counselling from a number of perspectives, I now propose to consider briefly the questions 'What is the future of counselling?' and 'What might counselling ideally become?'. I intend to look briefly at some possible short-term, mid-term and long-term futures.

Short-term

One of the most pressing questions currently facing counselling is professionalisation and the criteria and means of qualifying or accrediting counsellors. Whatever my own and others' reservations about the processes of accreditation or licensure, I think this tendency is an inevitability. I believe this is the way of the world and that as a profession we had better 'render unto Caesar' the qualifying hours and tokens he requires. At the same time, more positively, we may say that if the job of counselling is worth doing, it is worth doing well, which means that genuine core professional skills may be identified and hopefully strengthened. However, I concur with Rogers (1980) that the real, or infinitely more important quest is for effective practitioners, whoever they are and however they are or are not qualified. I am wary of a professionalising approach that would give all the power to those peddling and measuring atomistic counselling skills and overlook the need for wisdom and social and spiritual sensitivity (Friedman, 1993; Sternberg, 1990). The vitality of a thriving self-help and mutual aid sector testifies to the fact that unprofessionalised but skilled help-giving is effective and appreciated by millions.

Training courses in the short term will inevitably become acutely conscious of accreditation needs and will offer more of what the overseeing bodies require of them. I believe that the whole question of what counselling is and what purpose it serves in the context of social health, must be reviewed. If the trend towards installing counsellors in medical settings continues, then serious questions must be asked about the identity of counselling and, sooner or later, policies must be devised for the future training of counsellors to agreed national standards. I think this could involve some upheaval and a change in the structure of the helping professions (particularly medicine, psychiatry, psychotherapy and social work) generally.

I have no doubt that the emerging profession of counselling will continue for some time to be engaged in debates over its differentiation from other activities. In the meantime, other urgent debates include the problem of the proliferation of therapeutic models and the possible eclectic or integrative solutions; the scope and identity of counselling – honest, anti-panaceaic definitions and trade descriptions must surely replace misleading publicity; and the problem of effectiveness, which includes reference to finite resources and the debate as to how realistic long-term psychotherapy models are, weighed against models of brief counselling and therapy. Training courses will need to pay more attention to these issues, for example by challenging the idea of pure, core theoretical models and by taking research, and critiques of counselling, seriously. A better informed public will begin to ask exactly what is being taught on training courses and whether it matches what consumers need. A sharp distinction needs to be made, in my opinion, between counselling or therapy as a kind of personal growth hobby ('recreational therapeutics'), a substitute religious confessional, and counselling as a state-funded or state-regulated health profession which responds to urgent mental health problems. There may well be a legitimate place for forms of freely chosen personal growth therapies, but it is difficult to see how the state could (or whether it should) fund these.

Mid-term

In the mid-term I look forward, probably naively, to the dissolution of the counselling–psychotherapy pseudo-differentiation and to the establishment of a single profession. Others have already envisaged this as a kind of psychological general practice. I envisage a theory of psychological therapy purged of mystique and unhelpful traditional jargon; perhaps this might be facilitated by awarding prizes for translation into plain English of impenetrable psychoanalytic and behavioural texts, for example! I expect to see counsellors established in all GP surgeries and in other health, educational and occupational settings (although this process should also be critiqued – see, for example, Newton 1995). Along with such physical changes, I should like to see formal acknowledgement of the vital part that counselling can play in health care. I would expect neighbourhood health services to be significantly transformed by the presence of counselling facilities. At the same time, counselling practice would change both as it became more accepted and as it had to interact more with other disciplines and services. In this respect, the visionary work of pioneers like Pearse and Crocker (1943) and Pearse (1979) in community health might be fulfilled.

If counselling is to become a profession, then clearly a rationalized training format and curriculum must one day be devised. If society does one day come to value counselling widely, then the closest parallel to it as a profession in the UK is probably social work. Much social work education since the 1930s has included elements of relevant history, economics, public administration, sociology, law, political philosophy and psychology. Counselling might follow suit by adopting a suitably inter-disciplinary approach (Thorne and Dryden, 1993). Social work training is currently undergoing an upheaval, but already requires two to three years of full-time training. If counselling becomes recognised as being of similar value, then on health and economic grounds it should acquire similar training status as social work. The economics of this is hard to fathom, but since there is increasing recognition of the role of talking therapies, and certainly increasing demand from users of mental health services, marriage or relationship agencies and from other quarters, it seems likely that a diversion of funds from some areas to others would be justified. Medical and psychiatric practitioners, for example, are likely to experience fewer demands on their time when many of their clients are efficiently referred for counselling.

A study of the treatment of depression by Scott and Freeman (1992) showed that although counselling (here described as 'social work coun-selling') was more expensive than amitriptyline, cognitive-behaviour therapy and routine GP care, it was the most highly appreciated and desired by clients. Counselling is relatively expensive because of the time it takes, although counsellors are remunerated at a rate considerably lower than psychiatrists or GPs. What the Scott and Freeman study could not show was the long-term effects of differential treatments. It is a worthwhile hypothesis that clients who are given time in counselling, with the oppor-tunity for follow-up visits or mental health check-ups, will incur lower costs in the long run for health services. Developed models of brief therapy include, in the NHS in Britain, A. Ryle's (1990) cognitive-analytic therapy and the 'two-plus-one model' (Barkham, 1989), and in community settings in the USA, Budman and Gurman's (1988) and Cummings' (1988) brief therapy, which is offered as and when needed over the life cycle.

Long-term

Counselling encapsulates certain perennial concerns (the search for identity, how best to live, how to overcome adversity) and shares these with religion, education, philosophy and politics. As such, it is part of a project which Faber (1985: 158) refers to in these words:

> It may be suggested that all philosophy, religion, and psychoanalysis is, in the last reckoning, a struggle toward the evolution of a higher awareness, capable of detaching itself from the symbolic, transitional mode of perception which has dominated the life of the species for perhaps 50,000 years.

Counsellors witness the ravages of contemporary society on a daily basis in the microcosm of the counselling situation and cannot avoid imagining what a better world might look like. We may indeed consider that perhaps counsellors represent one of the compassionate edges of a slowly emerging new civilization. Zeldin (1994: 243) suggests that 'since the world began, compassion has been the most frustrated of emotions, perhaps more so than sex. . . . Impulses of generosity by tribes, nations or groups have repeatedly withered away.' Compassion and the construction of a sane society have always been major underlying concerns of religion, philosophy, politics and science, however much they have been distorted or forgotten. The essential compassion driving the talking therapies is currently thwarted by theoretical differences and professional battles. Surely what is called for is not only the integration of these approaches but the integration and transcendence of the many divisive political, philosophical, religious and psychological approaches. They all represented one and the same quest to Socrates and, more recently, to Buber and Krishnamurti. If Frankl can speak of an 'unconscious God', we may similarly conceive of a collectively unconscious yearning for an end to the millennia of human misery and confusion.

In the short to medium term, perhaps more acceptance of and funding for counselling would help. But in the long run, it is education and prevention that require attention. There is no reason why the findings of the counsellors, in combination with other contemporary and historical visions, should not be used to explore the construction of a psychologically informed and an ecologically sustainable society (Bohm and Edwards, 1991; Zohar and Marshall, 1993). Counselling and related interpersonal, dialogical activity in groups focuses attention on the benefits of open, intensive discussion and exploration, and a great deal could be achieved by bringing social problems into similar focus in neighbourhood groups, social ethics networks, people's parliaments, community-building enterprises and dialogue groups generally (Bohm, 1994; Friedman, 1993; de Maré et al., 1991; Newman, 1991; Peck, 1993; Sampson, 1993). Levin (1989) has examined philosophically the connections between the listening of the therapists and the potential inherent in a profound political and spiritual listening. Ultimately counselling cannot serve the community by being merely a narrow profession within it. Bertrand Russell warned against psychological knowledge being wielded by an aristocracy, a result that would be all the more lamentable when it has the power to contribute to greatly enhanced mental health (Russell, 1960).

Counselling is one of the softer parts of an often hard world. It is something that can be very difficult to justify on short-term cost–benefit grounds. But it is like green shoots that appear through cracks in concrete, signifying that human suffering and aspiration does not go away and that human compassion in its many guises never quite dies. If much of what is said in this book appears sceptical about what counselling is claimed to be, this is because compassion must be regarded as so precious that parodies of it deserve to be exposed. Institutionalised counselling and psychotherapy contain a good deal of nonsense, in common with much historical pseudoscience, hype and quackery, dogmatic and oppressive religion and politics, and dead-end philosophy. But at the heart of each of these ventures is a germ of truth, compassion and vision that perpetually seeks rediscovery. The ultimate concern of the counsellor is the promotion of mental health and the critique and elimination of all that diminishes mental and social health.

References

AHPP (1991) *Membership Directory*. London: AHPP.

Albee, G.W. (1990) The futility of psychotherapy. *Journal of Mind and Behavior*, 11 (3, 4), 369–384.

Aveline, M. (1992) *From Medicine to Psychotherapy*. London: Whurr.

BAC (1987) *Befriending and Counselling* (Information Sheet 2). Rugby: British Association for Counselling.

BAC (1992) *Code of Ethics and Practice for Counsellors*. Rugby: British Association for Counselling.

Bakan, D. (1990) *Sigmund Freud and the Jewish Mystical Tradition*. London: Free Association Books.

Bandura, A. (1982) The psychology of chance encounters and life paths. *American Psychologist*, 37, 747–755.

BAP (1992) *What is Psychotherapy?* London: British Association of Psychotherapists.

Barkham, M. (1989) Brief prescriptive therapy in two-plus-one sessions: initial cases from the clinic. *Behavioural Psychotherapy*, 17, 161–175.

Baron, J. (1994) In the manager's chair. *Counselling*, 5 (1), 13–15.

Bartley, W.W. (1978) *Werner Erhard: the Transformation of a Man*. New York: Clarkson N. Potter.

Beier, E.G. and Young, D.M. (1980) Supervision in communications analytic therapy. In A.K. Hess (ed.), *Psychotherapy Supervision*. New York: Wiley.

Belfrage, S. (1981) *Flowers of Emptiness*. London: The Women's Press.

Bellack, A.S. and Hersen, M. (eds) (1985) *Dictionary of Behavior Therapy Techniques*. New York: Pergamon Press.

Berlin, I. (1969) *Four Essays On Liberty*. Oxford: Oxford University Press.

Bessell, R. (1971) *Interviewing and Counselling*. London: Batsford.

Bettelheim, B. (1989) *Freud and Man's Soul*. Harmondsworth: Penguin.

Bhaktivedanta, A.C. Swami Prabhupada (1975) *Bhagavad-Gita As It Is*. Los Angeles, CA: Bhaktivedanta Book Trust.

Biestek, F. (1957) *The Casework Relationship*. London: Unwin.

Bimrose, J. (1993) Counselling and social context. In R. Bayne and P. Nicolson (eds), *Counselling and Psychology for Health Professionals*. London: Chapman and Hall.

Blieszner, R. and Adams, R.G. (1992) *Adult Friendship*. Newbury Park, CA: Sage.

Bloch, S. (1982) *What is Psychotherapy?* Oxford: Oxford University Press.

Bohm, D. (1994) *Thought as a System*. London: Routledge.

Bohm, D. and Edwards, M. (1991) *Changing Consciousness*. New York: Harper Collins.

Bollas, C. (1986) The transformational object. In G. Kohon (ed.), *The British School of Psychoanalysis: the Independent Tradition*. London: Free Association Books.

Bond, T. (1989) Towards defining the role of counselling skills. *Counselling*, 69, 3–11.

Bond, T. (1993) *Standards and Ethics for Counselling in Action*. London: Sage.

Bourne, H. (1993) A billion pounds of psychotherapy. *Psychiatric Bulletin*, 17, 295.

BPS (1993) *Regulations for the Diploma in Counselling Psychology*. Leicester: British Psychological Society.

Brandon, D. (1976) *Zen in the Art of Helping*. London: Routledge and Kegan Paul.

Brandt, L.W. (1982) *Psychologists Caught: a Psycho-logic of Psychology*. Toronto: University of Toronto Press.

Brown, J.A.C. (1961) *Freud and the Post-Freudians*. Harmondsworth: Penguin.

Brown, D. and Pedder, J. (1979) *Introduction to Psychotherapy*. London: Tavistock/ Routledge.

Brown, J. and Mowbray, R. (1990) Whither the human potential movement? *Self and Society (European Journal of Humanistic Psychology)*, 28 (4), 32–35.

Browne, L. (ed.) (1962) *The Wisdom of Israel*. London: Four Square Books.

Buber, M. (1937) *I and Thou*. Edinburgh: T. and T. Clark.

Budman, S.H. and Gurman, A.S. (1988) *Theory and Practice of Brief Therapy*. London: Guilford.

Bugental, J.F.T. (1992) *The Art of the Psychotherapist*. New York: Norton.

Buirski, P. (ed.) (1994) *Comparing Schools of Analytic Therapy*. Northvale, NJ: Aronson.

Cade, B. and O'Hanlon, W.H. (1993) *A Brief History of Brief Therapy*. New York: Norton.

Campbell, B. (1974) Emotion and survival: an evolutionary perspective. *Journal of Primal Therapy*, 1 (3), 236–249.

Capretta, P.J. (1967) *A History of Psychology in Outline*. New York: Dell.

Chaplin, J. (1988) *Feminist Counselling in Action*. London: Sage.

Charlton, W. (1988) *Weakness of Will: a Philosophical Introduction*. Oxford: Blackwell.

Chasseguet-Smirgel, J. and Grunberger, B. (1986) *Freud or Reich?: Psychoanalysis and Illusion*. London: Free Association Books.

Chesler, P. (1990) Twenty years since *Women and Madness*: toward a feminist institute of mental health and healing. *Journal of Mind and Behavior*, 11 (3, 4), 313–322.

Clare, A. and Thompson, S. (1981) *Let's Talk about Me: a Critical Examination of the New Psychotherapies*. London: British Broadcasting Corporation.

Clare, P. (1992) Post-traumatic stress disorder: offender, victim and colleague as survivors. *Probation Journal*, 39 (4), 175–181.

Clarkson, P. (1987) The bystander role. *Transactional Analysis Journal*, 17 (3), 82–87.

Clarkson, P. (1990) A multiplicity of psychotherapeutic relationships. *British Journal of Psychotherapy*, 7 (2), 148–161.

Clarkson, P. (1994) The nature and range of psychotherapy. In P. Clarkson and M. Pokorny (eds), *The Handbook of Psychotherapy*. London: Routledge.

Collins, G.R. (1986) *Innovative Approaches to Counselling*, vol. 1. Milton Keynes: Word (UK) Ltd.

Corsini, R.J. (1989) Introduction to R.J. Corsini and D. Wedding (eds), *Current Psychotherapies*, 4th edn. Itasca, IL: Peacock.

Craib, I. (1994) *The Importance of Disappointment*. London: Routledge.

Craighead, L.W., McNamara, K. and Horna, J.J. (1984) Perspectives on self-help and bibliotherapy: you are what you read. In S.D. Brown and R.W. Lent, *Handbook of Counseling Psychology*. New York: Wiley.

Cummings, N. (1988) Emergence of the mental health complex: adaptive and maladaptive responses. *Professional Psychology, Research and Practice*, 19 (3), 308–315.

Dale, N. (1988) Jews, ethnicity and mental health. In H. Cooper (ed.), *Soul Searching: Studies in Judaism and Psychotherapy*. London: SCM Press.

Davar, B.V. and Bhat, P.R. (1995) *Psychoanalysis as a Human Science*. London: Sage.

Davenport, D.S. (1992) Ethical and legal problems with client-centred supervision. *Counselor Education and Supervision*, 31 (4): 227–231.

Deikman, A. (1982) *The Observing Self: Mysticism and Psychotherapy*. Boston, MA: Beacon.

Deitch, R. (1974) Casework and counselling. *Counselling News*, Winter, 6–8.

Deurzen-Smith, E. van (1988) *Existential Counselling in Practice*. London: Sage.

Dreyfus, H.L. and Rabinow, P. (1982) *Michel Foucault: Beyond Structuralism and Hermeneutics*. Brighton: Harvester.

Dryden, W. (1991) *A Dialogue with Arnold Lazarus: It Depends*. Buckingham: Open University Press.

Dryden, W. (ed.) (1992) *The Dryden Interviews*. London: Whurr.

Dryden, W. and Feltham, C. (1992a) *Brief Counselling: a Practical Guide for Beginning Practitioners*. Buckingham: Open University Press.

Dryden, W. and Feltham, C. (eds) (1992b) *Psychotherapy and its Discontents*. Buckingham: Open University Press.

Durlak, J.A. (1979) Comparative effectiveness of paraprofessional and professional helpers. *Psychological Bulletin*, 86 (1), 80–92.

EAC (1994) *Newsletter*. June. (Rugby: European Association for Counselling.)

Efran, J.S. and Clarfield, L.E. (1992) Constructionist therapy: sense and nonsense. In S. McNamee and K.J. Gergen, *Therapy as Social Construction*. London: Sage.

Egan, G. (1990) *The Skilled Helper*, 4th edn. Pacific Grove, CA: Brooks/Cole.

Ellenberger, H.F. (1970) *The Discovery of the Unconscious*. New York: Basic Books.

Ellis, A. (1986) Do some religious beliefs help create emotional disturbance? *Psychotherapy in Private Practice*, 4 (4), 101–106.

Ellis, A. (1988) *How To Stubbornly Refuse To Make Yourself Miserable About Anything – Yes, Anything!* Secausus, NJ: Lyle Stuart.

Ellis, A. and Yeager, R. (1989) *Why Some Therapies Don't Work: the Dangers of Transpersonal Psychology*. Buffalo, NY: Prometheus.

Esterson, A. (1988) Judaism and wholeness. In H. Cooper (ed.), *Soul Searching: Studies in Judaism and Psychotherapy*. London: SCM Press.

Eysenck, H.J. (1992) The outcome problem in psychotherapy. In W. Dryden and C. Feltham (eds), *Psychotherapy and its Discontents*. Buckingham: Open University Press.

Eysenck, H.J. and Martin, I. (eds) (1987) *Theoretical Foundations of Behavior Therapy*. New York: Plenum.

Faber, M.D. (1985) *Objectivity and Human Perception*. Edmonton, Alberta: University of Alberta Press.

Farrell, B.A. (1981) *The Standing of Psychoanalysis*. Oxford: Oxford University Press.

Feltham, C. and Dryden, W. (1993) *Dictionary of Counselling*. London: Whurr.

Fish, J.M. (1973) *Placebo Therapy*. San Francisco: Jossey-Bass.

Foster, J.G. (1971) *Enquiry into the Practice and Effects of Scientology*. London: HMSO.

Foucault, M. (1975) *The Archeology of Knowledge*. London: Tavistock.

Foucault, M. (1988) *The Care of the Self*. Harmondsworth: Penguin.

Frank, J.D. (1963) *Persuasion and Healing: a Comparative Study of Psychotherapy*. New York: Schocken.

Frankfort, H.F., Frankfort, H.A., Wilson, J.A. and Jacobsen, T. (1964) *Before Philosophy*. Harmondsworth: Pelican.

Frankl, V.E. (1977) *The Unconscious God*. London: Hodder and Stoughton.

Freeman, L. (1990) *The Story of Anna O*. New York: Paragon House.

Freespirit, J. (1976) Open letter to my former shrinks. In H. Wyckoff (ed.), *Love, Therapy and Politics*. New York: Grove Press.

Freud, S. (1930) *Civilisation and its Discontents*. London: Hogarth.

Freud, S. (1974) *Introductory Lectures on Psychoanalysis*. Harmondsworth: Pelican.

Freud, S. (1978) *The Question of Lay Analysis*. New York: W.W. Norton.

Friedman, M. (1982) *Martin Buber's Life and Work: the Early Years, 1878–1923*. London: Search Press.

Friedman, M. (1993) *Religion and Psychology: a Dialogical Approach*. New York: Paragon House.

Friedrich, O. (1975) *Going Crazy: an Inquiry into Madness in Our Time*. New York: Avon

Fromm, E. (1963) *The Sane Society*. London: Routledge and Kegan Paul.

Fromm, E. (1980) *Beyond the Chains of Illusion*. London: Abacus.

Fromm, E. (1986) *Psychoanalysis and Zen Buddhism*. London: Unwin.

Gardiner, M. (ed.) (1973) *The Wolf-Man and Sigmund Freud*. Harmondsworth: Pelican.

Gardner, M. (1957) *Fads and Fallacies in the Name of Science*. New York: Dover.

Gazzaniga, M.S. (1992) *Nature's Mind*. Harmondsworth: Penguin.

Gellner, E. (1985) *The Psychoanalytic Movement*. London: Paladin.

Gellner, E. (1992) Psychoanalysis, social role and testability. In W. Dryden and C. Feltham (eds), *Psychotherapy and its Discontents*. Buckingham: Open University Press.

Gergen, K.J. (1990) Therapeutic professions and the diffusion of deficit. *Journal of Mind and Behavior*, 11 (3, 4), 353–367.

Gilbert, P. (1989) *Human Nature and Suffering*. London: Lawrence Erlbaum Associates.

Goldberg, C. (1977) *Therapeutic Partnership: Ethical Concerns in Psychotherapy*. New York: Springer.

Goldberg, C. (1992) *The Seasoned Psychotherapist*. New York: Norton.

Greenwald, H. (1974) *Active Psychotherapy*. New York: Aronson.

Grierson, M. (1990) A client's experience of success. In D. Mearns and W. Dryden (eds), *Experiences of Counselling in Action*. London: Sage.

Grossinger, R. (1982) *Planet Medicine: From Stone-Age Shamanism to Post-Industrial Healing*. London: Shambala.

Grunbaum, A. (1984) *The Foundations of Psychoanalysis*. Berkeley, CA: University of California Press.

Guy, J.D. (1987) *The Personal Life of the Psychotherapist*. New York: Wiley.

Hall, M.P. (1979) *Buddhism and Psychotherapy*. Los Angeles, CA: The Philosophical Research Society.

Halmos, P. (1965) *The Faith of the Counsellors*. London: Constable.

Harmer, J. and Arnold, J. (1978) *Advanced Speaking Skills*. Harlow: Longman.

Harris, C.M. (1987) Let's do away with counselling. In D.J.P. Gray (ed.), *Medical Annual*. Bristol: Wright.

Harrison, S. (1990) *Cults: the Battle for God*. Bromley, Kent: Helm.

Hart, J., Corriere, R. and Binder, J. (1975) *Going Sane: an Introduction to Feeling Therapy*. New York: Delta.

Hattie, J.A., Sharpley, C.F. and Rogers, H.J. (1984) Comparative effectiveness of professional and paraprofessional helpers. *Psychological Bulletin*, 95, 534–541.

Heaton, J.M. (1993) The sceptical tradition in psychotherapy. In L. Spurling (ed.), *From The Words of my Mouth: Tradition in Psychotherapy*. London: Routledge.

Herman, N. (1987) *Why Psychotherapy?* London: Free Association Books.

Herman, N. (1988) *My Kleinian Home: A Journey through Four Psychotherapies*. London: Free Press Association Books.

Heywood, J. (1967) *Casework and Pastoral Care*. London: SPCK.

Hillman, J. and Ventura, M. (1992) *We've Had a Hundred Years of Psychotherapy and the World's Getting Worse*. San Francisco, CA: Harper Collins.

Hogenson, G.B. (1994) *Jung's Struggle with Freud*. Wilmette, IL: Chiron.

Holmes, J. and Lindley, R. (1989) *The Values of Psychotherapy*. Oxford: Oxford University Press.

Honderich, T. (1993) *How Free Are You?: The Determinism Problem*. Oxford: Oxford University Press.

Horney, K. (1950) *Neurosis and Human Growth*. New York: Norton.

Houston, G. (1991) Ouch ouch stop it: a personal view. *British Journal of Guidance and Counselling*, 19 (2), 209–212.

Howard, A. (1992) What, and why, are we accrediting? *Counselling*, 3 (2), 90–92.

Howard, A. (1995) *Challenging Counselling and Therapy*. London: Macmillan.

Howe, D. (1993) *On Being a Client*. London: Sage.

Hubbard, L.R. (1950) *Dianetics: the Modern Science of Mental Health*. Los Angeles, CA: The Church of Scientology.

Humphreys, C. (1951) *Buddhism*. Harmondsworth: Pelican.

Hurding, R. (1985) *Roots and Shoots: a Guide to Counselling and Psychotherapy*. London: Hodder and Stoughton.

Hymer, S. (1988) *Confessions in Psychotherapy*. New York: Gardner.

Ivey, A.E., Ivey, M.B. and Simek-Downing, L. (1980) *Counseling and Psychotherapy: Integrating Skills, Theory and Practice*. Englewood Cliffs, NJ: Prentice Hall.

Iyengar, B.K.S. (1966) *Light on Yoga*. London: George Allen and Unwin.

Jackins, H. (1978) *The Upward Trend*. Seattle, WA: Rational Island.

Jacobs, M. (1994) Psychodynamic counselling: an identity achieved? *Psychodynamic Counselling*, 1 (1), 79–92.

James, W. ([1902] 1982) *The Varieties of Religious Experience*. Harmondsworth: Penguin.

Janov, A. and Holden, E.M. (1975) *Primal Man: the New Consciousness*. New York: Crowell.

Johnstone, L. (1989) *Users and Abusers of Psychiatry*. London: Routledge.

Jourard, S.M. (1971) *The Transparent Self*, 2nd edn. New York: Van Nostrand Reinhold.

Jung, C.G. ([1933] 1984) *Modern Man in Search of a Soul*. London: Ark.

Kakar, S. (1984) *Shamans, Mystics and Doctors*. London: Unwin.

Kegan, R. (1994) *In Over Our Heads: the Mental Demands of Modern Life*. Cambridge, MA: Harvard University Press.

Kelleher, A. (1993) *Decisions, Decisions*. London: Channel 4 Television.

à Kempis, Thomas (trans. 1952) *The Imitation of Christ* (trans. L. Sherley-Price). Harmondsworth: Penguin.

Kiesler, D.J. and Denburg, T.F. van (1993) Therapeutic impact disclosure: a last taboo in psychoanalytic theory and practice. *Clinical Psychology and Psychotherapy*, 1 (1), 3–13.

Kiev, A. (ed.) (1964) *Magic, Faith and Healing*. New York: Free Press.

Kirschenbaum, H. and Henderson, V.L. (eds) (1990) *Carl Rogers Dialogues*. London: Constable.

Koerner, K. and Linehan, M.M. (1992) Integrative therapy for borderline disorders: dialectical behavior therapy. In J.C. Norcross and M.R. Goldfried (eds), *Handbook of Psychotherapy Integration*. New York: Basic Books.

Kopp, S. (1972) *If You Meet The Buddha On The Road, Kill Him!* New York: Science and Behaviour Books.

Kottler, J.A. (1993) *On Being a Therapist*. San Francisco, CA: Jossey-Bass.

Kovel, J. (1988) *The Radical Spirit: Essays on Psychoanalysis and Society*. London: Free Association Books.

Kramer, P.J. (1989) *Moments of Engagement*. New York: Norton.

Krishnamurti, J. (1975) *Life Ahead*. New York: Harper and Row.

Krishmanurti, J. and Bohm, D. (1985) *The Ending of Time*. London: Gollancz.

La Barre, W. (1964) Confession as cathartic therapy in American Indian tribes. In A. Kiev (ed.), *Magic, Faith and Healing*. New York: The Free Press.

Lake, F. (1981) *Tight Corners in Pastoral Counselling*. London: Darton Longman and Todd.

Lambrias, C. (1994) Soul retrieval: a bridge between shamanism and therapy. *Cahoots*, 46, 38–39.

Landsman, T. (1982) Not an adversity but a welcome diversity. In M.R. Goldfried (ed.), *Converging Themes in Psychotherapy*. New York: Springer.

Lazarus, A.A. (1989) *The Practice of Multimodal Therapy*. Baltimore, MA: Johns Hopkins University Press.

Levin, D. (1989) *The Listening Self: Personal Growth, Social Change and the Closure of Metaphysics*. London: Routledge.

Levin, F.M. (1991) *Mapping the Mind: the Intersection of Psychoanalysis and Neuroscience*. Hillsdale, NJ: The Analytic Press.

Lindner, R. (1986) *The Fifty-Minute Hour*. London: Free Association Books.

Lomas, P. (1987) *The Limits of Interpretation*. Harmondsworth: Penguin.

London, P. (1986) *The Modes and Morals of Psychotherapy*, 2nd edn. Washington, DC: Hemisphere.

Luborsky, L., Singer, B. and Luborsky, L. (1975) Comparative studies of psychotherapies: is it true that 'everyone has won and all must have prizes'? *Archives of General Psychiatry*, 32, 995–1008.

Lukes, S. (1973) *Individualism*. Oxford: Blackwell.

Maeder, T. (1989) *Children of Psychiatrists and Other Psychotherapists*. New York: Harper and Row.

Mahrer, A.R. (1989) The postdoctoral plan for the education and training of counsellors. *Canadian Journal of Counselling*, 23 (4), 388–399.

Mair, M. (1989) *Between Psychology and Psychotherapy: a Poetics of Experience*. London: Routledge.

Mair, K. (1992) The myth of therapist expertise. In W. Dryden and C. Feltham (eds), *Psychotherapy and its Discontents*. Buckingham: Open University Press.

Maré, P. de, Piper, R. and Thompson, S. (1991) *Koinonia: From Hate, Through Dialogue, to Culture in the Large Group*. London: Karnac.

Malan, D. (1979) *Individual Psychotherapy and the Science of Psychodynamics*. London: Butterworth.

Maslow, A. (1968) *Towards a Psychology of Being*. New York: Van Nostrand Reinhold.

Masson, J. (1988) *Against Therapy*. New York: Atheneum.

Masson, J. (1991) *Final Analysis: the Making and Unmaking of a Psychoanalyst*. London: Harper Collins.

May, R.M. (1988) *Physicians of the Soul: the Psychologies of the World's Great Spiritual Teachers*. Amity, NY: Amity House.

May, R. (1992) *The Art of Counselling*. London: Souvenir.

Mays, V.M. and Albee, G.W. (1992) Psychotherapy and ethnic minorities. In D.K. Freedheim (ed.), *History of Psychotherapy: a Century of Change*. Washington, DC: American Psychological Asociation.

McCall, R.J. (1983) *Phenomenological Psychology*. Madison, WI: University of Wisconsin Press.

McGuire, W. (ed.) (1991) *The Freud/Jung Letters*. Harmondsworth: Penguin.

McLennan, J. (1991) Formal and informal counselling help: students' experiences. *British Journal of Guidance and Counselling*, 19 (2), 149–159.

McLeod, J. (1993) The research agenda for counselling. *Counselling*, 5 (1), 41–43.

McNamee, S. and Gergen, K.J. (1992) *Therapy as Social Construction*. London: Sage.

Mearns, D. and Thorne, B. (1988) *Person-Centred Counselling in Action*. London: Sage.

Mehta, G. (1990) *Karma Cola*. London: Minerva.

Meier, C.A. (1967) *Ancient Incubation and Modern Psychotherapy*. Evanston, IL: Northwestern University Press.

Messer, S.B. (1992) A critical examination of belief structures in integrative and eclectic psychotherapy. In J.C. Norcross and M.R. Goldfried (eds), *Handbook of Psychotherapy Integration*. New York: Basic Books.

Miller, A. (1987) *For Your Own Good: the Roots of Violence in Child-rearing*. London: Virago.

Mirowsky, J. and Ross, C.E. (1989) *Social Causes of Psychological Distress*. New York: Aldine de Gruyter.

Mozak, H.H. (1989) Adlerian psychotherapy. In R. Corsini and D. Wedding (eds), *Current Psychotherapies*, 4th edn. Itasca, IL: Peacock.

Naylor-Smith, A. (1994) Counselling and psychotherapy: is there a difference? *Counselling*, 5 (4), 284–286.

Needleman, J. (1982) *The Heart of Philosophy*. London: Routledge and Kegan Paul.

Nelson-Jones, R. (1988) *Practical Counselling and Helping Skills*. London: Cassell.

Newman, F. (1991) *The Myth of Psychology*. New York: Castillo.

Newton, T. (1995) *'Managing' Stress: Emotion and Power at Work*. London: Sage.

Noll, R. (1994) *The Jung Cult: Origins of a Charismatic Movement*. Princeton, NJ: Princeton University Press.

Norcross, J.C. and Goldfried, M.R. (eds) (1992) *Handbook of Psychotherapy Integration*. New York: Basic Books.

Norman, R. (1983) *The Moral Philosophers*. Oxford: Clarendon Press.

Nowell-Smith, P.H. (1954) *Ethics*. Harmondsworth: Penguin.

Oldfield, S. (1983) *The Counselling Relationship*. London: Routledge and Kegan Paul.

Onions, C.T. (1983) *The Shorter Oxford English Dictionary*. London: Guild Publishing.

Orlinsky, D.E. (1989) Researchers' images of psychotherapy: their origins and influences on research. *Clinical Psychology Review*, 9, 413–41.

Pagels, E. (1982) *The Gnostic Gospels*. Harmondsworth: Pelican.

Patten, M.I. and Walker, L.G. (1990) Marriage guidance counselling: 1. What clients think will help. *British Journal of Guidance and Counselling*, 18 (1), 28–39.

Pearse, I.H. (1979) *The Quality of Life*. Edinburgh: Scottish Academic Press.

Pearse, I.H. and Crocker, L.H. (1943) *The Peckham Experiment*. London: Allen and Unwin.

Peck, M.S. (1993) *A World Waiting to be Born: Civility Rediscovered*. New York: Bantam.

Pedder, J.R. (1989) Courses in psychotherapy: evolution and current trends. *British Journal of Psychotherapy*, 6 (2), 203–221.

Perls, F.S. (1969) *Gestalt Therapy Verbatim*. New York: Bantam.

Persaud, R.D. (1993) The 'career' of counselling: careering out of control? *Journal of Mental Health*, 2, 283–285.

Phillips, A. (1993) *On Kissing, Tickling and Being Bored*. London: Faber and Faber.

Pilgrim, D. (1990) British psychotherapy in context. In W. Dryden (ed.), *Individual Therapy: a Handbook*. Milton Keynes: Open University Press.

Pilgrim, D. (1992) Psychotherapy and political evasions. In W. Dryden and C. Feltham (eds), *Psychotherapy and its Discontents*. Buckingham: Open University Press.

Pilgrim, D. and Treacher, A. (1992) *Clinical Psychology Observed*. London: Routledge.

Pirani, A. (1988) Psychotherapy, women and the feminine in Judaism. In H. Cooper (ed.), *Soul Searching: Studies in Judaism and Psychotherapy*. London: SCM Press.

Pistrang, N. and Barker, C. (1992) Clients' beliefs about psychological problems. *Counselling Psychology Quarterly*, 5 (4), 325–335.

Progoff, I. (1975) *At a Journal Workshop*. New York: Dialogue House.

Purton, C. (1993) Philosophy and counselling. In B. Thorne and W. Dryden (eds), *Counselling: Interdisciplinary Perspectives*. Buckingham: Open University Press.

Quilliam, S. and Grove-Stephensen, I. (1990) *The Best Counselling Guide*. London: Thorsons.

Raimy, V. (1950) *Training in Clinical Psychology*. New York: Prentice Hall.

Rand, A. (1982) *Philosophy: Who Needs It?* Harmondsworth: Signet.

Reynolds, D.K. (1980) *The Quiet Therapies: Japanese Pathways to Personal Growth*. Honolulu: University of Hawaii Press.

Rhinehart, L. (1994) *The Search for the Diceman*. London: Harper Collins.

Richardson, F.C. (1989) Freedom and commitment in modern psychotherapy. *Journal of Integrative and Eclectic Psychotherapy*, 8 (4), 303–319.

Richter, H.E. (1974) *The Family as Patient*. London: Souvenir.

Rieff, P. (1973) *The Triumph of the Therapeutic*. Harmondsworth: Penguin.

Robinson, L.H. (ed.) (1986) *Psychiatry and Religion: Overlapping Concerns*. Washington, DC: American Psychiatric Press.

Robinson, P. (1990) *The Freudian Left*. Ithaca, NY: Cornell University Press.

Rogers, C.R. (1951) *Client-Centred Therapy*. London: Constable.

Rogers, C.R. (1980) *A Way of Being*. Boston, MA: Houghton-Mifflin.

Roiphe, K. (1994) *The Morning After: Sex, Fear and Feminism*. London: Hamish Hamilton.

Rose, N. (1989) *Governing the Soul: the Shaping of the Private Self*. London: Routledge.

Rowan, J. (1983) *The Reality Game*. London: Routledge.

Rowan, J. (1994) What is counselling about? *Counselling News*, 14, 14–16.

Rusk, T. (1991) *Instead of Therapy*. Carson, CA: Hay House.

Russell, B. (1960) *Sceptical Essays*. London: Allen and Unwin.

Russell, J., Dexter, G. and Bond, T. (1992) *Differentiation Between Advice, Guidance, Befriending, Counselling Skills and Counselling*. Discussion Paper 1. Welwyn, Herts: The Advice and Guidance Lead Body.

Russell, J. and Dexter, G. (1993) 'Ménage à Trois: Accreditation, NVQs and BAC'. *Counselling*, 4 (4), 266–269.

Ryle, A. (1990) *Cognitive-Analytic Therapy*. Chichester: Wiley.

Ryle, G. (1990) *The Concept of Mind*. Harmondsworth: Penguin.

Saltzman, N. and Norcross, J.C. (eds) (1990) *Therapy Wars: Contention and Convergence in Differing Clinical Approaches*. San Francisco, CA: Jossey Bass.

Sampson, E. (1993) *Celebrating the Other: a Dialogic Account of Human Nature*. New York: Harvester Wheatsheaf.

Samuels, A. (1993) *The Political Psyche*. London: Routledge.

Samuels, A., Shorter, B. and Plaut, F. (1986) *A Critical Dictionary of Jungian Analysis*. London: Routledge and Kegan Paul.

Sargant, W. (1957) *Battle for the Mind*. London: Heinemann.

Sayers, J. (1991) *Mothering Psychoanalysis*. Harmondsworth: Penguin.

Schechtman, M. (1994) The truth about memory. *Philosophical Psychology*, 7 (1), 3–18.

Schutz, W. (1979) *Profound Simplicity*. London: Turnstone.

Scott, A.I. and Freeman, C.P. (1992) Edinburgh primary care depression study: treatment outcome, patient satisfaction, and cost after 16 weeks. *British Medical Journal*, 304, 883–887.

Sennett, R. (1986) *The Fall of Public Man*. London: Faber and Faber.

Sieghart, P. (1978) *Statutory Regulation of Psychotherapists: a Report of a Professions Joint Working Party*. Cambridge: Plumridge.

Simpson, J.A. and Weiner, E.S.C. (eds) (1989) *Oxford English Dictionary*, 2nd edn. Oxford: Oxford University Press.

Slife, B.D. (1993) *Time and Psychological Explanation*. New York: State University of New York Press.

Smail, D. (1987) *Taking Care: an Alternative to Therapy*. London: Dent.

Smart, N. (1971) *The Religious Experience of Mankind*. London: Fontana.

Smith, D.L. (1990) Psychodynamic therapy: the Freudian approach. In W. Dryden (ed.), *Individual Therapy: a Handbook*. Milton Keynes: Open University Press.

Southgate, J. and Randall, R. (1978) *The Barefoot Psychoanalyst*. London: Association of Karen Horney Psychoanalytic Counsellors.

Spilka, B. (1986) Spiritual issues: do they belong in psychological practice? *Psychotherapy in Private Practice*, 4 (4), 93–100.

Spinelli, E. (1994) *Demystifying Therapy*. London: Constable.

Spires, A. and Dryden, W. (1988) Visions of reality in different approaches to counselling and psychotherapy. *Counselling*, 64, 9–14.

Spurling, L. (1993) *From the Words of My Mouth: Tradition in Psychotherapy*. London: Routledge.

Stafford-Clark, D. (1952) *Psychiatry Today*. Harmondsworth: Pelican.

Sternberg, R.J. (ed.) (1990) *Wisdom: Its Nature, Origins and Development*. Cambridge: Cambridge University Press.

Stevenson, L. (1987) *Seven Theories of Human Nature*, 2nd edn. Oxford: Oxford University Press.

Storr, A. (1988) *Solitude*. London: Fontana.

Strawbridge, S. (1992) Counselling, psychology and the model of science. *Counselling Psychology Review*, 7 (1), 5–11.

Strupp, H.H. (1982a) Critical comments on the future of psychoanalytic therapy. In M.R. Goldfried (ed), *Converging Themes in Psychotherapy*. New York: Springer.

Strupp, H.H. (1982b) Psychotherapists and (or versus?) researchers. In M.R. Goldfried (ed.), *Converging Themes in Psychotherapy*. New York: Springer.

Sue, D.W. and Sue, D. (1990) *Counseling the Culturally Different*, 2nd edn. New York: Wiley.

Sutherland, J.D. (1972) *Some Reflections on the Development of Counselling Services*. National Council of Social Service.

Sutherland, S. (1991) *Macmillan Dictionary of Psychology*. London: Macmillan.

Sutherland, S. (1992) What goes wrong in the care and treatment of the mentally ill. In W. Dryden and C. Feltham (eds), *Psychotherapy and its Discontents*. Buckingham: Open University Press.

Sutton, C. (1989a) The evaluation of counselling. In W. Dryden (ed.), *Key Issues for Counselling in Action*. London: Sage.

Sutton, C. (1989b) Counselling in the personal social services. In W. Dryden, D. Charles-Edwards and R. Woolfe (eds), *Handbook of Counselling in Britain*. London: Routledge.

Symington, N. (1986) *The Analytic Experience*. New York: St Martin's Press.

Szasz, T. (1988) *The Myth of Psychotherapy*. New York: Syracuse University Press.

Szasz, T. (1991) Diagnoses are not diseases. *Lancet*, 338, 1574–1576.

Talmon, M. (1990) *Single Session Therapy*. San Francisco, CA: Jossey-Bass.

Tannen, D. (1984) *Conversational Style: Analyzing Talk Among Friends*. Norwood, NJ: Ablex.

Taylor, C. (1991) *The Ethics of Authenticity*. Cambridge, MA: Harvard University Press.

Taylor, D.M. (1970) *Explanation and Meaning: an Introduction to Philosophy*. Cambridge: Cambridge University Press.

Temperley, J. and Himmel, S. (1986) Training for psychodynamic social work. *Journal of Social Work Practice*, 2 (3), 4–14.

Thomas, K. (1971) *Religion and the Decline of Magic*. London: Weidenfeld and Nicolson.

Thorne, B. (1990) Person-centred therapy. In W. Dryden (ed.), *Individual Therapy: a Handbook*. Milton Keynes: Open University Press.

Thorne, B. (1991) *Person-Centred Counselling: Therapeutic and Spiritual Dimensions*. London: Whurr.

Thorne, B. (1992) Psychotherapy and counselling: the quest for differences. *Counselling*, 3 (4), 244–248.

Thorne, B. and Dryden, W. (eds) (1993) *Counselling: Interdisciplinary Perspectives*. Buckingham: Open University Press.

Tillich, P. (1962) *The Courage To Be*. London: Fontana.

Timms, N. and Timms, R. (1982) *Dictionary of Social Welfare*. London: Routledge and Kegan Paul.

Tyndall, N. (1993) *Counselling in the Voluntary Sector*. Buckingham: Open University Press.

Urmson, J.O. and Ree, J. (1992) *The Concise Encyclopaedia of Western Philosophy and Philosophers*. London: Routledge.

Varah, C. (1985) *The Samaritans*. London: Constable.

Vicinczey, S. (1969) *The Rules of Chaos*. London: Macmillan.

Vilayat, P.G. (1993) *Counselling and Therapy: the Spiritual Dimension*. London: Souvenir.

Vitz, P. (1977) *Psychology as Religion: the Cult of Self Worship*. Tring: Lion.

Vitz, P. (1993) *Sigmund Freud's Christian Unconscious*. Grand Rapids, Mich.: Eerdmans.

Wachtel, P.L. (1987) *Action and Insight*. New York: Guilford Press.

Walker, M. (1990) *Women in Therapy and Counselling*. Milton Keynes: Open University Press.

Ward, E. and Ogden, J. (1994) Experiencing vaginismus – sufferers' beliefs about causes and effects. *Sexual and Marital Therapy*, 9 (1), 33–45.

Watts, A. (1975) *Psychotherapy East and West*. New York: Vintage.

Weatherhead, L.D. (1952) *Psychology, Religion and Healing*, 2nd edn. London: Hodder and Stoughton.

Weatherill, R. (1991) The psychical realities of modern culture. *British Journal of Psychotherapy*, 7 (3), 268–274.

Weinrach, S.G. (1992) An American perspective. *Counselling News*, 8, 20–21.

Whiteley, J.M. (1984) A historical perspective on the development of counseling psychology as a profession. In S.D. Brown and R.W. Lent (eds), *Handbook of Counseling Psychology*. New York: Wiley.

Wilber, K., Engler, J. and Brown, D.P. (1986) *Transformations of Consciousness*. Boston, MA: Shambala.

Winmill, M. (1994) Letter to the editor. *Counselling*, 5 (4), 256.

Winnicott, D.W. (1988) *Human Nature*. London: Free Association Books.

Wolberg, L.R. (1977) *The Technique of Psychotherapy*, vol. 1. New York: Grune and Stratton.

Wood, G. (1984) *The Myth of Neurosis*. London: Macmillan.

Wyckoff, H. (ed.) (1976) *Love, Therapy and Politics*. New York: Grove Press.

Yalom, I. (1989) *Love's Executioner and Other Tales of Psychotherapy*. London: Penguin.

Zeldin, T. (1994) *An Intimate History of Humanity*. London: Sinclair-Stephenson.

Zohar, D. and Marshall, I. (1993) *The Quantum Society*. London: Bloomsbury.

Index

What is counselling?